16 BIT
MICROPROCESSORS

MICHEL AUMIAUX

Translated from the original French by
JOHN C. C. NELSON

*Department of Electrical and Electronic Engineering
University of Leeds*

PRENTICE HALL

NEW YORK   LONDON   TORONTO   SYDNEY   TOKYO

First published 1988 by
Prentice Hall International (UK) Ltd,
66 Wood Lane End, Hemel Hempstead,
Hertfordshire, HP2 4RG
A division of
Simon & Schuster International Group

Printed and bound in Great Britain at the
University Press, Cambridge.

Library of Congress Cataloging-in-Publication Data

Aumiaux, Michel.
  16 bit microprocessors.

  Translation of: Microprocesseurs 16 bits.
  Includes index.
1. Microprocessors   2. Intel 8086 (microprocessor)
3. Motorola 68000 (microprocessor)   I. Title.
II. Title: Sixteen bit microprocessors.
QA76.5.A7895413   1988   004.165   87-29252

1 2 3 4 5   91 90 89 88

The original edition of this work was published in France by
Masson, Editeur, Paris, under the title
Microprocesseurs 16 Bits
© 1985 by Masson Editeur.

ISBN 0-13-811613-X

16 BIT
MICROPROCESSORS

CONTENTS

PART III THE 68000

PART I
GENERAL PRINCIPLES OF 16 BIT MICROPROCESSORS

1. GENERAL

1.1 History

The first 16 bit microprocessor was the National Semiconductor PACE. Its performance was similar to that of 8 bit microprocessors such as the 8085A, 6800 and Z80. Other 16 bit microprocessors appeared subsequently – the General Instrument CP100, the Texas 9900, the Western Digital WD16, the Panafacom 1610, the Ferranti F100L and the Fairchild 9440. All these first generation 16 bit microprocessors had a maximum address capacity of 64 kilobytes which is also the case with all the 8 bit microprocessors. The progress of MOS technology and the experience obtained with both 8 bit microprocessors and minicomputers permitted the development of a second generation of 16 bit microprocessors. The Intel 8086 appeared first in 1978 and in the following few years the Zilog Z8000, the Motorola 68000 and the National Semiconductor NS16032 appeared. While the Motorola 6800 8 bit microprocessor integrates around 5,000 transistors, the 8086 integrates 29,000, the 68000 almost 70,000, the APX432 of the order of 120,000 and the 32 bit Hewlett Packard around 450,000. These figures show that in the ten years from 1974 to 1984 the number of transistors integrated on to a single chip has been multiplied by a factor close to 100. This rapid progress led directly to the arrival of 16 bit microcomputers on a single chip.

1.2 Requirements which justify the concept of 16 bit microprocessors

All second generation 16 bit microprocessors result from an improvement of 8 bit microprocessors combined with simplified minicomputing concepts.

In some applications the performance of 8 bit microprocessors is not sufficient on account of the ever-increasing requirements of users which will now be discussed.

■ Requirement for an addressable memory space greater than 64 Kbytes
In the case of practical applications, the trend is towards increasing complexity which leads, in the case of a microcomputer application, to longer and longer programs and hence a large read only memory (ROM) capacity. The relatively recent use of micro-processors in small management systems leads to data files of non-negligible size and hence to a large random access memory (RAM) capacity. This requirement occurs equally in teleprocessing and telecommunications applications. It follows that the 64 Kbytes available for both ROM and RAM, and sometimes for ROM, RAM and input/output (I/O), are no longer sufficient. The above relates to the present state of microprocessor system exploitation. This requirement for a larger memory space is much more marked at the design and application stage using a development system. In fact the latter, which must be designed with the same microprocessor as that of the

practical application, monopolizes several tens of kilobytes of memory to accommodate the editor or assembler, in the case of an assembly language program, and the
compiler, in the case of a high level language. A compiler occupies more space than an
editor or an assembler but the use of high level languages is another present trend,
notably in the area of small management systems. Also, second generation 16 bit
microprocessors, the only ones which will be covered in this book, all have an
addressable memory space greater than that of 8 bit microprocessors which is 64
Kbytes. This addressable memcˑy space is

> 384 Kbytes for the Z8002, the 40 pin version of the Z8000, by using status lines
> allowing six spaces of 64 Kbytes
> 1 megabyte for the 8086
> 8 megabytes for the Z8001, the 48 pin version of the Z8000
> 16 megabytes for the 68000 and the NS16032.

■ Requirement for higher processing speed

Some sections of industry (which are large users of microprocessors) such as aviation,
telecommunications, data processing and oil prospecting companies, have to carry
out many calculations particularly 16 or 32 bit multiplication and division. This is also
the case with process control companies where the processing of control loops is
realized more and more by means of a microprocessor. Now 8 bit microprocessors,
with very few exceptions, have neither multiplication nor division in hardware, that
is, they have no multiplication or division instructions. It is possible to perform these
operations with 8 bit microprocessor programs but the execution time is much too
long. Furthermore, these 8 bit microprocessors process bytes which is clearly less
rapid than processing words of 16 or even 32 bits. Also, all second generation 16 bit
microprocessors have multiplication and division instructions. Moreover, their
powerful instruction set, inspired by that of minicomputers, allows a much greater
speed for processing of all kinds.

■ The need for security

Longer and longer user programs involve an increased requirement for security of
operation. In fact, as the programs become longer the risk of anomalous behavior is
increased. Multitask processing, in which it is important to avoid interference
between tasks, is also a present trend. This involves frequent access to one or more
common memory areas, a compiler program for example. Also, access to different
memory areas must be regulated. To ensure the required security of operation,
second generation 16 bit microprocessors have often made use of certain concepts
which have been proved with minicomputers.

    The concepts of 16 bit microprocessors in respect of security will be studied in
detail later, here it will merely be noted that these concepts lead to a special circuit,
called a memory management unit (MMU) whose two objectives are:

(a) Transfer of areas of memory when the memory is of increased capacity.
(b) Protection of these areas of memory (memory consists most often of a program

area, a data area and a stack area for each task) against all attempts by a user to access an area which does not belong to him or which does not correspond to the operation which he wishes to execute, for example an attempt to write into a ROM.

1.3 The pin-out of 16 bit microprocessors

Most 8 bit microprocessors are in the form of a 40 pin package. The change from an 8 to a 16 bit data bus required eight more pins. The increase of the address field dictated an address bus of more than 16 bits and the need for several additional address lines. To allow these extensions, the designers had three possibilities.

(a) Choose packages of more than 40 pins, principally 48 or 64 pins, without any multiplexing. This is the choice which was made by Motorola for the 68000 which has a 16 bit data bus and a 24 bit address bus, one of these bits A_0 being specified in a special way. This microprocessor is produced in a 64 pin package.

(b) Retain a 40 pin package and multiplex certain signals. In this case two signals share the same pin, each of the two signals being active at a different time. This solution requires at least one additional state line to specify to the peripheral circuits which is the active signal. It almost always also requires a latch to store the information sent first on the multiplexed lines. This additional memory slightly reduces the speed of operation. Multiplexing also has the disadvantage of generating transient interference on the multiplexed lines. Intel chose this signal multiplexing solution for the 8086, having already adopted it several years previously for the 8085. For the 8086, multiplexing occurs at address and data levels; an address, which is then stored in a latch by the address latch enable (ALE) signal, is transmitted first on the 16 bus lines followed by data which is latched within the microprocessor. Zilog also adopted this solution and the same type of multiplexing for the Z8002 version of the Z8000 (Figure 1).

(c) Combine the first and second possibilities. The Zilog Z8001 and the National Semiconductor NS16032 both have a 48 pin package and multiplexing of 16 address and data lines (Figure 1).

Comment. A frequently used technique to reduce the number of pins is coding of the internal states of the machine. Decoding of these states, which is necessary, is achieved explicitly by an additional circuit or in a special circuit associated with the microprocessor. In this way the Zilog Z8002 microprocessor sends 7 state bits to its memory management unit (MMU) which decodes them internally.

As always, each of these three possibilities has its advantages and disadvantages. If the provision of separate address and data buses is the most satisfactory solution for the user, it has the disadvantage of requiring a 64 pin package which makes future extension of the component difficult. This separation of the address and data buses, in theory, allows the microprocessor to generate the address and data simultaneously,

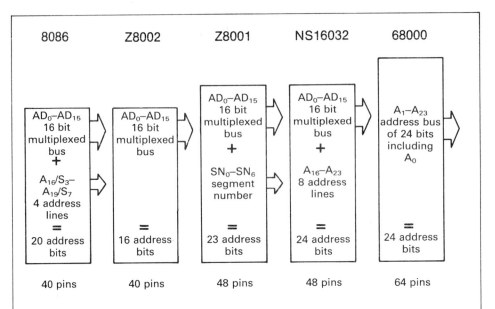

(a) Number of pins and address bits of 16 bit microprocessors

Characteristics	8086	Z8000	68000	NS16032
Number of bits of the internal data bus	16	16	32	32
Number of bits of the external data bus	16	16	16	16
Memory space without MMU	1 Mbyte	8 Mbytes	16 Mbytes	1 Mbyte
Memory space with MMU	1 Mbyte	48 Mbytes	16 Mbytes	16 Mbytes
I/O space separated from memory space	64 Kbytes	64 Kbytes	none	none
Instruction queue	6 bytes	yes	no	8 bytes
Management circuit for virtual memory	no	no	no	yes
Number of instruction types	111	110	56	86
Total number of instructions taking account of addressing modes, registers and the length of operands	300	410	> 1000	> 1000
8 bit version of the microprocessor	8088		68008	NS16008

(b) Characteristics of the four 16 bit microprocessors compared

FIGURE 1 *Characteristics of the 8086, Z8000, 68000 and NS16032 microprocessors*

which is not possible in the case of multiplexed address and data lines. The theoretical advantage is not as appreciable as might be imagined. In fact this simultaneity can be a bonus for write instructions but not for read instructions in which the data is received by the microprocessor and not sent. Writing is an operation which, statistically, occurs approximately eight times less frequently than reading. Furthermore, most memory circuits are incapable of receiving and processing the address and data at the same time. It is, however, beyond doubt that memory with multiplexed addresses suffers a delay which does not exist in the case of separate buses.

2. STANDARDIZATION OF REGISTERS

Certain concepts of 16 bit microprocessors are a successful generalization of the characteristics of 8 bit microprocessors, even if this generalization is not always complete, as in the attempt at 'standardization' of registers which will now be explained.

One of the weak points of 8 bit microprocessors, in connection with their programming, is the restricted number of registers and the specialization of these registers: a single accumulator for the 8080 and the 8085, a single index register for the 6800 and the 6802 and a single stack pointer for most of these 8 bit microprocessors. This weakness leads the programmer to frequent saving and restoration of the contents of a register. In addition to the regrettable lengthening of the program and its execution time, another disadvantage is the loss of continuity of the program which is no longer a faithful translation of the practical application. The power of the instruction set of 16 bit microprocessors, allowed principally by the availability of numerous multipurpose registers, causes this tedious aspect of programming of 8 bit microprocessors to disappear and is a bonus of 16 bits even when the application does not require the speed. The ideal solution is a set of general purpose registers, that is registers which can be used as data registers, accumulators, address registers, index registers and finally as pointers. In the case of such a structure, the registers are said to be 'generalized'. Specialized registers, in the case of the ideal solution, must be added to these generalized registers – a program counter, two or more stack pointers and a state register. Although no 16 bit microprocessor offers this ideal generalized register architecture, two of them are very close.

(a) The TMS9900, a first generation microprocessor designed by Texas, has sixteen general purpose 16 bit registers which can serve as data registers, accumulators, address registers and index registers but not as pointers. A feature of these registers is that they are located in RAM.

(b) The Z8000, a second generation microprocessor designed by Zilog, is even nearer to the ideal. Its architecture is globally generalized with a few small exceptions. It has sixteen general purpose 16 bit registers of which fifteen are generalized. Only the first register cannot be used as an index register or a pointer.

Two other second generation 16 bit microprocessors, the 16032 and the 68000, tend strongly towards the concept of a generalized architecture, without equalling the Z8000, which considerably eases the work of the programmer. The NS16032 has eight general purpose registers of 32 bits and some specialized registers. The 68000 has eight 32 bit registers intended for the manipulation of data (which can serve as auxiliary registers, accumulators and index registers) and seven registers of 32 bits intended for general addresses which can particularly serve as index registers. Of the second generation 16 bit microprocessors, the 8086 is the only one which does not offer a more or less generalized architecture; it has eight 16 bit registers which can serve as accumulators but each of these registers has a specialized function.

3. ORGANIZATION OF DATA

3.1 Organization of data in the registers

Normally, 8 bit microprocessors process data of 8 bits and exceptionally of 16 bits. With second generation 16 bit microprocessors the length of the data is much more varied since it can be, for optimum performance:

the bit;
the half byte or BCD digit (4 bits);
the byte (8 bits);
the 16 bit word which is understood as the traditional length of a 'word' without indicating its length, thereby implying 16 bits;
the 32 bit word or double word, called a 'long word' by Motorola (Figure 2);
exceptionally, a 64 bit word.

The organization of this data in the registers is an important point which arises in programming and which is illustrated with the help of Figures 2 and 3 from which several conclusions follow.

The 8086 is relatively poor in data registers. However, these registers replicate those of the 8080 and 8085 8 bit microprocessors, the 8086 being compatible, at source code level, with these two 8 bit microprocessors.

Second generation 16 bit microprocessors, except the 8086, process data of 8, 16 or 32 bits. The data length is defined by a letter added to the instruction's mnemonic expression for the 68000 and the NS16032 and integrated with the mnemonic expression for the Z8000.

The 68000 and the NS16032 have 32 bit data registers of which only the lower part is used for data of 8 or 16 bits. The part of the register which is not concerned is unchanged. This register architecture has the objective of 'orthogonality', that is a generalization of registers with respect to addressing modes and data length. Such a

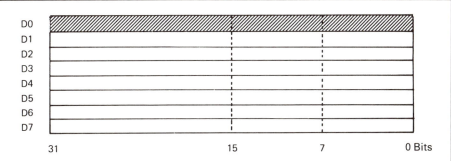

AX	AH	AL
BX	BH	BL
CX	CH	CL
DX	DH	DL

15 bits   7   0 bits

The four 16 bit registers enable formation of:
   4 registers of 16 bits
   or 8 registers of 8 bits
   or any possible combination

The length of the data is defined implicitly by the name of the register

8086

D0			
D1			
D2			
D3			
D4			
D5			
D6			
D7			

31   15   7   0 Bits

The eight 32 bit registers enable formation of:
   8 registers of 32 bits
   or 8 registers of 16 bits
   or 8 registers of 8 bits
   or any possible combination

The length of the data is defined explicitly by a suffix added to the operation code of the instruction if it is not contained implicitly.
B for 8 bits (byte), W for 16 bits (word) and L for 32 bits (long word).

Comment

Data of 8 or 16 bits is always stored in the low order part of the register. Each data register Dn can consist only of a single register whatever the length of the data, 8, 16 or 32 bits. This apparently inefficient use of data registers has been chosen by Motorola to make the instructions simple and powerful. Consequently, the mnemonic of an instruction for processing data is the same for the three types of data: byte, word or double word. Only the suffix changes.

68000

FIGURE 2 *Organization of data in the registers for the 8086 and the 68000*

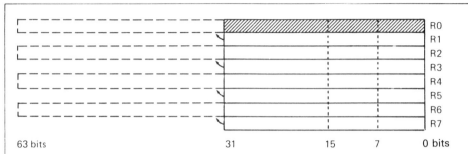

63 bits   31   15   7   0 bits

The eight 32 bit registers enable formation of:
  4 registers of 64 bits by associating the registers in pairs, e.g. R0–R1
  or 8 registers of 32 bits
  or 8 registers of 16 bits
  or 8 registers of 8 bits
  or any possible combination

The length of the data is defined by a suffix added to the operation code of the instruction:
B (8 bits), W (16 bits), D (32 bits); it is implicitly defined by the instruction when it is 64 bits.

As for the 68000, data of 8 or 16 bits is stored in the low order part.

NS16032

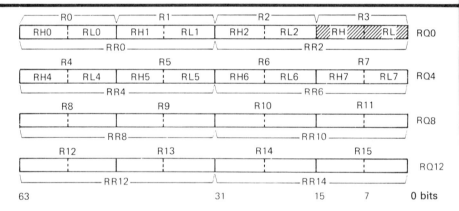

63   31   15   7   0 bits

The sixteen 16 bit registers, R0 to R15, enable formation of:
  4 registers of 64 bits by associating the registers in fours, e.g. RQ0 = R0–R1–R2–R3
  or 8 registers of 32 bits by associating the registers in pairs, e.g. RR0 = R0–R1
  or 16 registers of 16 bits, R0 to R15
  or 16 registers of 8 bits; each register R0 to R7 can be considered as two registers of 8 bits
  or any possible combination

When 2 or 4 registers R0 to R15 are associated to make a register of 32 or 64 bits, the register of lowest number contains the most significant bits.

The length of the data is defined by the mnemonic of the instruction.

Z8000

FIGURE 3 *Organization of data in the registers for the NS16032 and the Z8000*

philosophy leads to a large number of instructions from a small number of mnemonics. Hence each mnemonic expression corresponding to a data operation can almost always be combined with each of the data registers and with each of the operand lengths which give numerous instructions for a single mnemonic term. The result is evidently helpful to the programmer who has little to remember. By way of example, the instruction set of the 68000 reduces to only 56 types of instruction while that of the 6800 is 68. However the total number of instructions of the 68000 is greater than a thousand while that of the 6800 is 192.

3.2 Organization of data in memory

With second generation 16 bit microprocessors the organization of data in memory is carried out according to the following principles:

■ The unit of memory space addressing is always the byte
Thus if the address bus is of 20 bits (as in the case of the 8086), the hexadecimal address occurs between 00000 and FFFFF, which corresponds to a total number of 100000 bytes in hexadecimal notation or 16^5, that is 1,048,576, bytes in decimal.

■ The unit of transfer is the word or the byte
To achieve this the memory space is always organized as two memory subspaces of identical size. Thus an addressable memory space of 16 million bytes (as in the cases of the 68000 and the NS16032) is organized as two memory subspaces each of 8 million bytes. One of the subspaces corresponds to even addresses and the other to odd addresses. When the unit of transfer is a word, each memory subspace transfers a byte at the same time.

■ The 16 bit word can be represented in two ways
This organization of the memory space in two subspaces of which the addressing unit is the byte, gives two possibilities for storing a 16 bit word in memory. The more significant byte of the 16 bit word can be stored in the subspace relating to the even or odd address. In the first case, the data is represented in its natural order; this solution has been chosen for the 68000 and the Z8000. In the second case, the representation of data is inverted; to write 1984 in BCD it is necessary to write 84 first then 19. This solution has been retained for the 8086 and the NS16032. Figure 4 illustrates the organization of data in memory for second generation 16 bit microprocessors; a method for writing BCD words 1234 and 5678 is shown where the even addresses have been placed on the left (Figure 4(a)).

■ 16 bit words are aligned in memory space
This signifies that the addresses of words are even (Figure 4(b) and 4(c)); the address bit A_0 is therefore not used. The addresses of double words, if they exist, are also even. The four second generation 16 bit microprocessors follow this principle.

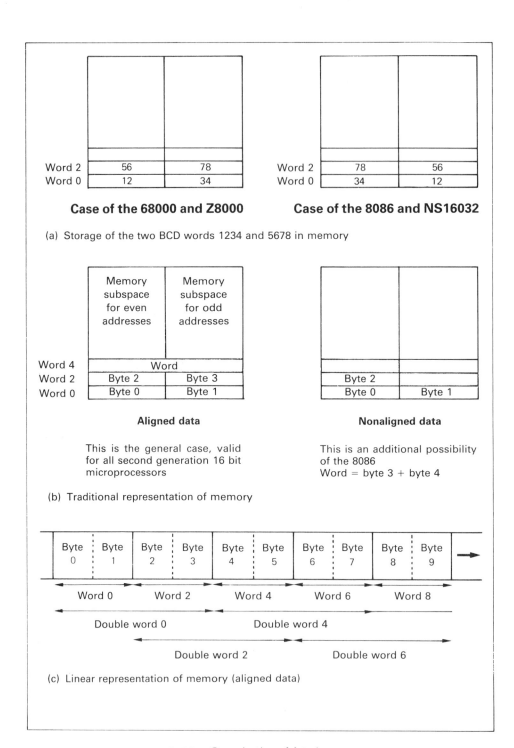

	56	78
Word 2	56	78
Word 0	12	34

Case of the 68000 and Z8000

	78	56
Word 2	78	56
Word 0	34	12

Case of the 8086 and NS16032

(a) Storage of the two BCD words 1234 and 5678 in memory

	Memory subspace for even addresses	Memory subspace for odd addresses
Word 4	Word	
Word 2	Byte 2	Byte 3
Word 0	Byte 0	Byte 1

Aligned data

This is the general case, valid for all second generation 16 bit microprocessors

	Byte 2	
	Byte 0	Byte 1

Nonaligned data

This is an additional possibility of the 8086
Word = byte 3 + byte 4

(b) Traditional representation of memory

| Byte 0 | Byte 1 | Byte 2 | Byte 3 | Byte 4 | Byte 5 | Byte 6 | Byte 7 | Byte 8 | Byte 9 | → |

Word 0   Word 2   Word 4   Word 6   Word 8

Double word 0   Double word 4

Double word 2   Double word 6

(c) Linear representation of memory (aligned data)

FIGURE 4 *Organization of data in memory*

However, and this is the only exception, the 8086 also accepts words of which the first byte is the odd address. In this case the two bytes of the 16 bit word are 'astride' the two aligned words (Figure 4(b)) which necessitates two successive transfers. The 8086 automatically controls the necessary number of transfers: one transfer if the address of the word is even and two transfers if it is odd. This internal operation is transparent to the programmer but transfer of a nonaligned word requires twice as long as that of an aligned word.

■ Each microprocessor provides two enabling signals for the memory subspaces
In order to enable one or both of the two memory subspaces, each microprocessor provides two signals of which one is often the address bit A_0. These signals must be connected to one of the enabling inputs of the memory devices if these have several. In Figure 5 the connections to be realized for the 8086, the Z8000, the 68000 and the NS16032 are shown assuming that the memory devices have enabling inputs CS (chip select) of which CS0 is used. These memory devices must receive at least one other CS command to define the writing area within the memory space.

4. INTERRUPTS AND THE TRACE MODE

The new features, in relation to interrupts, supported by 16 bit microprocessors are as follows.

■ Generalized vectoring of external inputs
In general, the microprocessor has several hierarchical interrupt pins of which one is vectored and valid for numerous external devices which can raise an interrupt demand.

This concept requires that each interrupt demand, arising from a peripheral or an external device must be followed on the data bus by a number which identifies the peripheral or external device.

This number, called the 'vector', can be generated either directly by the peripheral or its associated circuits or indirectly by an interrupt controller if this is designed to generate a vector, which is the case for the Intel 8259A. If an interrupt controller is not used, the peripherals or external devices must be equipped with a hierarchical priority structure, for it is strictly prohibited that two numbers should be deposited on the data bus at the same time followed by two simultaneous interrupt demands. One possible solution is 'daisy chaining'. The peripherals or external devices are connected together in series in a manner resembling the links of a chain. One of the ends of the chain has the highest priority. In the wait state, that is when there is no demand for an interrupt action, any peripheral or external device can raise an interrupt. But as soon as one has raised a demand, all possible interrupts originating from peripherals or external devices of lower priority are inhibited. One other possible solution is to use a priority encoder which provides the code of the demand of highest priority.

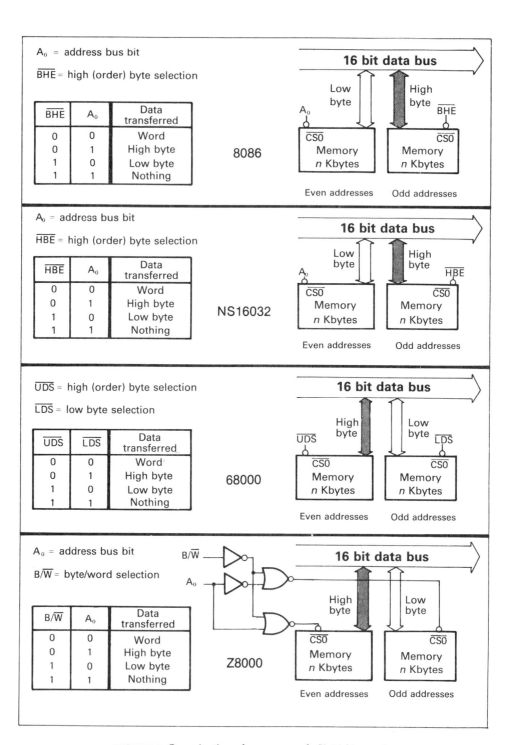

FIGURE 5 *Organization of a memory of nK 16 bit words*

The theoretical number of peripherals or external devices which can be connected in this way to the same interrupt pin is of the order of two hundred, which is considerable. When one of the peripherals activates its 'interrupt demand' output, the microprocessor, after executing the current instruction, saves the contents of the stack, the status register and the program counter in the usual way and then obtains the vector which identifies the peripheral which raised the interrupt demand from the data bus. Using this vector the microprocessor reads a subroutine address table relating to this vector and hence to the peripheral which raised the interrupt demand. Figure 6 explains the rerouting to subroutine SR2.

■ Generalization of a nonmaskable interrupt demand
Priority of a vectored interrupt demand is useful to indicate serious external events such as sector cutting, parity error, memory error, etc.

■ Extension of internal interrupts to exceptions
Apart from external interrupts, 8 bit microprocessors have an internal interrupt system of only one or a few software interrupts for which the demand initiative remains with the programmer. All second generation 16 bit microprocessors have been designed to generate an interrupt on their own initiative; this is new relative to 8 bit devices, when certain exceptional events occur which are external or internal to the microprocessor. These exceptional events are called 'traps' or 'exceptions'. The most common exceptions are:

  division by zero
  overflow
  abnormal access to a memory area
  an instruction which cannot be executed on account of the addressing mode or the
  operands.

Each exception is treated as an interrupt, that is it reroutes the program to a subroutine specific to the exception. This concept is of use to the programmer who is informed of his errors and can therefore foresee a consequent action at the subroutine level. An interrupt vector is assigned to each exception. The higher performance 16 bit microprocessors also allow the programmer to create his own exceptions. For example, for the 68000 all instructions whose operation code starts with 1010 or 1111 initiate an exception. The specific subroutine can act as a macro-instruction, that is a super-instruction consisting of a short program of several instructions. Furthermore, the 8086, the 68000 and the NS16032 have a 'trace mode' which does not exist with the classical 8 bit microprocessors such as the 8080, 8085, 6800, 6802, 6809, Z80, etc. After each instruction, the microprocessor tests a specific bit of the status register internally – the 'trace' bit. If this bit is zero it executes the following instruction, but if this bit is in the '1' state, it branches to a specific subroutine. In this subroutine the programmer can examine the registers in order to examine the operation 'step by step'. For the 68000 the trace mode in association with the 'halt' line allows 'cycle by cycle' operation. For the Z8000 the trace mode is obtained by activating one of the

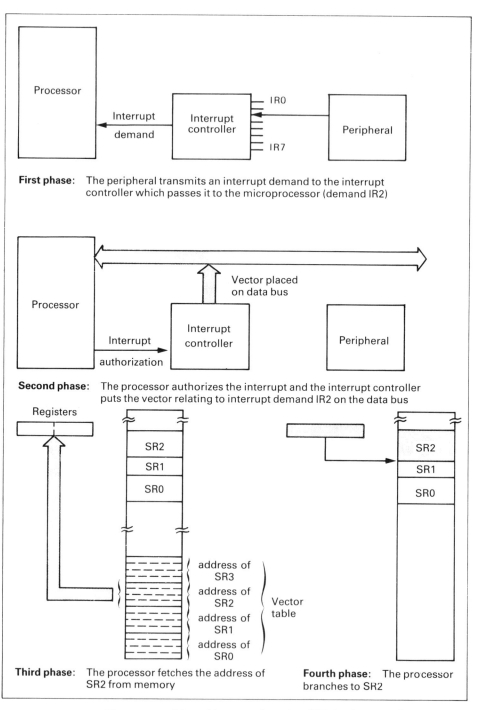

First phase: The peripheral transmits an interrupt demand to the interrupt controller which passes it to the microprocessor (demand IR2)

Second phase: The processor authorizes the interrupt and the interrupt controller puts the vector relating to interrupt demand IR2 on the data bus

Third phase: The processor fetches the address of SR2 from memory

Fourth phase: The processor branches to SR2

FIGURE 6 *The process of branching to subroutine SR2 in the case of an external interrupt (IR2 vector)*

microprocessor pins.

■ Grouping of the interrupt vectors in a table (Figure 6)
For the 8086 and the 68000 this table consists of 256 positions of 4 bytes starting from address zero. For the Z8000 and the NS16032 the position of the table in memory is defined by the contents of a pointer register. It is therefore the programmer who determines the location of this table.

5. THE OPERATING SYSTEM AND SUPERVISOR MODE

5.1 *The need for an operating system*

The software for a small practical application based on a microprocessor contains three distinct parts:

> The main program stored in ROM, PROM or EPROM.
> The data stored in RAM.
> The stack also stored in RAM.

The occupied part of the memory space, which is 64 Kbytes for an 8 bit microprocessor, is divided into three areas. A physical address, that is one of the 64K addresses, is allocated once and for all to these three areas (Figure 7). Notice that these areas can be extended if necessary. This division of the memory space into three areas assumes that the inputs and outputs (I/O) are processed by specific instructions as is the case for the 8085A and 8086. Otherwise a quarter of the memory space is allocated to I/O. In this section the former case will be assumed in order to simplify the notation which will be developed.

Returning to the small application where the memory space is divided into three areas, it is necessary to keep in mind the fact that during the execution cycle and operation of the application these three areas are stored in RAM. The problems which arise when the length of the practical application increases greatly, which is generally the case with 16 bit microprocessors, will now be discussed.

The established and continuing trend is for the complexity of applications in 'microprocessor systems' to increase. This complexity arises from one or more of the following points:

■ The large size of a single task single user application
Following the increasing complexity of microprocessor systems, a typical application which includes a program block, a data block and a stack block (area) has become much larger both at the program and data levels. In order to solve the problem most easily, the user (this term is used in the widest sense and includes the designer and the programmer) will divide the program into functional modules, thereby ensuring a

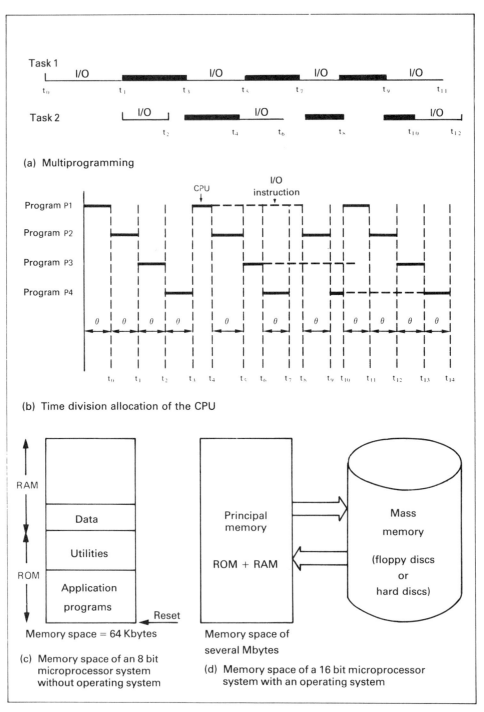

FIGURE 7 *Some operating system tools; multiprogramming, time division and mass memory*

function which is well defined and easy to implement. This can lead to a regrouping of data in files. A distinct memory area must be allocated to each module and to each file.

■ A single user multitask environment

The user may wish to process two or more tasks at the same time. As soon as a task requires numerous transfers between memory and a peripheral, the microprocessor becomes occupied for only a very small percentage of the time. Also, the user may wish to use this idle time profitably in order to carry out another task. This is particularly true at the design and commissioning stage of programs using a development system. Editing of a program from the console leaves the microprocessor free 99 percent of its time so it is tempting to profit from this situation by carrying out another task. This multitasking environment leads to at least one program area, one data area and one stack area per task being stored in memory. If a task is large, the user may separate it into modules and files, as mentioned, with a distinct memory area allocated to each. Figure 7(a) shows the benefit of multiprogramming in a multitasking environment for the case of two tasks T1 and T2.

■ A multiuser single task environment

The unoccupied time of the microprocessor in this case is used to allow several users to share the same microprocessor (Figure 7(b)). It is evident that, in the simple case where the task is sufficiently small not to be separated into modules and files, each user must have three distinct memory areas available: one for the program, one for the data and one for the stack. Each user may require several modules and files for his task. It follows that the memory must again be organized in numerous sections or areas.

The result, as has been seen, is that the memory must accommodate numerous program modules, numerous data areas and numerous stack areas. Each one of these elements to be accommodated in memory, program modules, files and stacks, can be given the general name of 'object'. The allocation of a memory area to each object cannot, of course, be carried out by the object itself; a program is necessary which must be located at a higher level and whose reliability must have been thoroughly tested. This program is called the 'operating system' or 'system' but it takes the more specific name of 'real time monitor' when it is used to control a process in 'real time'. This latter expression signifies that the response time to any event, an interrupt for example, must be adapted to this event, that is sufficiently short so that the process is not affected. This frequent use of the word 'system' in different senses makes it useful to recall certain definitions in order to avoid confusion.

A microprocessor system. This general term denotes a practical application controlled by one or more microprocessors.

An operating system. This is specialized software used to facilitate the operation of a complex or real time microprocessor system. It is software which is different from the user program. Companies which have designed microprocessors have also designed operating systems which they have marketed.

A development system. This is a microcomputer and associated peripherals whose purpose is to facilitate the design and application of a microprocessor system. The user normally makes use of several service programs to design and commission his microprocessor system, for example an editor, an assembler and one or more compilers.

5.2 Use of the operating system

An operating system is always involved in the design stage of a microprocessor system but may also be used at the operating stage.

5.2.1 Use of a monitor

■ Use of a monitor during design and commissioning
Microprocessor kits and personal computers using 8 bit microprocessors all have a small operating system called a 'monitor' whose length is often a few kilobytes. It is stored in ROM or EPROM and it provides the following four functions.

(a) Initialization of the processor when the RESET button is pressed. This function is essentially programming of the serial interface and supervision of supporting devices at the touch of a key.
(b) Making available to the user several basic functions called 'primitives' which are control subroutines for the peripherals and which are stored in memory at addresses called 'entry points'. Thus, there is a subroutine which returns the ASCII code of the character pressed on the keyboard to the accumulator. Another subroutine displays the character whose ASCII code has previously been loaded into the accumulator, or other register, on the console screen.
     Each primitive is a small piece of operating software for a peripheral without which the peripheral cannot be used. From these two primitives, the user can create other primitives which are used to control the microcomputor; one for program or data input into RAM, one for program execution, another for displaying the contents of an area of memory, etc.
(c) Servicing interrupts.
(d) Help in commissioning user's programs (debugging) by displaying the contents of registers after execution of an instruction by means of a subroutine specifically associated with a software interrupt.

■ Use of a monitor during operation of a microprocessor application
Most designs based on an 8 bit microprocessor do not use a monitor. Pressing RESET

automatically sets the program to its first address and this program boots itself. In contrast, in real time applications, it can be desirable or necessary to control the tasks by a real time monitor. The small memory space of 8 bit microprocessors does not necessitate an operating system to control the application; memory management does not pose any difficulty since the memory areas are fixed and therefore allocated once and for all. The programs and data together are often much less than the possible 64 Kbytes and there is therefore no need for mass memory (Figure 7(c)).

5.2.2 Use of an operating system

■ Use of an operating system during design and commissioning
Unlike kits and personal microcomputers which use a monitor, practical microprocessor applications are almost always designed with the help of a development system. The latter is a microcomputer equipped with peripherals and controlled by an operating system (OS) or disc operating system (DOS). In the case of a DOS a mass memory, consisting of a floppy or hard disc, is associated with the principal memory (RAM + ROM). The total memory space is considerably increased which allows some 40 Kbytes of DOS to be accommodated without difficulty (Figure 7(d)).

The operating system provides the basic functions of a monitor but also allocates resources to different tasks and schedules, the latter for activation either by an external interrupt or by the program. The basic software of a development system, in addition to the DOS, contains utilities such as a text editor, an assembler, a line editor, a loader, an interpreter, a compiler and an emulator (Figure 8). These service programs are long and consequently stored in mass memory.

The DOS commands and utilities are a very useful tool for microprocessor system design and application. However, the DOS of one manufacturer can have a better or worse performance than that of another.

■ Use of the operating system when the application is operational
With 16 bit microprocessor applications, the use of an operating system is necessitated by the length of the programs, dynamic memory management made necessary by the existence of mass memory and the desired protection of tasks operating in multitasking (multiprogramming) or multiuser mode (time-division). The operating system can take one of two forms – a real time monitor or an 'in-house' operating system.

A real time monitor is used in the following cases.

(a) Process control: response to events in an industrial process must be sufficiently rapid to guarantee security, equilibrium and correct operation of the process.
(b) File interrogation systems: these are characterized by a frequent interrogation of a large data file called a 'data base' and by the need for a real time response, that is a delay acceptable to the interrogator (of the order of a minute).

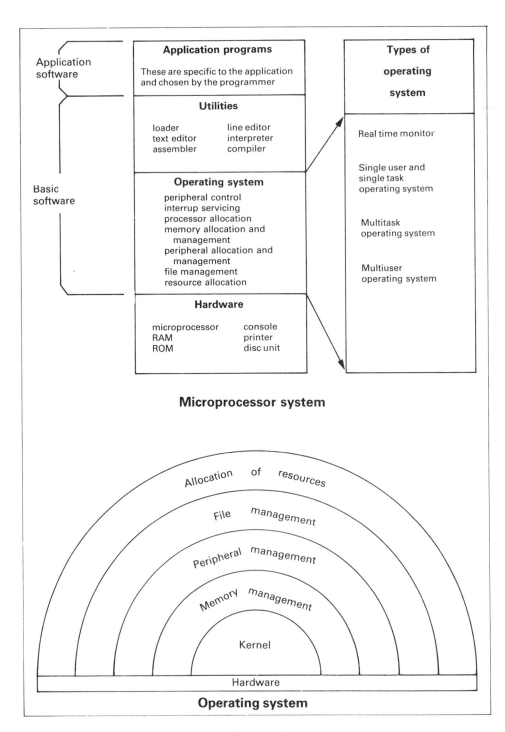

FIGURE 8 *Hierarchy of programs*

(c) Transaction systems characterized by very frequent use and numerous terminals, such as place reservation. It is imperative that a given place cannot be reserved at the same time by two agents. A response with a delay acceptable to the customer is of course necessary.

An in-house operating system is used in the following cases.

(a) Batch processing: the tasks to be executed are stored in order of their arrival for processing in a batch without interruption of a task which is being executed.
(b) A multitask environment: multiprogramming and allocation of resources are necessary, two complex functions which necessitate a DOS.
(c) A multiuser environment: time division allocation of the processor necessitates an operating system. There is apparent simultaneity of operation, each user has the impression that he is the sole user of the system.
(d) A multiprocessor environment: the various tasks are allocated to several microprocessors, which at times involves use of the same peripheral by several microprocessors. There is real simultaneity of processing. Here again only an operating system can manage the complex functions such as control of priorities and allocation of resources.

In Figure 8 the hierarchy of programs for a microprocessor application with an operating system is given. The latter has the highest priority and the user programs the lowest priority. A common representation of an operating system with the hierarchy of the different software is also given.

The 'kernel' consists essentially of the synchronization primitive for the running of tasks in multitasking systems and of a processor allocation primitive. It has the highest priority.

5.3 The semaphore concept

5.3.1 Historical evolution of operating systems

■ Channels and multiprogramming

The principal reason which motivated the concept of operating systems is the large difference in processing speed between the central processing unit and the peripherals. Although the central processing unit executes an instruction in less than a microsecond, a peripheral requires 2 to 10 milliseconds to receive or transmit data. This factor of 10,000 leads to a very poor rate of utilization of the central processing unit when the program contains numerous input/outputs. An initial remedy to this problem has been to construct highly developed interface circuits between the central processing unit and each peripheral. These circuits called 'channels' are really special processors containing buffer memories. The channel can read or write into a buffer memory while the central processing unit processes data from another buffer memory. The second remedy is 'multiprogramming' where the principle is to profit from an input/output transfer of one program to execute central processing of a second program. If the latter also requires an input/output transfer, the central processing unit is transferred to a third program. But two programs can require the same peripheral or the same memory space; it is therefore necessary that the operating system ensures allocation of resources which include the processor, the memory and the peripherals.

■ Multiprocessing and communication between tasks

With multiprocessor systems, matters become complicated since several processors can request access to the same peripheral or memory area.

For certain resources it is essential that the service required, during execution of a task, should be completely finished before another processor can gain access to the same resource. In a place reservation system it could happen that two agencies request the same place at a given instant. If a place remains available, interrogation of the file by the two agencies apparently simultaneously leads each one to reserve the seat. To avoid such a conflict, access to the memory area which contains the available places and which is in continuous operation must not be possible for a second processor unless the first has signalled that it no longer requires this memory area. In the case described, the service required of the memory consisted of the following procedures.

(a) A read operation to determine whether a place is available and under what conditions.
(b) An unoccupied time of the memory when no other processor can gain access. During this time the agency consults its customer to determine whether he wishes to make the reservation.
(c) Final modification of the memory area if the customer accepts the place.

Such resources which are not accessible to several processors with apparent simultaneity are called 'indivisible'; these are peripherals, files available for writing and data areas which can be modified. It follows that access to an indivisible resource by a task must involve exclusion of all other access to this resource; this is the principle of 'mutual exclusion'. One more function for the operating system!

In the context of multiprocessing, to which a multiprocessor system leads, tasks executed truly simultaneously are asynchronous. However, when these tasks require a common resource, the processors must synchronize their activities. Consider the example of processor A executing a task which consists of making calculations then outputting listings which include the results of these calculations. When processor A requires the printer it is possible that it is already occupied by another processor B. In this case it is necessary to wait until processor B finishes using the printer.

According to the execution of tasks by these two processors, the situation can reverse, B having to wait until A has finished. This new function which must be added to the operating system is 'synchronization'.

Multiprocessing can lead to a 'blocking' situation when two processors A and B both need resources 1 and 2 at the same time. If resource 1 had been allocated to processor A at a moment when resource 2 was not available, processor A must wait until resource 2 is free. If this had been specifically allocated to processor B, the latter must wait until resource 1 becomes available. The situation is therefore blocked.

To ensure mutual exclusion functions and synchronization of the processors while avoiding blockages in a multiprocessor environment, Dijkstra in 1965 proposed the concept of 'semaphores' which have since been used in operating systems and will now be examined.

5.3.2 Definition and function of a semaphore

A semaphore, in simplified form, is a logical variable S associated with a critical, that is indivisible, resource and with which the following are associated.

(a) A queue F to store the tasks which have required the resource without being able to obtain it.
(b) An operation P which sets the semaphore to '1' ('wait' operation).
(c) An operation V which sets the semaphore to '0' ('signal' operation).

A '0' value of the semaphore indicates that the resource is available, a '1' value indicates, of course, that the resource is occupied. Each task which requests the resource does so starting with operation P which is in practice controlled by a primitive.

This operation P carries out the following:

(a) The task which requires the resource tests S.
(b) If S = 0, S is set to one and the resource is allocated to the task with the highest priority, that is the first in the queue if this is not empty or the task which requested the resource in the case when the queue is empty.

If S – 1 the file is put in the queue and blocked. Each task which releases the critical resource after having used it does so by operation V which is a primitive and which carries out the following:

(a) S is set to '0', which means the end of use of the resource.
(b) The task of highest priority is extracted from the queue and activated.

In practice, putting a task into, and extracting it from the queue are controlled by two other primitives.

Figure 9 illustrates an example of the use of a semaphore with a queue containing up to two tasks B and C.

Comment. Gaining of a resource by operation P is normally an indivisible 'read' sequence (of the value of the semaphore) – 'modification' (setting to '1' of this value in the accumulator) – 'write' (of the value '1' into the semaphore which can be a register or a memory location).

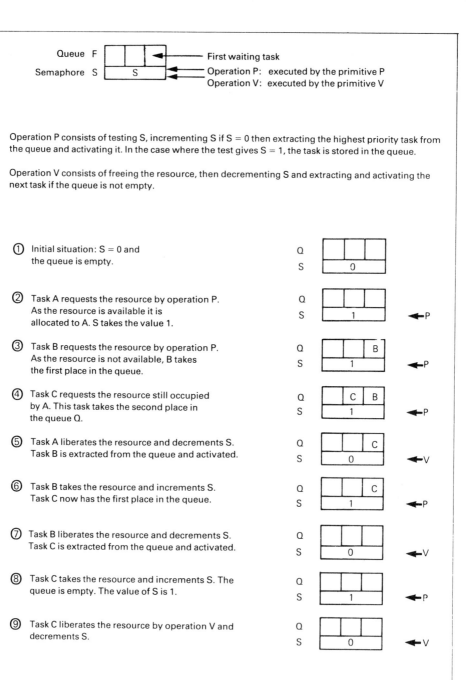

Queue F — First waiting task
Semaphore S — Operation P: executed by the primitive P
Operation V: executed by the primitive V

Operation P consists of testing S, incrementing S if S = 0 then extracting the highest priority task from the queue and activating it. In the case where the test gives S = 1, the task is stored in the queue.

Operation V consists of freeing the resource, then decrementing S and extracting and activating the next task if the queue is not empty.

① Initial situation: S = 0 and the queue is empty.

② Task A requests the resource by operation P. As the resource is available it is allocated to A. S takes the value 1.

③ Task B requests the resource by operation P. As the resource is not available, B takes the first place in the queue.

④ Task C requests the resource still occupied by A. This task takes the second place in the queue Q.

⑤ Task A liberates the resource and decrements S. Task B is extracted from the queue and activated.

⑥ Task B takes the resource and increments S. Task C now has the first place in the queue.

⑦ Task B liberates the resource and decrements S. Task C is extracted from the queue and activated.

⑧ Task C takes the resource and increments S. The queue is empty. The value of S is 1.

⑨ Task C liberates the resource by operation V and decrements S.

Semaphore, S; queue, Q; operator, P; operator, V

FIGURE 9 *Example of operation of a semaphore in the simplified case where it reduces to one logical variable*

■ Different states of a task

The concept of the semaphore arose in order to guarantee the integrity of the system when a task requests a resource in a multiprocessor environment. This integrity is assured only by regulating all resource demands which means that a task must wait and 'take the queue' before being serviced. Also a task can be in one of several states which will now be defined.

(a) An 'active task' is one which makes the required resources available to a processor. In other words, it is a task being executed.
(b) An 'eligible task' is one to which all the required resources are available except one – the processor.
(c) A 'blocked task' has a processor but waits for the availability of a resource which it needs at the end of an operation. The task is said to be 'waiting'.
(d) A 'dormant task' is not waiting for anything and is not running.

An active task goes to the blocked state after an unsatisfied resource demand. It goes to a state which can be activated when it is obliged to free the processor for the benefit of a task of higher priority (preemption). Figure 10 shows all the possible state transitions.

The information necessary to activate a task, that is to put it into an active state, is called the 'context'. The context clearly includes the address of the first instruction to be executed to start or restart the task and, if necessary, other information such as the contents of the processor registers. The information relating to a task, that is the name of the task, its state and its context are stored in a memory area called 'task description'.

■ Mutual exclusion and the semaphore

Indivisible resources are protected from apparently simultaneous access by several tasks if the following three conditions are observed

(a) All sections of a program which authorize access to an indivisible resource are declared to be 'critical sections'.
(b) Each critical section is allocated a semaphore exclusive to that section.
(c) Each critical section must start with the primitive P allocated by the semaphore to this section and finish with the primitive V which applies to the same semaphore.

In this way as soon as a task A has been allocated to a critical resource it sets the semaphore of this resource to '1', prohibiting any other task B from taking the resource. Only restoration of the resource by the task setting its semaphore to '0' allows another task to gain access. The critical section must, of course, be executed without any interruption. This can be achieved in several ways.

(a) By prohibiting all interrupts during execution of primitives P and V and the critical section.
(b) By a latching function 'lock'. Thus, for the 8086, all instructions preceded by the

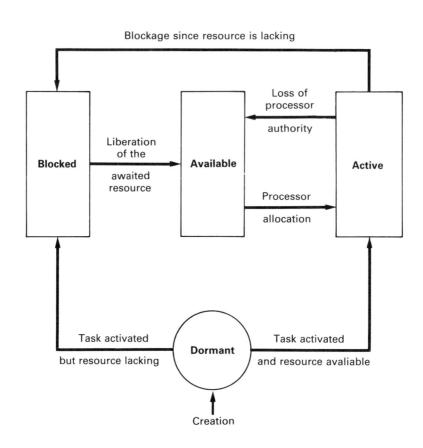

A task is dormant if it is neither being executed nor in a wait state for a resource or a processor.

A task is blocked (or 'waiting') if a resource is lacking. In this case a processor is not allocated to it.

A task is available (or 'activatable') if it has the required resource but a processor is not available.

A task is active if the awaited resource (or resources) and a processor are available to it.

A dormant task is activated by an operating system command.

FIGURE 10 *The various states of a task (or 'process')*

8086

```
              MOV         AL, 1           ;  ⎫ The value of the semaphore is
Wait  :       LOCK XCHG   AL, SEMAPHORE ; ⎪ tested and set to 1 to prohibit all
              TEST        AL, AL          ;  ⎬ other access to the resource
              JNZ         WAIT            ;  ⎪ If the semaphore was already at
                                             ⎭ '1' wait in a loop
              _____  ⎫                       Otherwise use the resource
              _____  ⎪ critical section      (critical section)
              _____  ⎬
              _____  ⎪ (use of the resource)
              _____  ⎭

              MOV         SEMAPHORE, 0    ;  Reset the semaphore to '0' to
                                             free the resource
```

(a) Access to a resource protected by a semaphore in the case of the 8086

68000

```
Wait          TAS         Semaphore
              BNE         Wait

              _____  ⎫
              _____  ⎪ Use of the resource
              _____  ⎬
              _____  ⎭
              CLR         Semaphore
```

(b) Access to a resource protected by a semaphore in the case of the 68000

FIGURE 11 *Program for access to a resource protected by a semaphore for the 8086 and 68000 microprocessors*

prefix 'lock' forbid every processor except that which has control of the bus to access the bus and hence all system resources. Figure 11(a) gives an example of the use of this function to allocate a resource under the control of a semaphore. The latter is a memory location initialized to '0' and given the name 'semaphore'.

(c) By a 'test and set' instruction which, in a single operation, tests and modifies the contents of a memory location and hence of a semaphore if this is represented by a memory location. During execution of the instruction, access to this memory location is automatically prohibited to all processors other than that which is executing the instruction. The 68000 microprocessor provides this instruction whose mnemonic code is TAS. Figure 11(b) gives an example of the use of this instruction to allocate a resource under the control of a semaphore. The latter is a memory location called 'semaphore'.

■ Synchronization and semaphores

Use of the semaphore concept allows tasks which use the same indivisible resource to be synchronized. To be specific, consider as an example the printing of the contents of a memory area using a printer with two buffer memories each having the capacity of one line of text. While the content of one memory buffer is printed, the processor can write another line into the other buffer memory. Thus, at a given instant, one buffer is being read and the other is available for writing; then when the latter is full it is read while the first becomes available for writing. There is an alternation of role of the two buffers with each printing of a line of text, this alternation is realized by electronic circuits. Let the buffer which is available for writing at a given instant be called the 'write buffer'. Let the buffer which is being read at the same time by the printer, or is available for this function, be called the 'read buffer'.

The pair of buffers forms a unit with a single input/output bus; a single task can have access to this pair at a given instant either for writing or reading but not for both operations simultaneously.

To ensure a mutual exclusion of these two operations a semaphore which will be called S-FREE (buffers free) is allocated to the buffers. A second semaphore which will be called S-WBE (write buffer empty) is allocated to the state of the write buffer. A third and last semaphore which will be called S-RBF (read buffer full) is allocated to the state of the read buffer.

These semaphores are initialized as follows:

S-FREE = 0,   S-WBE = 0,   S-RBF = 1

The part of the program which relates to writing a line into the write buffer is declared to be a critical section, as is that which relates to reading a line into the read buffer.

These critical sections are presented in the following form:

```
; Write program                      ; Read program
BEGIN 1                              BEGIN 2
    PRIMITIVE P (S-WBE)                  PRIMITIVE P (S-RBF)
    PRIMITIVE P (S-FREE)                 PRIMITIVE P (S-FREE)
      write one line                       read one line
      into the write                       from the read
      buffer                               buffer and print
    PRIMITIVE V (S-FREE)                 PRIMITIVE V (S-FREE)
    PRIMITIVE V (S-RBF)                  PRIMITIVE V (S-WBE)
    JUMP BEGIN 1                         JUMP BEGIN 2
```

A mechanism for interrogating interrupts must be added to these critical sections.

■ Blocking and the semaphore

It has been seen that the concept of the semaphore yields a satisfactory solution to the first two problems of multiprocessing or the multiprocessor environment; mutual exclusion and synchronization. The third problem, knowledge of blocked tasks, is much more difficult to resolve. However, certain algorithms have been proposed to provide a solution to this problem:

To prevent blockages by making them totally impossible.

To detect and correct blockages.

To anticipate a possible blockage and allocate resources in order to avoid it.

5.4 Software and the operating system functions

5.4.1 The kernel

■ Programs forming the kernel

The service programs closest to the hardware are very often used; they must be as short as possible which is the reason why they are always written in assembler language. These are described below.

The module which controls interrupts. This control most often includes the saving of registers and the process of branching to appropriate subroutines.

The primitives P and V associated with the semaphores. These primitives are a useful tool for the protection of resources and particularly memory areas.

The scheduler. This module, also called a 'low level distributor', has the function of sharing the available processor time between the different tasks which are being executed 'apparently' at the same time (apparent simultaneity). It has been seen that these tasks can be in one of the three following states: active, available or blocked. It has also been seen that the information relating to a task is contained in a description of the task also called the state vector. The active tasks are grouped in the form of an ordered queue of decreasing priorities called the 'operation queue'. An interrupt destined to activate a task involves modification of the state of this task in its description and a change in the operation queue.

The role of the scheduler is to find the task with the highest priority in the operation queue and to update the task descriptions. Thus, if a task passes from an active to an available state the scheduler must save the contents of the program counter and other registers in its description, that is the context.

■ Storing the kernel in memory

The operating system is too important to be stored in active memory. It is stored in mass memory (backing memory) where it is divided into modules consisting of 'objects', in the general sense which has been given to this term. As a program or data file cannot be used in mass memory the operating system transfers the objects which it needs at a given time into random access memory (RAM). But for this it is necessary that the program which operates the transfer should be in RAM. Also when an operating system is used there are always two distinct parts.

(a) A 'resident' part, that is stored in ROM. It is called the 'supervisor' and consists at least of the kernel and the 'loader' which has the task of transferring objects from the mass memory into RAM (Figure 12).

(b) A 'non-resident' part stored in RAM. Modules of this part are transferred into RAM when necessary. Similarly, certain new or modified files are transferred from RAM to the mass memory. These changes are called 'swapping' (Figure 12).

Comment 1. The term 'supervisor' has been used from the creation of the first operating systems. Since then the size of the supervisor has continuously increased. When this size is large, only the essential part is resident.

Comment 2. The resident part can equally be stored in RAM. In this case a small program called the 'initial loader' is stored in ROM. The only function which it can fulfill is to transfer into RAM the loader program which has been defined above and which is itself capable of transferring any object into RAM. When the RESET button is activated the processor automatically branches to the first instruction of the 'initial loader' program.

■ Hardware mechanisms associated with the kernel

It has already been seen that the kernel is the software closest to the hardware. To ensure reliability of the functions which are the responsibility of the kernel, some hardware mechanisms are integrated on to the chip of second generation 16 bit microprocessors. They will be considered in turn.

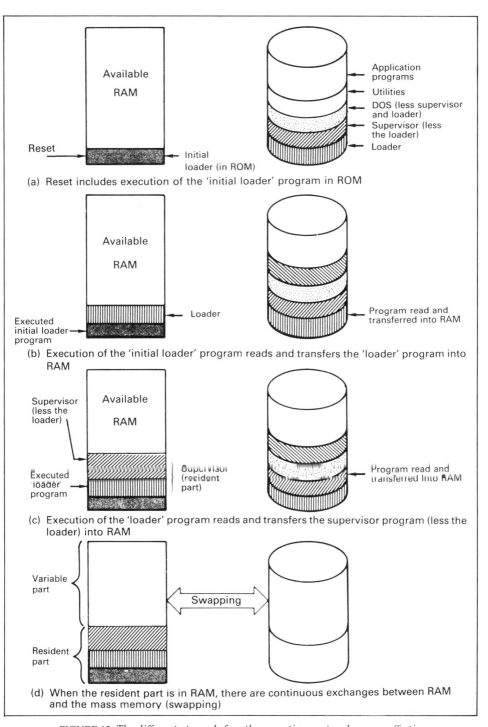

(a) Reset includes execution of the 'initial loader' program in ROM

(b) Execution of the 'initial loader' program reads and transfers the 'loader' program into RAM

(c) Execution of the 'loader' program reads and transfers the supervisor program (less the loader) into RAM

(d) When the resident part is in RAM, there are continuous exchanges between RAM and the mass memory (swapping)

FIGURE 12 *The different stages before the operating system becomes effective*

The interrupt mechanism. This already existed with 8 bit microprocessors; it has been improved for 16 bit microprocessors by the inclusion of a vector table and the existence of internal interrupts.

Memory protection. This is achieved by separation of the memory space into distinct address spaces (program, data, stack) and by giving the operating system a higher level of service and priority – the 'supervisor mode' – in contrast to the lower level of service which the user must accept and which is called 'user mode'.

Privileged instructions. A set of privileged instructions is reserved for the supervisor by a hardware mechanism which determines the mode of service from the instruction code at each instant: supervisor or user. Every instruction can be used by the operating system in supervisor mode. When the user tries to use a privileged instruction there is a 'violation of privilege' which generally leads to an internal interrupt and hence a rerouting of the program. Notice that every interrupt puts the system into supervisor mode. Equally there are calling instructions for the supervisor which switch the processor into supervisor mode and which are accessible to the user.

5.4.2 Memory management software

The design of 16 bit microprocessors allows for elaborate memory management: segmentation or virtual memory. It is the operating system which ensures transfer of objects from the mass memory to RAM or the reverse in the case of writing to disc from a file. It is also the operating system which will manage the storing in physical memory of different objects which are transferred there, a function known as 'memory allocation' which will be discussed later.

5.4.3 Peripheral management software

There are 'indivisible' peripherals which must not be interrupted during execution of their application subroutine. The printer is one example. Other peripherals are divisible, this is the case with a disc unit. In a multiprocessor environment a semaphore will always be associated with a peripheral. The control of this semaphore will be slightly different in the case of divisible and indivisible resources.

Control of the physical mechanism of a peripheral is realized by a special primitive called a 'device handler'. This primitive also controls the semaphore of the associated queue, following various P operations (also called 'wait operations') and V operations (also called 'signal operations').

The user calls an I/O subroutine (more frequently called an 'input/output procedure') using a 'call-supervisor'. This is an operating system command with the necessary parameters: name of the procedure, type of operation, source or destination if any, possible number of characters and address of the semaphore which must indicate the end of the procedure. These parameters are stored in the task description associated with the I/O procedure (the latter being a type of task).

5.4.4 File management software

When the peripheral is a printer or a magnetic tape store, the associated task description parameters are sufficient. In contrast, in the case of a disc unit more information is necessary and it is preferable to group the programs or data in 'files' by associating a file description with each one. This contains the drive number, the side of the disc, the number of the sector and track where the first character is stored, the number of characters to be transmitted, the first memory address where the first byte is to be read or written, etc. A catalogue of files, called the 'directory', is set up to give the corresponding physical address of each filename.

The existence of files is controlled by numerous commands which are again procedures:

The procedure for opening a file.
The procedure for closing a file.
The procedure for erasing a file.
The procedure for changing the name of a file.
The procedure for copying a file, etc.

5.4.5 The scheduler

As would be expected, the abundance and complexity of the operating system software makes a general coordination of the execution of tasks and the allocation of resources necessary by means of particular software. Interruption of a task following a demand of higher priority means that at a given instant several tasks are waiting for service. Managing the priority of these concurrent tasks as a function of available resources and avoiding blocking situations as far as possible is a difficult task which is accomplished by other operating system software, the 'scheduler'. Several algorithms have been proposed for this function such as priority of the shortest task, rotating priority and a two level queue. These algorithms cannot be described in this work.

In this brief description of an operating system an attempt has been made to acquaint the reader with the computing concepts which are found with 16 bit microprocessors – the supervisor mode and privileged instructions, semaphores and specific instructions (prefixed by 'lock' for the 8086 and the 'test and set' (TAS) instruction of the 68000).

Comment. A trend in microprocessor design is to include a read only memory containing either a small operating system or the kernel of a larger operating system in the microprocessor itself. These software instructions in the silicon (one speaks of 'siliconized' software!) have been included in the Intel APX432 32 bit microprocessor and the Texas Instruments 99120 microprocessor. The designers have also tended to include the compiler or interpreter of a high level language in the silicon, on the microprocessor chip. In this way National Semiconductor has integrated a BASIC interpreter on to the chip of its 8073 8 bit microcontroller.

6. MEMORY ALLOCATION

6.1 Static and dynamic memory allocation

The problem of memory allocation arises when the user's object code and the operating system occupy a space greater than that of the physical memory. Although 16 bit microprocessors allow a physical memory of several million bytes, it is often preferable to associate a mass memory with a read/write memory of reasonable size and the problem of memory allocation arises.

Read/write memory occupies the largest part of the physical memory space and it is use of this read/write memory which constitutes memory allocation. At initialization the operating system transfers a certain number of objects into the read/write memory. Afterwards some of these objects become unused while other objects situated in the mass memory become necessary in read/write memory. Also, the system tries to exploit memory areas made available by objects which become unused by putting necessary objects in their place. This 'reallocation', or 'relocation', of the memory does not involve the return of unused objects from read/write memory to the mass memory. In fact all the objects in mass memory remain permanently stored since mass memory is nonvolatile. Furthermore, to write something into RAM it is not necessary that the initial contents of the RAM should be zero; the new program overwrites its predecessor. In the course of time this first 'reallocation' of the memory will be followed by several others. Two possible solutions to the problem will now be examined; static and dynamic memory allocation.

6.1.1 Static memory allocation

The first approach to the problem of memory allocation is to allocate a memory area to each object at the time of initialization by assigning a physical address to each object which defines the first real address of this object. Since the allocated memory areas are fixed, 'reallocations' are made by loading objects which have become necessary in place of objects which have become unused. This simple approach has two principal problems – the risk of access to forbidden memory and fragmentation of the memory. These will be explained for a simple case, that of a single user application. It is evident that in a multitask or multiuser environment the magnitude of these problems is increased.

■ The risk of access to forbidden memory
Assuming that program and data are located sequentially from the first address, it is customary to locate the stack area starting from the last address since it extends towards lower addresses.

A modification of the program can extend this area by several instructions and hence erase data. Larger extensions of the program and data often occur when the program is put to use. If the memory is just sufficient it can happen that the stack erases some data in memory. To avoid such forbidden access, it is possible to provide software protection but that makes a test necessary at the time of each memory access or at least at the time of each access to the stack. The result is a higher design cost and a lower speed.

■ Fragmentation of memory

Assume, for a single user application, that the read/write memory is filled by five objects of which some are part of the operating system. Assume also that objects 2 and 5 are no longer useful and that it is required to transfer objects 6 and 7, which have sizes as indicated in Figure 13(a), into RAM. Object 6, which is shorter than object 2, leaves a free memory area which is not negligible but not big enough for object 7. The latter cannot take the place of object 5 which was smaller than object 7. However, the total of the two unoccupied memory areas is greater than the length of object 7. The unoccupied memory area is fragmented (Figure 13). As more objects are transferred into RAM, the unoccupied memory space becomes more fragmented. The solution is to place certain objects in several linked sub-blocks, each one containing references to the following sub-block. Extension of an object can also be made by the overlay technique. These two problems of static memory allocation are avoided by dynamic memory allocation.

6.1.2 Dynamic memory allocation

This concept implies the possibility of relocating an object anywhere in read/write memory after the initial loading of the program into memory. Partitioning of the memory is no longer fixed; it changes as the programs run. For this the operating system tries to make best use of the memory space by locating objects necessary for the execution of tasks end to end in memory.

The unoccupied area of memory is therefore in a single block and the problem of memory fragmentation disappears. Of course dynamic allocation depends on the possibility of moving objects within read/write memory relatively easily.

6.2 Translation of programs

Dynamic allocation of read/write memory can be made all the more easily because translation of programs is easy. There are several stages in this movement facility which at times seem to be confused. To avoid this confusion, the different stages will be defined in this section by giving the characteristics, requirements and finally an example of each one. A relocatable program will first be defined in order to distinguish it from a translatable program. This is then followed by a translatable program, a program 'with code independent of its position in memory' (PIC), a reentrant program and a recursive program.

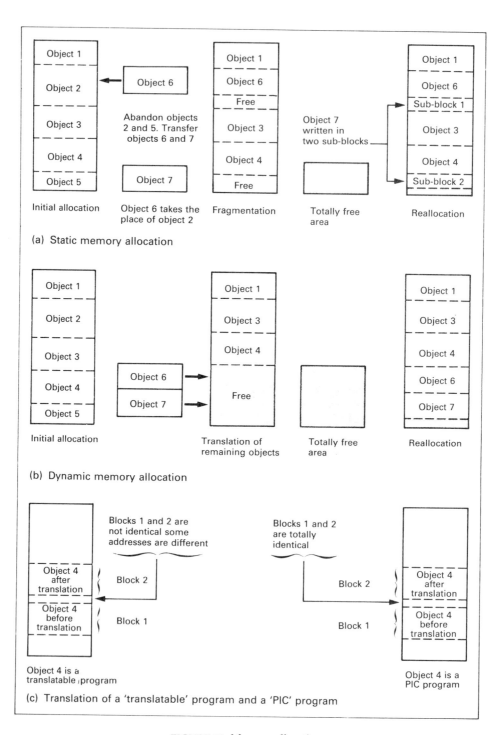

FIGURE 13 *Memory allocation*

■ Relocatable programs

The concept of relocatable programs is generally associated with that of the linking editor which is a useful facility offered by some development systems. The user can design his microprocessor system in a modular fashion, each module being part of the program or possibly data. These modules can be edited, assembled or compiled separately but the resulting object code is not executable. The reference address of the module, that is its first address, is zero. All other addresses relating to the module are expressed with respect to the zero reference. However, the module can contain references to addresses situated in other modules and recognized by their name, as in the case of a unique program. The linking program editor carries out the following operations.

(a) It groups the 'program' and 'data' parts of the different modules by putting them end to end according to an order imposed by the programmer.
(b) It converts the relative addresses of each module into absolute addresses by adding the absolute address attributed to the module to each relative address; that is the value zero, arbitrarily allocated to the first address of the module, is replaced.
(c) It calculates the absolute address of module names; the addresses of these names are situated in other modules and form entry points.

This translation of addresses relative to absolute addresses is carried out by a special small program called a 'relocatable loader'. After this translation the program and data exist as executable object code in read/write or read only memory. The purpose of the linking editor is to allow the programmer a modular design for his application. Reassembly of a module, necessitated for example by a modification to the program, does not involve the need to reassemble all the modules.

■ Translatable programs

In a translatable program all branches, whether conditional or not, are made to an address with respect to the value of the program counter at the time of execution of the branch instruction. This address mode exists in certain 8 bit microprocessors, the 6800 for example, but the displacement is limited to -128 and $+127$ which necessitates the use of absolute addresses. In contrast, 16 bit microprocessors offer a relative address with respect to the program counter with a displacement from $-65,535$ to $+65,534$, which is favorable to the concept of translatable programs.

The addresses of the I/O ports are absolute and fixed, whether or not they are part of the memory space. They do not cause any difficulty. In contrast, a program uses data and its translation is less simple than for branch addresses. It is the same for the addresses of memory locations used to store intermediate or final results. For clarification these addresses will be treated in the same way as data. There are several possibilities.

(a) The data are expressed by the absolute addresses whose location in physical memory is unalterable. In this case translation of a program with its data addresses does not pose any difficulty. However, this solution is a constraint since it reduces the memory space available for dynamic allocation of objects.

(b) The data are expressed by absolute addresses whose location in physical memory can be modified by the operating system. Translation of a program then necessitates recalculation of all absolute addresses which does not facilitate dynamic memory allocation. However, it is possible to group all the data at adjacent addresses in one memory area and to access this data by indexed addressing. For this an index register is allocated to this area and it contains the first address of the area. Access to the nth data in the area is obtained by taking $n - 1$ as the displacement. Thus the instructions

$$\text{LDA } 0,X \quad \text{and} \quad \text{LDA } 4,X$$

read the first and fifth data values respectively. Translation of all the data is simply achieved by changing the value of the index X.

(c) The data are contained in a memory area and their addresses are expressed relative to a base address contained in a base register. This is the case of pagination and segmentation, two techniques used with 16 bit microprocessors which will be examined in subsequent sections. Furthermore, with these techniques branch addresses can also be expressed relative to another base register. The relative address is contained in the program counter. As for the preceding case, translation of a program involves only a change of the contents of the two base registers to modify the addresses.

(d) This case consists of two subroutines (or procedures) for which the true data, called 'parameters' or 'arguments', are transmitted by registers. Intermediate and final results are stored either in registers or in the stack. Translation of subroutines does not require any address modification; it is therefore very easy.

(e) This consists of subroutines for which the parameters are transmitted by the stack. Intermediate and final results are also stored on the stack. For this the address of the stack pointer is transferred to an index register and the memory locations of this stack constitute a working area (scratch pad memory) addressed by the index register. As in the preceding case, translation of subroutines does not require any address modifications which greatly facilitates dynamic memory allocation.

■ 'Position independent code' programs
These are translatable programs for which the object code is unchanged after translation. In the literature these programs are described as 'PIC' or 'ROMable'. The latter arises from the fact that these programs can be put into a ROM which can be located anywhere in the physical memory. The CS address of the ROM package determines the address location of the ROM. Cases (a), (c) (on condition that the programs do not contain instructions to load the base registers), (d) and (e) belong to this category of programs. The condition to be satisfied is, of course, that no address modification should be involved during translation.

■ Reentrant programs
Consider a subroutine called by the main program and interrupted during execution by a priority interrupt whose routine calls this same subroutine. If the latter can be

interrupted and continue to be executed as if it had not been interrupted, it is described as 'reentrant'. This situation can occur in the context of hierarchical interrupts and also in a multiuser environment as a consequence of time-division processing. If this subroutine is long, only a part is executed during the time slot allocated to one user. It could be that the following user is also using this subroutine in his time slot.

Reentrance assumes that the parameters and the working area are stored in registers and/or in a memory area situated in the stack and unique to each calling program. In 16 bit microprocessors the programmer, using pagination or segmentation, is allowed to choose as many stacks as he wishes. It is therefore possible to allocate a stack area to each calling program. This multiple structure, which is a novelty of 16 bit microprocessors in comparison with 8 bits, considerably facilitates the reentrance of programs.

However, reentrance requires the contents of registers used by the subroutine to be stored on the stack. If other registers are used for the transmission of arguments it is necessary either to save the contents of these registers also, or to forbid interrupts during the transmission of arguments. Let SPN be the value of the stack pointer of the program PN just before execution of the subroutine calling sequence. This sequence then proceeds through the following phases.

Phase 1. Saving the contents of the registers used in the reentrant subroutine and for the transmission of arguments via the stack. The stack pointer then takes the value SPN_1. This saving could also be carried out at the beginning of the subroutine.

Phase 2. Loading the arguments of the subroutine and possible reservation of working memory locations. The stack pointer takes the value SPN_2. None of these arguments must be lost in the case of an interrupt at the time of their transmission. If necessary, interrupts should be forbidden during this transmission so that no argument is lost

Phase 3. Calling of the reentrant subroutine. The stack pointer takes the value SPN_3. It can change during execution of the subroutine but it retakes the value SPN_2 after execution of the return from the subroutine.

Phase 4. Incrementing the contents of the stack pointer to return to SPN_1.

Phase 5. Restoring the contents of the registers saved on the stack during phase 1. The stack pointer retakes the value SPN_0.

Certain 16 bit microprocessors have a subroutine return instruction which increments the stack pointer by n units after restoring the return address, hence phase 4 becomes included in phase 3. This is the case with the 8086 RET N instruction. After examining the software of the 8086 and the 68000 an example of a reentrant program and its calling sequence will be given.

Reentrance remains possible, however, when there is only one stack as in the case of 8 bit microprocessors. The first instructions of the calling subroutine must reserve sufficient memory positions on the stack for proper execution of the subroutine. The stack pointer is therefore decremented as many times as is necessary and its last value is transferred into an index register. Each memory location reserved for data or storage of intermediate results is addressed by an address indexed by the fixed value of the index register and a displacement. This technique allows the subroutine to reserve a distinct area on the stack for the calling program which uses the subroutine and for the interrupted subroutine which also uses the reentrant subroutine. Figure 14 illustrates this case for the multiplication subroutine MUL in the case of the 6800. The most and least significant bytes of the multiplicand and the multiplier are assumed to be in memory at addresses CANDH, CANDL, IERH and IERL in an area unique to each of two programs called P1 and P2 (Figure 14).

■ Recursive programs

A program is recursive when it can call itself. A classic example is that of the calculation of factorial N, where N is a positive integer. The equation is:

$$FACT(N) = N \times FACT(N - 1) \text{ with } FACT(0) = 1$$

When the microprocessor evaluates this equation with $N = 4$ it is called on to calculate $FACT(N - 1)$ which is $FACT(3)$ which leads it to calculate $FACT(2)$, $FACT(1)$ and finally $FACT(0)$ which it knows. From this data it returns to $FACT(1)$, which it finds equal to 1, then to $FACT(2)$ for which the calculation gives 2, then $FACT(3)$ and finally to $FACT(4)$. Recursivity requires the contents of the registers before each subroutine call to be saved on the stack and restored afterwards.

7. MEMORY PARTITIONING AND PROTECTION

7.1 Memory partitioning into logical address spaces

■ 'Program', 'data' and 'stack' spaces

The relative ease of involuntarily overlapping two of the three distinct RAM areas (program, data and stack) has already been mentioned. It results in abnormal deletion of instructions, data or information saved on the stack. Although 8 bit microprocessors do not offer any protection in this respect, three of the higher performance 16 bit microprocessors namely the 8086, the Z8000 and the 68000 have been designed to offer the programmer a hardware separation of the 'program', 'data' and 'stack' spaces. This separation, integrated into the microprocessor itself, offers the highest level of security which is much better than all software separation.

The mechanism of selection of one of these address spaces occurs at the instruction level which implicitly contains the type of memory access. In this way, memory accesses intended to fetch the instruction byte or bytes will automatically

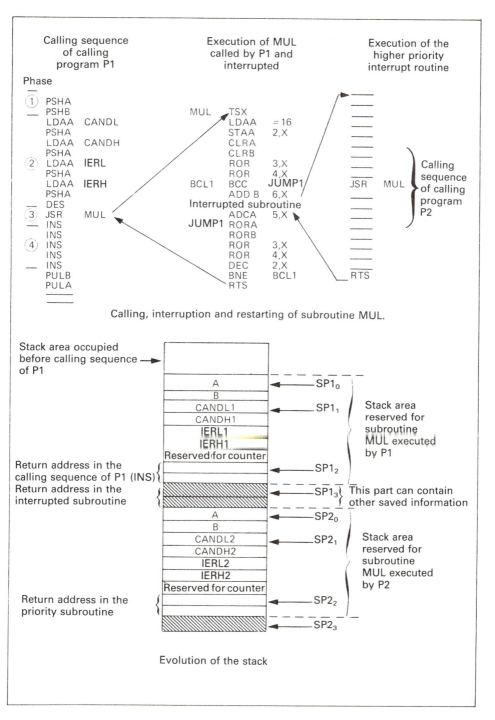

FIGURE 14 *Example of reentrant subroutine with an 8 bit microprocessor*

enable the 'program' address space. Instructions requiring a transfer of data from the memory to the registers or vice versa will enable the 'data' address space at the time of their execution. Instructions relating to the stack are very specific and their execution will enable the 'stack' address space without difficulty. However, this last memory space is not always separated from the other two.

The selection mechanism of an address space, intrinsic in the instruction, is represented, at the microprocessor level, by several status signals which indicate the selected address space in coded form. Decoding can be carried out by several supplementary logic circuits. The status signals are particularly intended to be used by a memory management unit associated with the microprocessor. This is the case for the Z8000 and the 68000. The 8086, however, has a rudimentary memory management unit integrated on to the chip and the status signals do not leave the microprocessor. The memory space of the 8086 is divided into four address spaces: one for the program, one for data, one for the stack and a supplementary one for data. Writing into physical memory in each of these spaces occurs by loading an address into a register assigned to each space. Also, selection of one of the four address spaces, determined from the instruction, leads directly to the choice of one of the four registers.

Protection of the spaces is achieved by control effected at microprocessor level for each memory access instruction. In this way the microprocessor initiates an 'exception' in the case of an anomaly: an invalid instruction, a nonexistent addressing mode, an access to a memory word with an odd address or an attempt to write into a protected area.

■ Separation of 'supervisor' and 'user' spaces

Another partitioning of memory space occurs with certain microprocessors (Z8000, 68000 and NS16032) at the 'supervisor' and 'user' mode level. Selection of one of the two spaces is made by one bit of the status register whose setting to '0' or '1' complies with strict rules governing the protection function imposed by this separation of the two modes. If a privileged instruction, that is one which can be executed only in supervisor mode, arises in the user program, it will not be executed and will cause an 'exception', that is an internal interrupt. The Z8000 and the 68000 combine the two types of address space separation which gives them five and six address spaces respectively. Figure 15 shows these spaces for each of the four second generation 16 bit microprocessors.

For the NS16032, separation of supervisor and user spaces is optional and this separation is the only one that this microprocessor realizes.

■ Separation of spaces extends the address field

In practice, separation of program, data and stack spaces provides an increase in the total addressable memory space. Thus the Z8002 microprocessor, a version of the Z8000 without the memory management unit, has a 16 bit address bus which corresponds to an address field of 64 Kbytes. But this 16 bit address bus remains

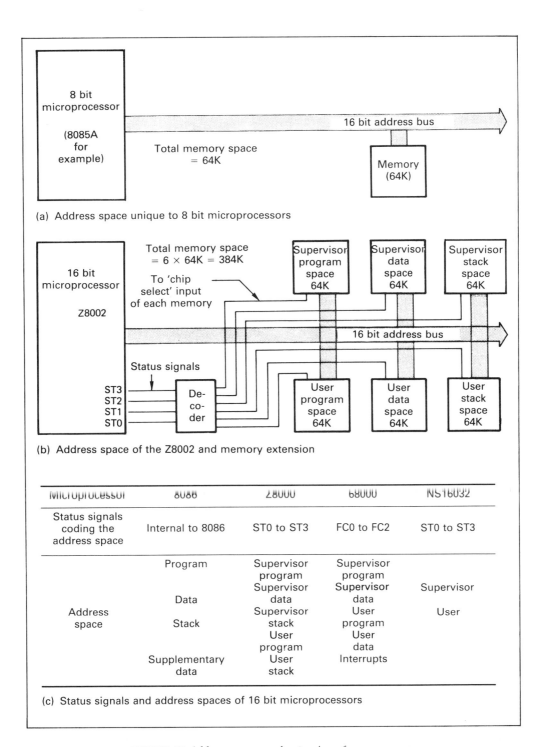

FIGURE 15 *Address spaces and extension of memory space*

available in full for each of the address spaces whose length can therefore be 64 Kbytes. As there are six address spaces for the Z8002 microprocessor, the total addressable memory space is $6 \times 64K$ or 384 Kbytes (Figure 15). Similarly the Z8001, a version of the Z8000 with a memory management unit, uses 23 bits to express its addresses which gives an address field of 8 million bytes. But separation of the memory space into six address spaces, as for the Z8002, means that the total memory field of the Z8001 is 6×8 or 48 million bytes. Finally, for the 68000 it would be possible to decode four address spaces. As the address bus has 24 bits, which allows 16 million bytes to be addressed, it would be possible to extend the total memory field to 4×16 or 64 million bytes.

7.2 Partitioning of the address space into pages or segments

■ The principle of partitioning

It has been seen that, for the Z8002 microprocessor, the total memory space consists of six address spaces each of 64 Kbytes. But for the other 16 bit microprocessors, the Z8001, the 68000 and the NS16032, the length of the address space can be much greater and can extend to 16 million bytes. Such memory spaces are awkward to manage. Also, the designers of 16 bit microprocessors have anticipated a partitioning of each of the address spaces into memory blocks of much shorter length which allows the programmer to develop his design in modular form. These memory blocks are called 'segments'.

A number is assigned to each segment and to access a memory location within a segment it is necessary to know:

(a) The address space concerned.
(b) The number of the segment within the address space.
(c) The relative address of the memory location within the segment, that is its 'displacement' with respect to the first address of the segment.

This first address can be taken as zero for any segment which facilitates programming and particularly modular programming, each programmer starting his program at address zero. Together these three pieces of information constitute the 'logical address' of the memory location. The first two pieces of information together allow a physical address to be assigned to the segment, that is a real address in the memory field; this is the 'base address' of the segment. This concept allows the programmer to manipulate only the displacement, generally expressed in 16 bits, within a segment, thus allowing one byte in the length of memory reference instructions to be gained. In contrast it necessitates calculation of the real address corresponding to the logical address; that is the 'physical address'. This calculation slightly increases the duration of a memory access.

The segments are either of fixed length or of variable length.

Fixed length. The partitioning mechanism of the memory space is called 'pagination' since the strict name of the segment is the 'page', but this term is not always used.

Variable length. The partitioning mechanism of the memory space is called 'segmentation'. But again this term is sometimes used to designate pagination. Since pages are of a fixed length they are easy to store in memory but it can be difficult for them to contain logical entities such as a user task, a compiler program, a data file, etc. Also it is difficult to provide protection at the page level. On the other hand this protection is relatively easy at the segment level where the variable length allows functional modules to be stored. But management of the segments is necessarily more complex.

■ The principle of pagination

The 8086 has a rudimentary form of pagination; this technique will also be explained using an associated memory management unit which has been produced by National Semiconductor for the NS16032. The very simple pagination of the 8086 will be shown. The NS16032 can operate with a single address space or with two, 'supervisor' and 'user', spaces. Whatever the choice made by the programmer, the total memory space is separated into 32,768 pages of 512 bytes. To be easily managed these pages are grouped into blocks of 128 pages called 'segments'. The address of a memory location requires three pieces of information:

> The number of the segment.
> The number of the page in the segment.
> The number of the byte in the page.

This information constitutes the logical address of the memory location. This logical address is converted to a physical address by a simple process which is explained in Figure 16 for the logical address 586 (segment 5, page 8, byte 6).

The first physical address of each segment is stored in a branch table called the 'segment table'. Thus for segment 5, the first address is assumed to be 895. A 'page table' is set up for each segment which is again a branch table; it contains the first physical address of each page of the segment. Thus the first address of page zero of segment number 5 is actually stored at address 895. The first address of page 8 of segment number 5 is stored at address 895 + 8 (8 being the number of the page) which is 903. This first address is assumed here to be 10200. The number of the byte in the addressed page is 6 so the physical address of the memory location of logical address 586 is 10200 + 6 or 10206.

Comment. In practice, for the NS16032 each word of the branch tables has a length of 32 bits which corresponds to 4 address bytes. Also, the address manipulation which has just been carried out is accompanied by a multiplication by 4 of the segment number and the page number. Furthermore, for the sake of simplicity it has been assumed that the branch tables are stored in read/write memory starting from

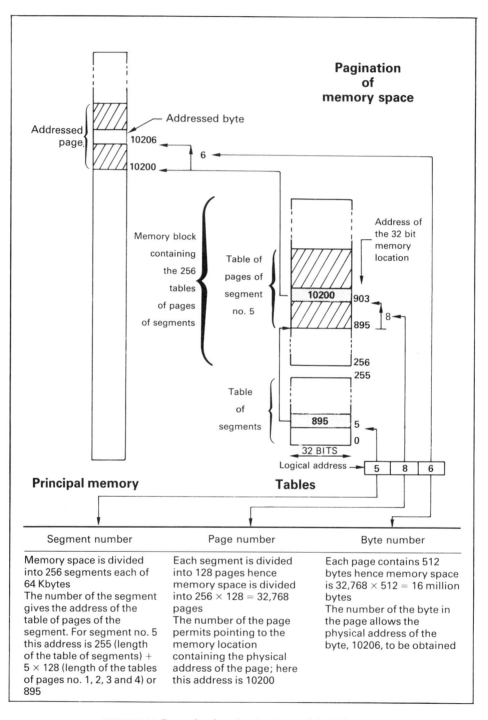

Pagination of memory space

Addressed byte

Addressed page

10206 — Addressed byte

10200

6

Memory block containing the 256 tables of pages of segments

Table of pages of segment no. 5

10200 — 903

895

256

255

Address of the 32 bit memory location

8

Table of segments

895 — 5

0

32 BITS

Logical address → | 5 | 8 | 6 |

Principal memory   **Tables**

Segment number	Page number	Byte number
Memory space is divided into 256 segments each of 64 Kbytes The number of the segment gives the address of the table of pages of the segment. For segment no. 5 this address is 255 (length of the table of segments) + 5 × 128 (length of the tables of pages no. 1, 2, 3 and 4) or 895	Each segment is divided into 128 pages hence memory space is divided into 256 × 128 = 32,768 pages The number of the page permits pointing to the memory location containing the physical address of the page; here this address is 10200	Each page contains 512 bytes hence memory space is 32,768 × 512 = 16 million bytes The number of the byte in the page allows the physical address of the byte, 10206, to be obtained

FIGURE 16 *Example of pagination (case of the NS16032)*

physical address zero. If this reference address is different from zero, the two calculations of the address tables may be extended.

For the 8086 the total memory space, which is 1 megabyte, is divided into N pages, called 'segments', each of 64 Kbytes. The programmer chooses the number N in terms of his application; but, of these N pages, only four can be addressed at a given time without changing the program. The programmer stores his N pages in physical memory and in order to be able to use the four addressable pages at any time, he transfers the first physical address of each of the four pages into four specialized base registers; each of these registers relates to one of the four address spaces of the 8086 – the program space, the data space, the stack space and the supplementary data space. In other words the physical address of a memory location, located in one of the four addressable pages, is determined by two pieces of information.

(a) The contents of the base register assigned to the segment.
(b) The address of the memory location with respect to the first address of the page which can be chosen to be zero. This address, called the displacement, is the only one which occurs in instructions. It expresses the displacement or 'offset' within the page. The base register to be used is determined implicitly in the instruction by its type.

The microprocessor incorporates a very simple memory management system which converts each logical address into a physical address. The conversion consists of adding the displacement within the page to the physical address of the start of the page according to the standard formula: base + displacement. Hence, for the 8086, pagination involves choosing at any time four pages of 64 Kbytes from N pages which have been determined and stored in memory by the programmer and which can be adjacent or overlayed. Among these four pages one contains a program, another contains the data, yet another contains the stack and finally one is reserved for supplementary data. Notice that the possible overlay of the pages allows the programmer to obtain pages of 'effective' length less than 64 Kbytes.

■ The principle of segmentation
Segmentation divides the memory space into N segments of variable length, which involves dividing some or all of the address spaces into several segments. A number is usually assigned to each segment of an address space. The logical address of a memory location, therefore, consists of the following.

The number of the address space.
The number of the segment within the address space.
(These two numbers must have a unique combination, as is the case for the Z8000.)
The displacement of the memory location in the segment.

The logical address is transformed to a physical address by calculating base + displacement; the base is the physical address of the segment, that is the first physical

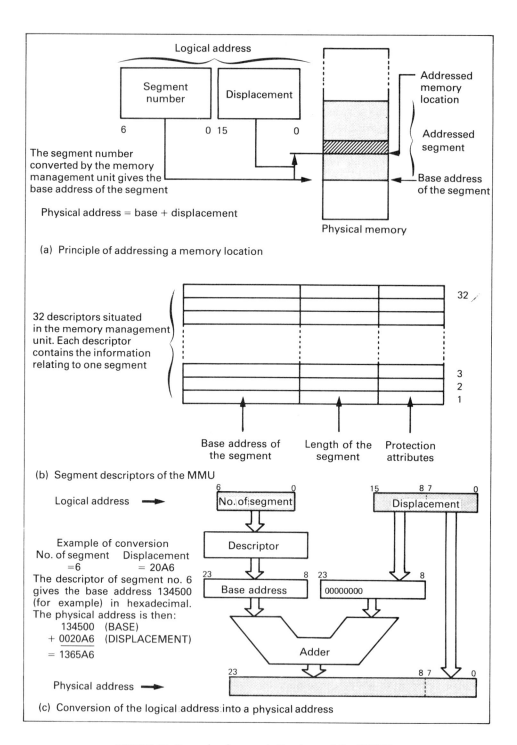

Logical address

Segment number | Displacement

6   0 15   0

The segment number converted by the memory management unit gives the base address of the segment

Physical address = base + displacement

Addressed memory location

Addressed segment

Base address of the segment

Physical memory

(a) Principle of addressing a memory location

32 descriptors situated in the memory management unit. Each descriptor contains the information relating to one segment

32

3
2
1

Base address of the segment   Length of the segment   Protection attributes

(b) Segment descriptors of the MMU

Logical address ➡

6   0
No. of segment

15   8 7   0
Displacement

Example of conversion
No. of segment   Displacement
=6   = 20A6
The descriptor of segment no. 6 gives the base address 134500 (for example) in hexadecimal. The physical address is then:
    134500   (BASE)
+ 0020A6   (DISPLACEMENT)
= 1365A6

Descriptor

23   8   23   8
Base address   00000000

Adder

23   8 7   0

Physical address ➡

(c) Conversion of the logical address into a physical address

FIGURE 17 *Example of segmentation (case of the Z8001)*

address of the segment (Figure 17(a)).

The variable length of the segments allows logical entities such as tasks to be stored in these segments. It is, therefore, easy to protect the tasks by assigning protection at the level of each segment. Also, characteristics, called 'attributes', will be imposed on each segment. For example the attribute 'read only' could be attributed to a segment containing part of a program. Also each segment has a number of pieces of information which belong to it alone, notably:

The physical address of the base of the segment.
The length of the segment.
The protection attributes.

The information relating to a segment is contained in a register of several bytes called the 'descriptor' (Figure 17(b)). The descriptors are located within the memory management unit associated with the microprocessor. Before being able to use segments the programmer must of course load each descriptor with the appropriate value.

Two of the second generation 16 bit microprocessors (the Z8000 and the 68000) use segmentation by means of an associated memory management unit. For the Z8000 the memory space is partitioned into 64 or 128 segments by associating one or two memory management units respectively with the microprocessor. The length of these segments can vary from 256 bytes to 64 Kbytes in increments of 256 bytes. For the 68000, the memory space is divided into 32 segments whose length varies between 256 bytes and 16 million bytes and is expressed as $2^n \times 256$ bytes, that is 256, 512, 1024, 2048, etc. bytes. To avoid the large loss of space to which this binary progression could lead, it is possible to describe a segment by means of two or more descriptors.

Hence, for a segment of 35 Kbytes, it is possible to consider the 35 Kbytes as two adjacent segments in physical memory, one of 32 Kbytes and the other of 4 Kbytes.

7.3 *The concept of virtual memory*

This concept involves considering the read/write memory and the mass memory as a single memory space. For this purpose, the latter is divided into pages which are grouped in segments. The user knows only the logical addresses; he is not concerned with the physical addresses. When the memory management system does not find the required information in read/write memory it calls the page or segment containing the information. This concept is, therefore, a pagination accompanied by an automatic test for the presence or otherwise in read/write memory of the page concerned and an automatic loading of the segment registers when it is necessary to transfer a segment from mass memory to read/write memory. Of course, in order to make space available in read/write memory it is often necessary to transfer some pages temporarily from read/write memory to mass memory. The resulting exchange process between these two memories is called 'swapping'.

7.4 The memory management unit

7.4.1 The need for a memory management unit

Separation of address spaces and partitioning of these spaces into pages or segments are two concepts which do not exist for 8 bit microprocessors and make second generation 16 bit microprocessors possible. Separation of address spaces is a concept which has been integrated into the microprocessor itself; it is, therefore, a separation offering the maximum security. Partitioning of memory space by pagination or segmentation is a concept for which the microprocessor has been designed, but hardware realization of this partitioning is not done by the microprocessor itself but by a special device specific to the microprocessor and called a 'memory management unit' (MMU). It has already been noted that the 8086 is an exception since the simplicity of the memory management unit which is associated with it has made its integration on to the microprocessor chip possible. Furthermore, when pagination or separation is used, the address space separation system, although totally integrated into the microprocessor, is associated with this pagination or segmentation. It is again the memory management unit which controls this association. Also, memory management units Z8010, 68451 and NS16082 are associated with the Z8000, 68000 and NS16032 microprocessors respectively. Several MMUs can be associated with the Z8000 and 68000.

7.4.2 The functions of memory management units

A memory management unit always ensures two fundamental functions:

Conversion of the logical address into a physical address.
Memory protection.

For some microprocessors management of virtual memory is an additional function. These functions will be examined in sequence.

■ Conversion of the logical address into a physical address
For all memory accesses, the microprocessor provides the logical address which generally consists of two parts:

The number of the segment.
The displacement within the segment, expressed as a 16 bit address.

The memory management unit receives this logical address from the microprocessor. It has also received the physical base address of each segment during programming, either by the programmer or by the operating system. It adds the displacement to this physical base address which gives the real address of the addressed memory location.
The detailed mechanism of the conversion of the logical address into a physical address is particular to each microprocessor. Figure 17(c) shows this mechanism for the

Z8000 microprocessor. The latter sends the logical address, consisting of a 16 bit displacement and a 7 bit segment number, to the memory management unit. The 8 low order bits of the displacement give the 8 low order bits of the physical address directly. The 8 high order bits of the displacement are transformed into a 16 bit word by the addition of insignificant zeros. The 16 bit word is then added to 16 bits of the address of the base of the segment. These 16 bits of the base address are actually the 16 high order bits of the physical address of the segment expressed in 24 bits, the 8 low order bits being forced to zero for each physical address of a segment. The result of the addition gives the 16 high order bits of the physical address.

■ Memory protection
This protection is made at several levels:

At address space level. The type of instruction to be executed informs the microprocessor of the address space concerned. If the operand does not conform to the address space assigned to the instruction, the latter is declared invalid and the microprocessor raises an internal interrupt (exception). For this purpose the microprocessor sends the status signals which encode the address space corresponding to the type of instruction which it is executing to the memory management unit. This protection includes, for most second generation 16 bit microprocessors, prohibition of access to certain memory areas in user mode and prohibition of priviliged instructions reserved for the operating system in supervisor mode.

At segment length level. The memory management unit always knows whether the segment is of fixed or variable length. It acts as a control and generates an internal interrupt in case of overflow. This protection therefore avoids all unintentional overflows from one area to another.

At the write level. The attributes of a segment allow all writing into the segment to be forbidden, which is useful for programs.

At the task level. Segmentation is ideal for assigning a segment to each task. In this case the microprocessor can access only the memory area of that task.

■ Management of virtual memory
This function is executed by the NS16082 memory management unit and that of the Intel 80286 microprocessor which is integrated into the 80286. It consists essentially of loading the appropriate base address into each segment register.

7.4.3 Integration of the memory management unit into its hardware environment

The memory management unit is connected, according to its functions, between the microprocessor and physical memory. From the microprocessor it receives:

(a) The address bus.
(b) The status signals which encode the address space.
(c) The number of the segment, in the case of the Z8000 which is designed for segmented addressing (address bus of 16 bits and segment number) in contrast to the 68000 and the NS16032 which provide a 24 bit address bus directly (linear addressing).
(d) The control bus.

Figure 18 shows the connection of the memory management unit associated with the 68000.

Comment. The possible extension of memory space by separation of address spaces has already been noted. This possibility may or may not be used by the memory management unit. It is partly used in the memory management unit associated with the Z8001 in which the memory space extends from 8 to 16 million bytes. In contrast this possibility is not used by the memory management unit associated with the 68000.

7.4.4 When should a memory management unit be used?

There is a general answer to this question which is valid for any microprocessor and a specific reply for each microprocessor. The general reply is that it is useful to use a memory management unit when:

The memory space to be managed is very large.
The problem of memory protection is vital even if the space is reasonable.

This general reply must always be modified in accordance with the specific details of each microprocessor. Thus for the 8086 this question is irrelevant since the 8086 operates only with its integrated memory management unit.

The Z8001 is designed for segmented addressing; its address bus, limited to 16 bits, is augmented by a 7 bit segment number and four status lines. It is, however, possible to decode the address spaces and to increase the memory space up to 6 × 64K. But in this case it is preferable to use the nonsegmented Z8002 version of the Z8000. Also, with some exceptions, the Z8010 memory management unit is normally associated with the Z8001 microprocessor.

The 68000 is designed with linear addressing, like 8 bit microprocessors, but with a 24 bit address bus. For a small application the memory management unit is necessary only if the protection problem is vital. The essential protection function can, however, be obtained without a memory management unit using logic circuits to ensure decoding and separation of the address spaces. In the case of a large application the memory management unit is very suitable since, in addition to protection, it has the benefit of modular program design.

The NS16032, designed like the 68000 for linear addressing, can address 16 million bytes. The reply to the question regarding the use of a memory management unit is the general reply given at the start of this section.

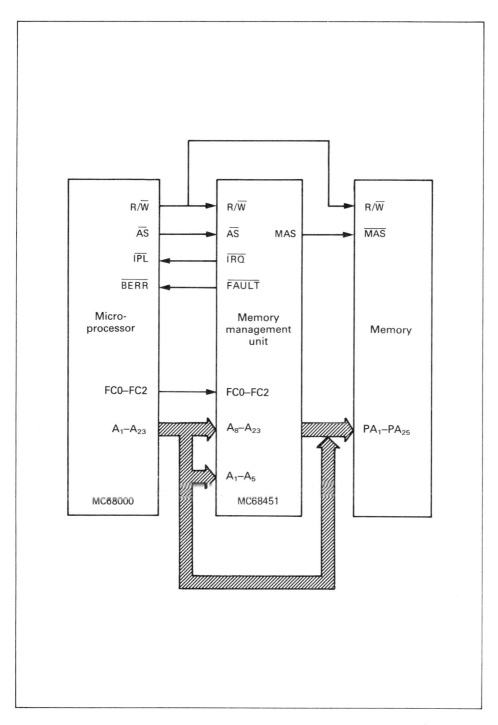

FIGURE 18 *Connection of the MC68451 memory management unit to the Motorola MC68000 microprocessor*

Comment. When a mass memory is used it is the operating system which carries out dynamic memory allocation, that is which manages transfers from mass memory to read/write memory and which translates objects in read/write memory to group them. This translation leads to the determination of a base address for each segment. Notice that for most of the time a segment is allocated to an object. The segment is therefore the container and the object is the contents. The memory management unit merely calculates the physical address of a memory location from the logical address. However, certain memory management units such as the 68451 and the NS16082 generate an interrupt when the logical address does not correspond to any segment or page which is directly addressable at that time. In such a situation the NS16082 similarly indicates to the processor, in practice to the operating system, the page which it is necessary to transfer from mass memory to read/write memory.

8. BUS ACCESS DEMAND

8.1 The nature of the problem

A microprocessor bus access demand is the activation of a specific signal for the microprocessor to disconnect itself from the address, data and control buses in order to allow another device to take command of the bus and hence of the memories and peripherals. All bus access demands pose the problem of bus allocation.

(a) Taking the buses must be done according to an established protocol allowing synchronization of operations within the microprocessor. This internal synchronization often allows asynchronous bus access demands to be made, which is useful. This effectively avoids the need for supplementary logic circuits in order to synchronize bus access demands. This is the case for the 8086, Z8000 and 68000 microprocessors.
(b) Only one circuit must access the bus at a given time; this necessitates a hierarchical priority mechanism in the case of simultaneous bus access demands.

For this purpose, microprocessor designers normally provide a specialized device which ensures arbitration of priorities. Thus Intel provides the 8289 for its 8086 microprocessor and Motorola provides the 68452 (Bus Arbitration Module) for its 68000 microprocessor.

Three possible situations give rise to a bus access demand. They will be considered in turn.

■ Bus access demand by a DMA controller
This is the simplest situation; it has been investigated with 8 bit microprocessors. There can, however, be several DMA controllers connected to the microprocessor. This first situation is a simple division of the microprocessor system resources. When

the microprocessor is active, the DMA controller or controllers are inactive. When a DMA controller is active the microprocessor and the other DMA controllers are inactive. There are no parallel functions.

■ Bus access demand by a processor other than the microprocessor

This situation occurs when one or more devices, associated with the microprocessor, can possibly take bus mastership. These devices can be microprocessors, the same as or different from the first. A typical example is that of 'coprocessor' circuits associated with a microprocessor, for example the 8087 arithmetic coprocessor and the 8089 input/output circuit associated with the 8086. In this situation the processors or coprocessors share the microprocessor buses which, at any time, are assigned only to a single device.

■ Bus access demand in a multiprocessor environment

The constant need for higher processing speed and the low cost of microprocessors encourage microprocessor system designers to arrange for different tasks to be executed by different processors. The latter operate in parallel and at times exchange information between each other or with a common memory. This multimicroprocessor environment requires that each microprocessor has its own bus and its own memory. Exchange of information between processors is made by a bus common to all the processors and called the 'system bus'.

The processors each have their own memory but they can also share a common memory and the peripherals. This environment leads to an increased performance but it requires a rigorous protocol for allocation of the system bus. The latter consists of:

The data bus.
The address bus.
The control bus including, particularly, the bus arbitration signals.
Several hierarchical interrupt levels.

The first two situations leading to bus access demands are solved by sharing the 'local bus'; this term relates to the buses of the microprocessor itself. The third situation requires hardware realization of a 'system bus' for which several standards have been proposed. Examples are the Intel 'Multibus', the Microprocess 'Makbus', the Motorola 'Versabus' and above all the 'VME bus' which resulted from an agreement between Motorola, Mostek and Philips/Signetics. Several months after this agreement Thomson adopted the VME bus followed by numerous other companies. The demand protocol for bus access will be examined for the case of a local bus and then for a system bus.

8.2 *Access demand for a local bus*

The exchange protocol between the microprocessor and the demanding circuit, this general term designating a direct memory access controller or processor and particularly a microprocessor, is based on several dialogue signals in accordance with the specific timing diagrams of each microprocessor. Figure 19 gives these timing diagrams for the four second generation 16 bit microprocessors. The protocol always begins with a request from the demanding circuit to the microprocessor by activating a signal which will be called 'bus access demand'. The microprocessor detects this demand and normally terminates the current machine cycle. Then it puts its bus into the high impedance state and activates a signal which will be called 'bus allocation'. When the demanding circuit deactivates its bus access demand, the microprocessor retakes control of its buses, grouped under the term 'local bus'.

Exceptionally, the two dialogue signals are combined in a single bidirectional signal for the 8086. The 68000 has an additional dialogue signal which is 'acknowledge receipt of the local bus' on the part of the demanding circuit.

The 'bus allocation' signal informs all demanding circuits that the microprocessor is disconnected from the local bus. The highest priority demanding circuit takes control of the bus, via a possible circuit for arbitrating priorities, and informs the microprocessor.

8.3 Access demand for a system bus

In the case of a multimicroprocessor environment with a system bus, the signals are of course used for dialogue between processors. But two processors cannot communicate directly by their dialogue signals. The latter are specific to the processor, also an interface circuit is often necessary to transform them into signals conforming to the standard adopted, Multibus, Makbus or VME standard, for example. Microprocessor designers provide such interface circuits, for example the 8289 to be associated with the 8086. Before examining the two most commonly used bus systems, Multibus and VME, the multimicroprocessor environment will first be defined.

The reliability and very low cost of microprocessors lead the designers of data processing systems to arrange for different tasks to be carried out by several microprocessors rather than a single large processor. It is therefore possible to use microprocessors below their maximum capabilities which allows a reconfiguration of the system in case of breakdown. This multiprocessor structure brings parallelism to the processing of tasks; microprocessors facilitate sharing of a given task or set of tasks. In the latter case the processors have access to a file of waiting tasks and are informed as soon as the file is not empty. Unoccupied processors take the tasks in order of their availability. In such a system, the only consequence of failure of a microprocessor is a reduction in the speed of execution of tasks. Reliability, modularity and low cost are the principal advantages of multimicroprocessor architectures. Several architectures exist.

Star structure. A processor can communicate with another only by way of a central processor or a central module consisting of a matrix of switches. A

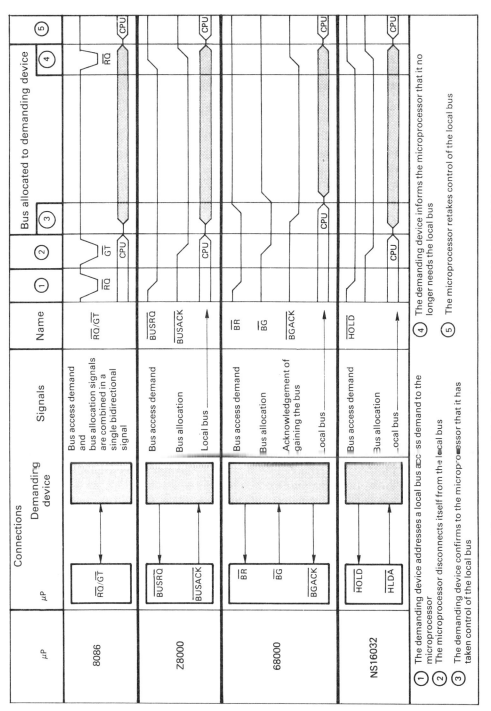

FIGURE 19 *Local bus access demand for the 8086, Z8000, 68000 and NS16032 16 bit microprocessors*

breakdown of the central processor or module paralyzes the whole system and this is the principal disadvantage of this architecture.

Multiplexed bus architecture. The processors are connected by a bus system. Exchanges are made either directly by the processors themselves or by a central processor. This architecture is useful when the processors are situated at the same location.

Loop structure. The processors are the links of a closed loop or chain. Each processor communicates only with the processor which precedes or follows it. Information transmission is serial and simplex (in one direction). Only a multiplexed bus structure will be examined. In this structure each processor most often has its own program memory (ROM) and working memory (RAM). But it can also make use of a memory or peripheral which is common to all the processors. In this case, exchange of data is made by means of the system bus.

8.4 Multibus and VME bus systems

Multibus was created by Intel for 171.5 × 304.8 mm single board computer (SBC) cards which had been the most widely sold in the world up to 1983 but were in danger of being overtaken by the Eurocards adopted for the VME bus system. These Eurocards are available in two sizes: the 160 × 100 mm single Eurocard format and the 160 × 233.4 mm double Eurocard format (see Figure 20).

In a multimicroprocessor environment, each microprocessor operates asynchronously and asynchronous access demands for the system bus must be synchronized. In the case of several simultaneous demands, priority arbitration is necessary; it is generally accomplished by a specific priority arbitration circuit. For an execution which includes several exchanges, it is important to observe the protocols rigorously on the basis of the dialogue signals which precede or follow the data transfers between a master and common memory or a common peripheral. It follows that a bus system involves several categories of signal.

(a) The data bus where the number of bits is 8 or 16 for the Multibus and 8, 16 or 32 for the VME bus. The latter can therefore accept 32 bit microprocessors.
(b) The address bus whose standard width is 20 bits for the Multibus and 24 bits for the VME bus with a possible extension to 24 bits for the Multibus and to 32 bits for the VME bus.
(c) Bus demand and arbitration signals. The Multibus has a single 'bus access demand' signal, the VME bus has four hierarchical levels for bus access demands.
(d) Interrupt demands: 8 hierarchical levels for the multibus, 7 for the VME bus.
(e) Power supplies +5 V, ±12 V and earth.

In addition to these fundamental signals each bus system has one or more secondary signals. The Multibus has a $\overline{\text{LOCK}}$ signal which permits the system to be

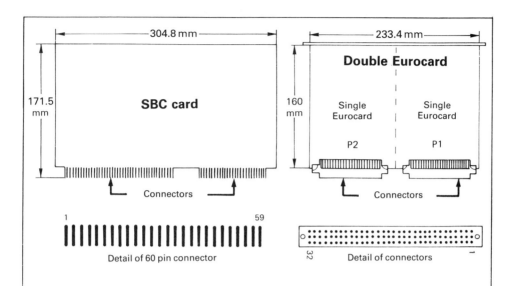

Comparison of multibus and VME bus systems

Characteristics	Multibus	VME bus
Type of bus	Asynchronous not multiplexed	Asynchronous not multiplexed
Data bus	8 or 16 bits	8, 16 or 32 bits
Address bus	20 bits as standard possible extension to 24	24 bits as standard possible extension to 32
Interrupt levels	8	7
Number of 'bus access demand' signals	1	1
Serial interprocessor connection	No	Yes
Special signals	Locking signal for the system bus activated by program	Signal indicating an error
Power supplies	+5 V and ±12 V	+5 V and ±12 V
Card format	SBC card 171.5 × 304.8 mm	Single Eurocard 100 × 160 mm or double Eurocard 160 × 233.4 mm
Connectors	2 edge connectors of 60 and 86 pins	2 mounted connectors each of 96 pins

FIGURE 20 *Cards and characteristics of the multibus and the VME bus*

locked, that is to prohibit allocation of this bus to a master other than that which is using it. This allows part of a program, which must not be divided, to be executed in a single block. The VME bus does not offer this possibility but it contains several error signals (loss of power, bus error, system failure) and one serial interprocessor link.

This set of signals is provided on two connectors for each of the two standard buses; 86 and 60 pins for the Multibus, 96 and 96 pins for the VME bus. Only 32 pins of the second connector are used for the VME bus, the other 64 being available for the user.

To compete with the success of the VME bus, Intel introduced Multibus II in 1984; this includes five buses which are interconnected and configurable by software.

(a) A synchronous parallel 32 bit system bus designated by PSB (parallel system bus).
(b) A local extension bus with a frequency of 12 MHz designated by LBX II (local bus extension).
(c) A serial system bus with a frequency of 2 MHz for the transfer of messages designated by SSB (serial system bus).
(d) Two other buses leading from the Multibus: a multichannel DMA bus and an input/output extension bus.

Intel has adopted the double Eurocard format but with one depth of 22 cm instead of 16 cm for VME bus cards. Several companies are associated with Intel in the promotion of this new bus system.

9. THE SIMPLICITY AND POWER OF THE INSTRUCTION SET

9.1 Orthogonality

Second generation 16 bit microprocessors have an instruction set which is much more powerful than that of 8 bit microprocessors. However, this power is not generally obtained by an increased number of instructions but by a highly regular instruction set allowed by an architecture based on several registers. The result is orthogonality.

This arises from the multiplicity of internal registers in conjunction with the addressing modes and instructions, which means that, with few exceptions, each instruction can use any register in any addressing mode. This regularity, which exists for the Z8000, the 68000 and the NS16032, is even greater for the latter two microprocessors for which any data format can be chosen for most of the instructions. The choice is made by adding a suffix to the instruction mnemonic; for example, B for byte, W for word and D for double word. The same mnemonic expression is therefore used for tens or even hundreds of different instructions. In this way with only 56 different mnemonic expressions the 68000 has a set of over a thousand instructions. This greatly facilitates programming.

9.2 Basic instructions with two operands

Eight bit microprocessors are 'one address processors'; that is the instruction provides only one operand address. As arithmetic operations use two operands, the one which is not indicated is implicitly the contents of the accumulator. Hence the instruction ADD 1000 signifies 'add the contents of memory address location 1000 (these contents are the second operand) to the contents of the accumulator (these contents are the first operand) and transfer the result into the accumulator'. The latter, therefore, contains the first operand initially, and the result of the calculation finally.

The NS16032 and 68000 microprocessors are 'two address processors'; that is the instruction provides two operand addresses. The architecture of these processors is described as 'memory to memory'. The 8086 and Z8000 microprocessors are not two address processors but can nevertheless work on two operands; one is the contents of a register and the other is indicated in the address field of the instruction. The register containing an operand is no longer a unique register, the accumulator, as it is for the majority of 8 bit microprocessors, but a register chosen from several possible ones and indicated in the instruction.

Hence the instruction ADD 1000, typical of an 8 bit microprocessor, becomes ADD 001000,D*n* for the 68000. This instruction signifies 'add the contents of register D*n* (one of registers D0, D1, ... D7) to the contents of memory address location 001000 and transfer the result into this register'. Also, the instructions of a 16 bit microprocessor can be classified with respect to the operands into three groups.

(a) Instructions without an explicit operand such as processor control or flag setting instructions.
(b) Instructions with an explicit operand such as conditional and unconditional branch instructions, rotation, shifting, incrementing and decrementing instructions.
(c) Instructions with two explicit operands such as arithmetic, logical and transfer instructions. The two operands are provided either by two registers or by a register and an address or, for the 68000 and the NS16032, by two addresses.

9.3 Bit manipulation instructions

Eight bit microprocessors do not normally allow the setting of a flag from the value of a single bit of a register or memory location. For this it is necessary to transfer the contents of the register or memory location into the accumulator and then to test the chosen bit either by one or more shifts into the 'carry' position or by masking. The group of instructions required for this test of one bit is available in the form of a single instruction with 16 bit second generation microprocessors except the 8086. These instructions act at bit level and also allow the bit to be set to '0' or '1'.

In general, for the Z8000, 68000 and NS16032 microprocessors, these instructions allow either:

setting the zero flag from the value of one of the bits of a register or memory location;
or setting a bit to the value '0' or '1';
or a combination of these two operations.

The instruction indicates both the register or memory location concerned and the number of the selected bit in the register or memory location. This number is indicated either directly in the instruction (static selection), or by the contents of a register (dynamic selection).

Thus, for the 68000 microprocessor, assuming the contents of register D2 to be 5, the instruction BTEST D0,D2 tests bit number 5 of register D0 by setting the Z flag with the complemented value of the tested bit. For bit manipulation instructions, the 8086 has the lowest performance of the 16 bit microprocessors since it does not possess any specific instructions. The Z8000 and the 68000 have four and the NS16032 has ten. These instructions are particularly important in signal processing applications.

9.4 *Instructions for manipulating strings of characters*

Manipulation of strings of characters is important in management applications where one important part of the work of the microprocessor consists of transferring or comparing blocks. Printing information, which occurs in all applications, is equally a manipulation of strings of characters. Although no provision has been made for processing strings with 8 bit microprocessors, specific instructions have been incorporated in most second generation 16 bit microprocessors. These instructions generally allow the following operations.

(a) Copying of an area of memory, containing a series of characters or words, into another area.
(b) Comparison of two strings of characters or words, the operation being repeated until there is a match.
(c) Searching for a character or word within a block, the character or word being stored in a register.
(d) Conversion of a block of data, for example conversion of data expressed in ASCII code into EBCDIC code.

This last operation is possible only with the Z8000 and the NS16032; the first three operations are offered by these two microprocessors and the 8086. The 68000 does not have specific instructions for processing strings of characters, in contrast to Z8000 which is richly provided with them.

Each of these specific instructions replaces a short program for an 8 bit microprocessor. Execution of one instruction necessitates initialization of several registers.

(a) A register which points to the source area.
(b) A register which points to the destination area if one exists.

(c) A register which contains the number of bytes or words in the source area.

(d) A register which points to the conversion table, if the operation to be repeated is a conversion; this is also called 'translation'. Character string manipulation instructions are interruptible. In this case the contents of initialization registers are saved, which allows processing of the string of characters to restart after execution of the interrupt routine.

9.5 Arithmetic instructions in fixed and floating point

■ Representation of a number in fixed point

In fixed point representation a number is represented by a sign, a value and a position of the decimal point which is permanently fixed. This mode of representation has two disadvantages: the first is that a reduced number of significant figures is not permitted for small numbers and particularly those which are less than 1 (Figure 21); the second is the impossibility of expressing very large numbers. Also as soon as calculations require more than a minimum of precision, they are performed in another mode, floating point. Like 8 bit microprocessors, 16 bit microprocessors do not have arithmetic instructions in floating point but some of them, such as the 8086 and the NS16032 have an arithmetic coprocessor which executes calculations in floating point. The result is a considerable gain in speed, of the order of 100 for example.

■ Representation of a number in floating point

In this mode a number N (for example, $+1200 = +0.1200 \times 10^{+4}$) is represented in the form $SM\alpha sE$ where

S represents the sign of the number: 0 for a positive number, 1 for a negative number.

M is the mantissa, that is the value of N expressed as a fraction less than 1 (the 0 before the decimal point is not represented).

α is the base of the numbering system used: 10 for the decimal system, 2 for the binary system.

s is the sign of the exponent: 0 for a positive exponent, 1 for a negative exponent.

E is the value of the exponent.

Thus, expressing the mantissa by 8 digits in the decimal system and the exponent by three digits, the number 2500.5 is represented by

$S = 0$ for a positive number

$M = 25000500$ (mantissa expressed by 8 decimal digits)

$\alpha = 10$ (decimal system)

$s = 0$ (positive exponent)

$E = 5$

hence

$$25000.5 = +0.25000500 \times 10^{+5}$$

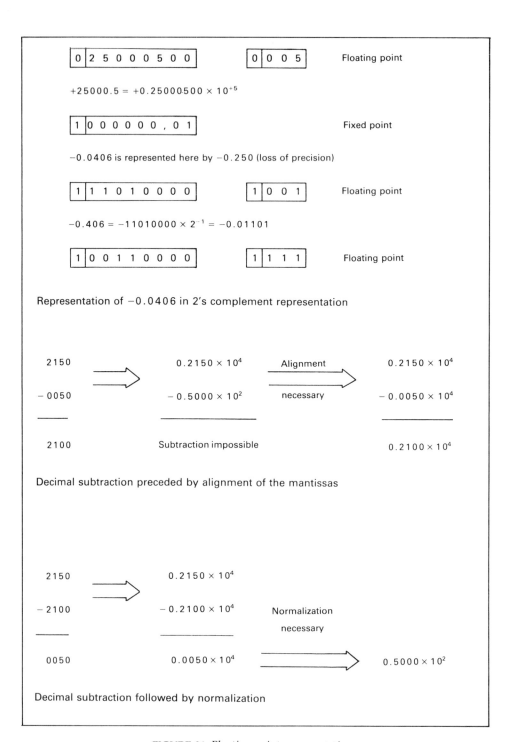

FIGURE 21 *Floating point representation*

Figure 21 shows the representation of this number and that of the number −0.0406 in the binary system, the mantissa and exponent being expressed by 8 and 3 bits respectively. Notice that negative binary numbers are normally represented in two's complement form.

■ The format of a floating point number

The arithmetic coprocessors associated with certain 16 bit microprocessors express the results of calculations in single or double precision. But the 8087 coprocessor associated with the 8086 can carry out calculations with a greater precision and express the results with a reduced precision. Thus in double precision the 8086 operates on 64 bit numbers (1 bit for the sign of the number, 11 bits for the exponent and its sign, 52 bits for the mantissa). But in 'temporary floating point' the calculation is carried out with a 64 bit mantissa which avoids a loss of precision when using intermediate results. The final result is nevertheless expressed in 64 bits.

■ Addition and subtraction of two floating point numbers

These calculations must often be preceded by an alignment of the mantissas and followed by a normalization of these mantissas.

Alignment of the mantissas. Bits of the same weight must be made adjacent, which leads to equality of the exponents. For this it is necessary to determine the number having the smallest exponent then to increment it as necessary by one while shifting the mantissa one place to the right for each increment of the exponent (Figure 21).

Normalization of the mantissas. The result of a subtraction can be expressed with a mantissa starting with one or more zeros. The result of an addition can also start with a zero if the capacity is exceeded. It is therefore necessary to 'normalize' the result by shifting the mantissa one or more places to the left until the leftmost digit of the mantissa takes the value 1. Each shifting is accompanied by decrementing the exponent by one.

■ Multiplication of two floating point numbers

Floating point multiplication involves multiplication of the mantissas and addition of the exponents. Alignment of the mantissas is not required. The two operands to be multiplied are assumed to be normalized and the value of their mantissas is assumed to be between $\frac{1}{2}$ and 1. The result of the multiplication is therefore between $\frac{1}{4}$ and 1. As a consequence, if normalization of the result is necessary this is reduced to a shifting of one place to the left.

■ Division of two floating point numbers

Floating point division involves division of the mantissas and subtraction of the exponents. Alignment of the mantissas is not required. The two numbers to be divided are assumed to be normalized and the division gives a result assumed to be between $\frac{1}{2}$ and 2. In consequence, if normalization of the result is necessary this is reduced to a shifting of one place to the right including the 'carry' in the shift.

PART II
THE 8086

10. INTERNAL AND EXTERNAL ORGANIZATION OF THE 8086

The first of the second generation 16 bit microprocessors to appear was the 8086 in 1978. This microprocessor is produced in HMOS technology, integrates about 29,000 transistors in a 40 pin package and uses a single power supply. The 8086 is actually the basic processor of a complete family of devices, APX86, which includes

The 8086 microprocessor which is the head of the family.
The 8087 arithmetic coprocessor.
The 8089 input/output coprocessor.
The 8288 bus controller which is necessary for the maximum 8086 configuration.
The 8289 priority arbitration circuit which is necessary for multiprocessor operation of the 8086.

The APX86 family was followed by the APX186 family, which resulted from an improvement of the 8086 giving the 80186, the APX286 family based on the 80286 microprocessor and designed for multitask, multiuser and real time applications and finally the APX386 family.

The general characteristics of the 8086 are as follows.

(a) A multiplexed address/data bus of 16 bits.
(b) Simplified page addressing; a rudimentary memory management unit is incorporated on the microprocessor chip. This results in 20 address bits which gives an addressable memory space of 1 Megabyte, divided into 16 pages of 64 Kbytes.
(c) Four separate address spaces, 'program', 'data', 'stack' and 'supplementary data', but the distinction between supervisor and user modes does not exist. The program can access any one of the four 64 Kbyte spaces without having to modify register contents in the memory management unit.
(d) A 16 bit data organization in memory which processes the less significant byte first. The 16 bits of data, or words, are normally aligned to provide the highest speed of transfer but can be nonaligned at the price of a reduction in speed (see Figures 4(b) and 4(c)).
(e) A limited number of internal registers which are also specialized. This weakness of the 8086 does not allow the orthogonality offered more or less totally by the other second generation 16 bit microprocessors.
(f) Two modes of operation, minimum and maximum; the latter is particularly intended for a multimicroprocessor environment.
(g) Two possible I/O structures, I/O by I/O instruction (the I/O space being separate from the memory space) and I/O by memory instruction (the I/O space being included in the memory space). In the first case the 8086 uses specialized I/O instructions allowing up to 64K 8 bit ports or 32K 16 bit ports to be addressed outside the memory space; the I/O space is not segmented. In the

second case I/O exchanges are made with the full range of memory instructions but at the price of a reduction in memory space. These two I/O structures are a strong point of the 8086.

(h) The possibility of operating in single step using trace mode.

(i) Adaptation to a multiprocessor environment by virtue of specific dialogue signals and a priority arbitration circuit.

(j) A relative addressing mode with respect to the program counter which allows any memory location in a 64 Kbyte segment to be accessed in the case of an unconditional branch but which is limited to $-128/+127$ for conditional jumps.

10.1 *Internal organization of the 8086*

As seen by the user the 8086 has four types of register: data registers, segment registers, pointer registers and the status register. There is also a program counter which is not accessible to the user (Figure 22).

■ Data registers

The four data registers AX, BX, CX and DX act as 16 bit accumulators and operand registers. Each of these registers can be separated into two 8 bit registers. The letter X is then replaced by H for the register containing the high order byte and L for the register containing the low order byte. Hence, the combination of AH and AL gives AX. Since the 8086 is compatible, at source code level, with the 8080A and the 8085A, the AL, BX, CX and DX registers serve as the AC, HL, BC and DE registers respectively of the 8080A and 8085A as indicated by shading in Figure 22. Since these four 16 bit registers of the 8086 can all operate as general purpose registers for arithmetic and logical operations and transfers, each one has a specific level of operation associated with particular instructions.

(a) AX is used for input/output operations, decimal corrections, multiplications, divisions and translations.

(b) BX serves as a base register for addressing memory locations in the indirect mode by base register addressing.

(c) CX counts data in character string manipulations.

(d) DX is used for multiplications and divisions in conjunction with AX, or as an indirect address register for addressing an input/output port.

■ Segment registers

The four segment registers CS, DS, SS and ES form part of the memory management unit integrated into the 8086. Each of these registers contain the physical base address of one of the four 64 Kbyte pages, called 'segments' by Intel, within which it is possible to address a memory location directly at any time. Each base address, which defines the physical location of the corresponding segment in memory, must have its four most significant bits at zero. Also the segment registers contain only the 16 most

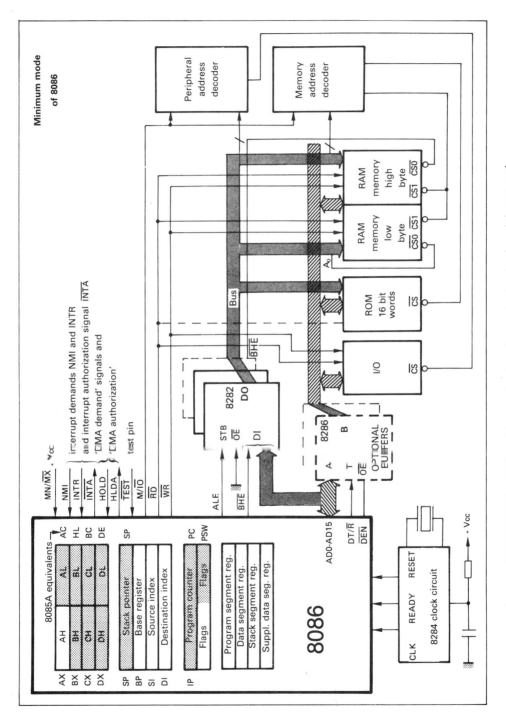

FIGURE 22 The 8086 registers and external organization in the minimum mode

significant bits of the base addresses. Each of the four registers contains the base address of the four current segments which are identified as four address spaces of the 8086.

(a) CS contains the base address of the program address space, here this space means a 64 Kbyte segment, called the 'code segment' by Intel. Every access to a memory location in the program segment is made with an address relative to the CS register. This signifies that the address of an instruction to access a memory location containing a program byte expresses the displacement with respect to the base address contained in CS. Notice that the displacement is the contents of the program counter, which Intel calls the 'instruction pointer' (IP). This IP register effectively points to the different bytes of the program.

(b) DS contains the base address of the data address space; this space corresponds to a 64 Kbyte segment, called the 'data segment' by Intel. Every access to data not on the stack is made with an address relative to the DS register.

(c) SS contains the base address of the stack address space which is another segment of 64 Kbytes, called the 'stack segment' by the manufacturer.

(d) ES contains the base address of the supplementary data address space which is the last of the four current segments of the 8086, that is the four segments whose interior can be accessed by the program at any time without changing the contents of the segment registers. This register is used in the manipulation of character strings. Execution of a program requires prior initialization of the segment registers.

■ Pointer registers

These are the SP, BP, SI and DI registers. As for the data registers, these four registers participate in arithmetic and logical operations. The first two are used by default to express a displacement within the stack segment, the latter two are used by default to express a displacement within the data segment except for operations on data strings.

■ The program counter

This register, designated by the mnemonic expression IP (instruction pointer), contains the displacement of the addressed memory location within the segment concerned. This displacement is added to the segment base address in order to obtain the physical address; the calculation is performed by the memory management unit integrated into the 8086. This displacement is expressed in 16 bits. Any program which does not cause any loading or manipulation of segment registers is dynamically relocatable. Such a program accepts interrupts and can be translated within memory space by modifying the values of the segment registers. This modification of values is accomplished by the operating system, or by the programmer if there is no operating system. For compatibility of the 8086 with the 8080A and the 8085A, the IP register plays the role of the PC (program counter) register of these two 8 bit microprocessors.

The set of registers of the 8086 is shown in Figure 22 where the 8086 registers representing those of the 8080A and the 8085A are indicated by a shaded area. This figure also shows the 8086 signals and their function, which will be examined.

■ The status register

This 16 bit register, of which only 9 bits are used, brings all the status indicators together (Figure 23).

Among these the five flags of the 8080A and the 8085A reappear:

AF (auxiliary carry flag) this is the forward carry of weight 2^4 used in the case of decimal arithmetic operations.

CF (carry flag), this is the forward carry.

PF (parity flag), this indicates the parity, it is set to '1' if the parity is even.

SF (sign flag) indicates the sign.

ZF (zero flag) indicates zero.

In addition to these five flags, the status register also contains the following:

(a) The OF (overflow flag) status bit; this is the overflow indicator which is set to '1' when the most significant bit of the data is lost after exceeding the available capacity.

(b) The DF (direction flag) control bit used for the manipulation of strings of characters. When set to '0' or '1' by the programmer, the string of characters is processed in the direction of increasing or decreasing addresses.

(c) the IF (interrupt flag) control bit. When set to '0' or '1' by the programmer, maskable external interrupts are inhibited or allowed. This bit does not have any effect on nonmaskable external interrupts (NMI) or internal interrupts.

(d) The TF (trace flag) control bit governs the trace mode. If the program sets this bit to '1' an internal interrupt, called a 'trap', is initiated after execution of each instruction. The program is then diverted to a 'trace' routine allowing the contents of the registers to be examined, thus providing 'step by step' operation.

■ The queue

The internal architecture of the 8086 consists of two parts:

(a) The execution unit (EU) executes the usual logic and arithmetic functions.

(b) The bus interface unit (BIU) stores 6 bytes of advance instructions in a queue consisting of a 6 byte memory (Figure 23).

Thus, while the arithmetic and logic unit executes an instruction, the bus interface unit finds the next instruction in memory. Of course this anticipation is useful only for sequential instructions and does not provide any increase in speed for jump instructions, but these are less numerous resulting in increased processing speed.

In the case of a jump instruction, the contents of the queue are no longer valid and it is restarted from the jump address. The queue is therefore an obligatory route between the bus interface unit and the execution unit.

This mode of operation, called the 'pipeline' mode, is widely used in data processing. However the 8086 was the first 16 bit microprocessor to use it.

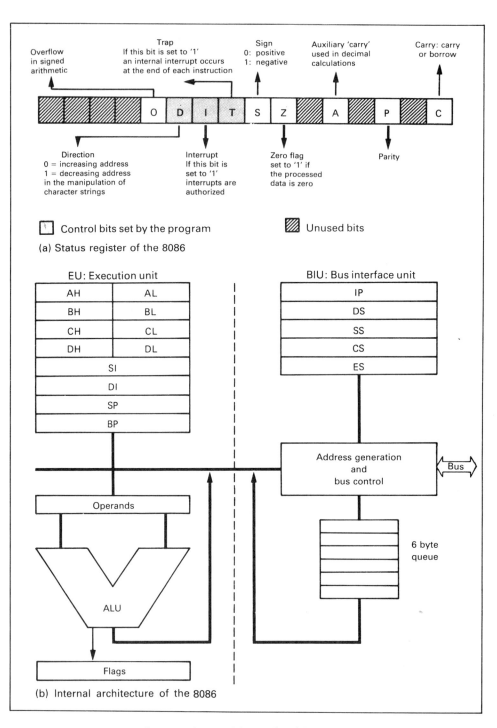

Overflow
in signed
arithmetic

Trap
If this bit is set to '1'
an internal interrupt occurs
at the end of each instruction

Sign
0: positive
1: negative

Auxiliary 'carry'
used in decimal
calculations

Carry: carry
or borrow

O D I T S Z A P C

Direction
0 = increasing address
1 = decreasing address
in the manipulation of
character strings

Interrupt
If this bit is
set to '1'
interrupts are
authorized

Zero flag
set to '1' if
the processed
data is zero

Parity

Control bits set by the program   Unused bits

(a) Status register of the 8086

EU: Execution unit

AH	AL
BH	BL
CH	CL
DH	DL
SI	
DI	
SP	
BP	

Operands

ALU

Flags

BIU: Bus interface unit

| IP |
| DS |
| SS |
| CS |
| ES |

Address generation
and
bus control

Bus

6 byte
queue

(b) Internal architecture of the 8086

FIGURE 23 *Status register and internal architecture of the 8086*

1.2 External organization of the 8086

The 8086 was designed to operate in two modes: the minimum and maximum modes. Some signals from the microprocessor are valid in both modes and others are specific to one mode. The choice of minimum or maximum mode is made by the MN/$\overline{\text{MX}}$ pin by connecting it to +5 V or earth respectively. In the minimum mode the microprocessor itself generates the control signals but these are produced by a special circuit, the 8288, in the maximum mode.

10.2.1 The signals used in the two modes

■ AD_0 to AD_{15}
These are the 16 address/data lines (Figure 24).

■ A_{16}/S_3, A_{17}/S_4, A_{18}/S_5, A_{19}/S_6
These are the four most significant lines of the address bus multiplexed in time with four status signals whose significance is given in Figure 25(a).

■ $\overline{\text{BHE}}/S_7$ (bus high enable)
This signal is provided by the CPU to select one of the bytes of a 16 bit word in conjunction with the address bit A_0 (see Figure 5). S_7 is a status signal available for a possible enhanced version of the 8086.

■ ALE (address latch enable)
This output signal is provided by the 8086 to lock the $\overline{\text{BHE}}$ signal and the 16 address bits available on the multiplexed address/data bus during a bus cycle state. It is therefore intended to be connected, as shown in Figures 22 and 26, to 8282 devices which are both latches and buffers. Three devices are necessary if more than 32 Kbytes are used, otherwise two are sufficient.

■ Ready
This input is used, as with the 8085A, to make asynchronous exchanges between the CPU and memory or input/output circuits. Hence, if the memory devices are fast enough for the 8086, this pin would be connected to +5 V. If they are not fast enough, one or more additional devices would be used to generate a signal which would be at the zero level as long as the memory is not ready to read or write data and which changes to the '1' level as soon as the memory is ready. This signal would be connected to the READY pin.

■ CLK
This input is the clock of the 8086.

■ RESET
Activation of this signal at the high level, during at least four clock pulses, initializes

Signals common to the two modes of the 8086

- • • AD_0 to AD_{15} multiplexed address/data bus
- • • A_{16}/S_3, A_{17}/S_4m A_{18}/S_5 and A_{19}/S_6. The µP provides the four high order bits of the address then the status signals on these four multiplexed outputs
- • • $\overline{BHE}/S_7$. The µP provides the $\overline{BHE}$ signal which enables the high order data byte then a status signal on this, multiplexed output
- • • $\overline{RD}$ Read signal
- • READY   Synchronization with slow memories or peripherals
- • CLK   8086 clock input
- • RESET   8086 initialization
- • NMI   Nonmaskable interrupt demand active on the rising edge
- • INTR   Maskable interrupt demand active at the high level
- • $\overline{TEST}$ Synchronization with a specialized processor

Signals specific to the minimum mode	Signals specific to the maximum mode

• • $M/\overline{IO}$ Selection of memory $(M/\overline{IO} = 1)$
        or a peripheral $(M/\overline{IO} = 0)$
 • • $\overline{WR}$ Write signal
 • • $\overline{INTA}$ Interrupt authorization
 • • $DT/\overline{R}$ } Signals required for
 • • $\overline{DEN}$ } data bus buffers
 •   ALE   Address latching signal
 •   HOLD Direct memory access demand
 •   HLDA Direct memory access authorization
	• • $\overline{S_0}$, $\overline{S_1}$, $\overline{S_2}$ Status signals decoded by the
	      8288
	 • $\overline{RQ}/\overline{GT_0}$, $\overline{RQ}$, $\overline{GT_1}$ Bus access demands
	     and authorization
	 • • $\overline{LOCK}$ Prevention of bus access
	     in multiprocessor operation
	 • QS_0, QS_1 Status of the queue

Characteristics of the two modes of the 8086 compared

	Minimum mode	Maximum mode
Connection of MN/$\overline{MX}$ signal	To +5 V	To ground
Devices forming the processor	8284 + 8086 + 2 × 8282	8284 + 8086 + 8288 + 3 × 8282
Maximum addressing capacity	1 Megabyte in theory most often 32 or 64 K	1 Megabyte
Addressing of I/O ports	By memory instructions or by I/O instructions in theory but most often by I/O instructions	By memory instructions or by I/O instructions
Number of I/O ports addressable by I/O instructions	64 K 8 bit ports in indirect mode by DX with AL or 32 K 16 bit ports in indirect mode by DX with AX or 256 8 bit ports in direct mode with AL or 128 8 bit ports in direct mode with AX	

Comment: Signals preceded by two dots are three state logic

FIGURE 24 *Signals and characteristics of the two modes of the 8086*

$\overline{S_2}$	$\overline{S_1}$	$\overline{S_0}$	Type of transfer in progress
0	0	0	Authorization of an interrupt
0	0	1	Peripheral read
0	1	0	Peripheral write
0	1	1	Halt
1	0	0	Instruction fetch
1	0	1	Memory read
1	1	0	Memory write
1	1	1	Nothing

S_4	S_3	Segment selected
0	0	'Supplementary data'
0	1	'Stack'
1	0	'Program'
1	1	'Data'

S_5 is a copy of the 'interrupt' status bit I
S_6 is at the zero level
S_7 is an unused status bit available for a future version of the 8086

QS_1	QS_0	Status of the queue
0	0	No operation in progress
1	0	The first byte of an instruction has been taken from the queue
0	1	The queue has been reinitialized
1	1	The following byte of an instruction has been taken from the queue

(a) Status signals of the 8086

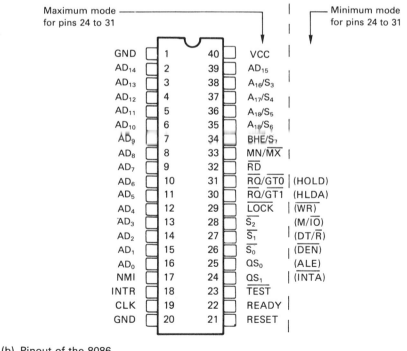

(b) Pinout of the 8086

FIGURE 25 *Status signals and pinout of the 8086*

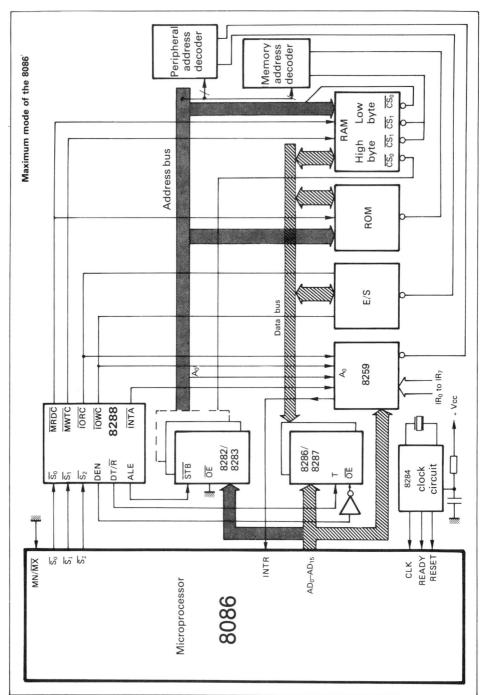

FIGURE 26 *Internal architecture of the 8086 and external organization in maximum mode*

the microprocessor, that is it branches to the subroutine relating to the reset vector.

This input is activated on the falling edge of a positive clock pulse. The three input signals above are provided by the 8284 clock circuit which receives the initialization signal $\overline{\text{RESET}}$.

■ $\overline{\text{RD}}$

This is the read signal.

■ NMI and INTR

These are the two interrupt demands. The first is nonmaskable and is activated by a low to high transition, it is vectored and of higher priority than INTR. The second is maskable, active at the high level and vectored; it is normally used with the 8259A interrupt controller which generates the vector.

■ $\overline{\text{TEST}}$

This input serves to synchronize a specialized processor with the 8086.

10.2.2 Signals specific to the minimum mode

These signals are generated or acted on directly by the 8086 on pins 24 to 31 (Figure 24).

■ DT/$\overline{\text{R}}$ (data transmit receive) and $\overline{\text{DEN}}$ (data enable)
The output of the data bus does not allow more than 6 to 8 devices to be connected. Interface buffers are used to increase the output drive. To facilitate this amplification the CPU provides DT/$\overline{\text{R}}$ and $\overline{\text{DEN}}$ signals. The interface circuits used are 8286 bidirectional buffers each of which handles eight signals. When not in use the outputs of these devices are in a high impedance state. When the bus is to be used, the microprocessor signals this by activating the $\overline{\text{DEN}}$ signal which acts as an enabling signal for the data bus and the outputs of the 8286s leave the high impedance state. The DT/$\overline{\text{R}}$ signal is provided by the CPU as the complement of $\overline{\text{DEN}}$ in order to select the direction of data transfer through the 8286s: towards the microprocessor for an input and towards the memory or a peripheral for an output.

■ $\overline{\text{WR}}$

This is the write signal.

■ M/$\overline{\text{IO}}$

This output is used, as in the 8085A, to distinguish a memory access (M/$\overline{\text{IO}}$ = 1) from a peripheral access (M/$\overline{\text{IO}}$ = 0).

■ $\overline{\text{INTA}}$

This output is the active low 'interrupt authorization' signal. When the 8259A is used, the 8086 generates two pulses on the $\overline{\text{INTA}}$ output if an interrupt demand has been addressed on INTR. These two pulses behave as two read pulses of the vector provided by the 8259A.

■ HOLD and HLDA

These signals are the direct memory access demand and authorization respectively. Putting HOLD into the high state activates this input. The microprocessor responds by setting the HLDA output to the high state and simultaneously putting the address/data bus, the four most significant bits of the address bus and the control signals $\overline{BHE}/S_7$, $\overline{RD}$, $M/\overline{IO}$, $\overline{WR}$, $\overline{INTA}$, $DT/\overline{R}$ and $\overline{DEN}$ into the high impedance state.

10.2.3 Signals specific to the maximum mode

Most of the signals are generated by the 8288 bus controller from the status signals $\overline{S}_0$, $\overline{S}_1$ and $\overline{S}_2$ whose significance is indicated in Figure 25(a).

■ $\overline{S}_0, \overline{S}_1, \overline{S}_2$

These are the status signals provided by the 8086 (Figure 25).

■ $\overline{RQ/GT}_0$, $\overline{RQ/GT}_1$

These two bidirectional signals are the bus access demand and bus access authorization. The first has the higher priority.

■ $\overline{LOCK}$

This output is activated during instructions preceded by the suffix LOCK when the $\overline{INTA}$ output is activated. It prohibits access to the bus by all devices other than that which controls the bus.

■ QS_0, QS_1

These two outputs define the activity of the queue; they are intended for coprocessors. Their significance is given in Figure 25 together with the pin connections of the 8086 in the two modes. The connections and signals for the maximum mode are given in Figure 26.

11. OPERATION OF THE BUS

■ The bus cycle

A bus cycle is a group of four microprocessor clock periods. The sequence of these four clock periods forms a set of four 'states' designated by T_1, T_2, T_3 and T_4 (Figure 27(a)). During a standard cycle the microprocessor:

(a) Puts the address of a memory location or an input/output port on the multiplexed bus in state T_1.

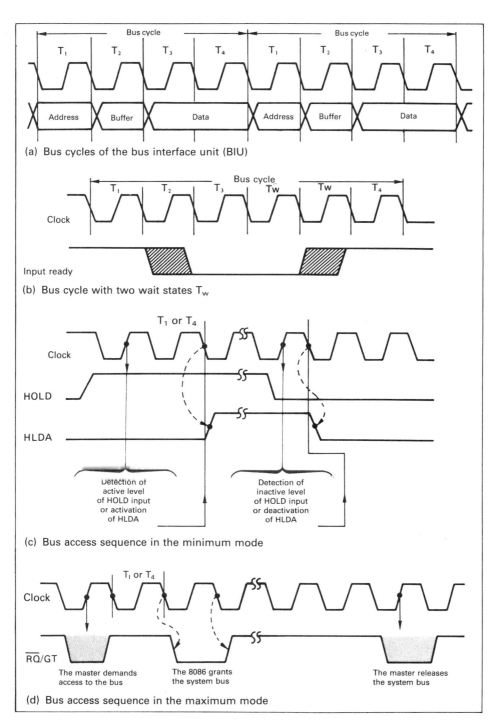

(a) Bus cycles of the bus interface unit (BIU)

(b) Bus cycle with two wait states T_w

(c) Bus access sequence in the minimum mode

(d) Bus access sequence in the maximum mode

FIGURE 27 *Dynamic operation of the 8086*

(b) Activates the read or write signal.

(c) In the case of a write cycle, puts data on the multiplexed bus from state T_2 to state T_4, or in the case of a read cycle receives data during cycles T_3 and T_4; the bus is in the high impedance state during state T_2.

The bus interface unit executes a bus cycle only in order to fill the queue in which the execution unit advances instruction words, in turn, during fetch cycles. During instruction execution cycles, the bus interface unit is unoccupied for several states which are 'BIU idle states'; they are denoted by T_I. Besides idle states T_I, the 8086 inserts wait states T_W under certain conditions during which the contents of the bus remain unchanged. These states, inserted between T_3 and T_4, are used when a memory or peripheral is not fast enough to put data on the bus in state T_4 in the case of a read operation.

■ Bus access sequence in the minimum mode

In the minimum mode, when a master demands access to the bus, it activates the HOLD input of the 8086.

In response to this demand, the microprocessor activates the HLDA output, which signifies bus access authorization for the master, and puts the multiplexed bus, address bits A_{16} to A_{19} and the control signals into the high impedance state. As the HOLD input is asynchronous, the 8086 tests the level of this input on the rising edge of each clock pulse. It then activates the HLDA output at the end of the present bus cycle, either at the end of state T_4 or at the end of an 'idle state T_I' if the bus interface unit is idle. Figure 27(c) shows the timing diagrams of these HOLD and HLDA signals. Bus access demand has priority over an interrupt waiting to be serviced.

■ Bus access sequence in the maximum mode

In the maximum mode, access to the bus is a sequence of three phases operating on a single bidirectional line $\overline{RQ}/GT_0$ or $\overline{RQ}/GT_1$. The sequence is initialized by a system bus access demand by a master, that is by a negative pulse (active at the zero level) sent on the $\overline{RQ}/GT$ input line. The level of this line is tested on the rising edge of each clock pulse. When the active level of $\overline{RQ}/GT$ has been detected, the 8086 responds at the end of the present bus cycle, or at the end of the present wait state if the bus interface unit is idle. The response involves sending another negative pulse on the $\overline{RQ}/GT$ line which becomes an output and putting the system bus into the high impedance state at the end of the next clock pulse. The third and last phase of the sequence occurs when the master which has taken control of the bus has finished its transfer; it then generates another negative pulse on the same line which becomes an input again. Figure 27(d) shows the timing diagram of the $\overline{RQ}/GT$ line. There must be at least one clock pulse before another bus access becomes possible. The two $\overline{RQ}/GT$ lines have priority over an interrupt waiting for service.

The time interval between receipt of a bus access demand by the 8086 and issue of bus access authorization is 3 to 6 clock pulses when the bus access demand arrives during execution of an instruction without the LOCK prefix. When this prefix exists the time interval is 15 clock pulses and 24 to 31 if the present instruction is XCHG.

■ Interfacing memory or a peripheral to the multiplexed bus

Interfacing memory or an input/output device can be done at the multiplexed address/data bus (local bus) level or at the demultiplexed address and data bus (system bus) level. In the first case the memory or input/output device must not disturb the address generated on the bus during T_1. To avoid this, the outputs of the memory or device, which are three state logic, must not be energized by the chip select signal. In fact, putting the address on the multiplexed bus at time T_1 activates the chip select signal and therefore connects the outputs of the memory or input/output device to the bus which conveys the address and then the data. There could be conflict on the bus. To avoid such conflict the three state outputs of the memory or input/output device must be controlled by the read signal as indicated in Figure 28(a). The timing diagram shows the time separation between the ALE signal (used to latch the address) and the read signal which enables the memory outputs.

However, this requires that the memory or input/output device has an 'output enable' (OE) pin. If this is not the case, several interfacing techniques are possible but they all have disadvantages. Figure 28(b) shows a possible interface arrangement in which the main disadvantage is the reduction of time available for decoding the address before accessing the data, as the corresponding timing diagram shows.

■ Interfacing memory or a peripheral to the system bus

The lines of the multiplexed bus cannot source more than 2 mA and the load capacitance of each line must not exceed 100 pF for the characteristics of the 8086 to be observed. This limits the number of devices which can be connected to the multiplexed bus, called the 'local bus', to 5 or 6. To overcome this restriction, Intel have provided the 8286 (noninverting buffer) and 8287 (inverting buffer) power interface devices. They use three state logic and each output can source 32 mA and accept a load capacitance of 300 pF.

These devices are controlled by the $\overline{\text{DEN}}$ and $\text{DT}/\overline{\text{R}}$ signals provided by the 8086. The duration of these signals has been designed in order to isolate the multiplexed bus from devices connected to outputs of the 8286s during state T_1. It has also been designed to avoid conflict on the 'buffered' bus, called the 'system bus', during a read or write operation.

However, a conflict on the system bus can still occur if the devices do not have an output enable control. In the case of a write operation, the outputs of the device are connected to the system bus on which the data to be written are already present between the time when the device is enabled by CS and the time when the WR signal is active. There is a conflict as shown in Figure 29.

12. MEMORY

12.1 *Organization of data in the memories*

Recall that the unit of memory addressing is the byte (also with 20 address bits the

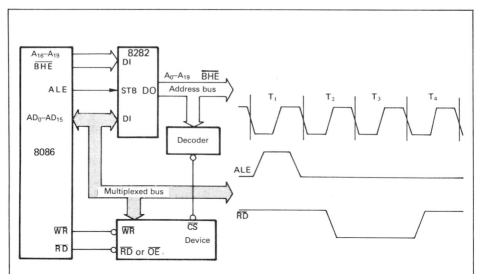

(a) Connection of a device with output enable control to the multiplexed bus

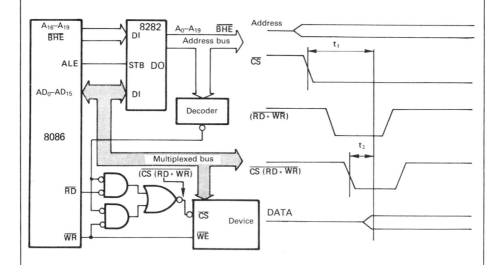

t_1 = access time when the device is selected directly by $\overline{CS}$

t_2 = access time when the device is selected by $\overline{CS}$ ($\overline{RD}$ + $\overline{WR}$)

(b) Connection of a device without output enable control to the multiplexed bus

FIGURE 28 *Interfacing of memory or peripherals to the multiplexed bus*

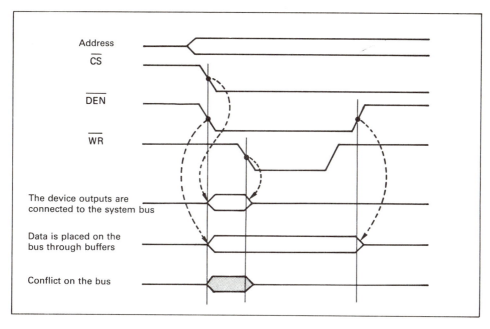

FIGURE 29 *Conflict on the system bus in the case of a device without output enable control*

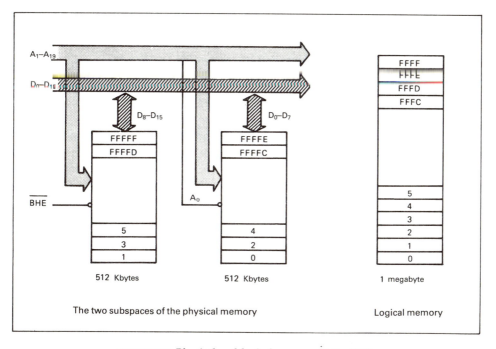

FIGURE 30 *Physical and logical memory of the 8086*

8086 can address up to one million bytes) and that the memory space is organized as two subspaces of identical length (512 Kbytes each). In the case of a word (two bytes) two memory addresses are necessary and the 8086 processes the low (less significant) byte first. The first address of the word, which is normally an even address, therefore corresponds to the low byte (Figure 30).

However, the 8086 also allows words whose first address is odd to be processed. In this case two transfers are necessary for one word; they are executed automatically by the 8086 at the cost of reduced processing speed. These two possible organizations of a 16 bit word in memory were illustrated in Figures 4 and 5 of Part 1.

12.2 *Memory interfacing*

■ Interfacing ROM, PROM and EPROM

These are the easiest devices to interface to the 8086 bus. Since the only operations with these devices are read operations, the A_0 and $\overline{BHE}$ signals need not be included in the address decoding for CS to enable these memories. The first address line used is A_1, and not A_0, and the number of lines used depends, of course, on the size of the memory. Figure 31 shows the interfacing of a 2732 EPROM of 4 Kbytes capacity. This memory has an output enable control, $\overline{OE}$.

■ Interfacing static RAM devices which have an
output enable control

When the memories have common inputs and outputs and an output enable control, the standard RAM interface is that of Figure 31(b) which requires two CS inputs. The diagram of Figure 31(c) requires only a single CS input since the A_0 and $\overline{BHE}$ signals are logically ANDed with $\overline{WR}$. The signals applied to the $\overline{WE}$ inputs of the memories are actually WR.A_0 and $\overline{WR.BHE}$. A 'CS address' signal, which is applied to the CS input, is one of the outputs of an address decoder.

The interfaces shown in Figures 31(b) and 31(c) relate to two memory packages. It is of course possible to increase the RAM capacity by increasing the number of memory packages. In this case the connections remain the same except for the 'CS address' signal which changes. This signal could be, for example, the output CS_0 of an address decoder for the two packages forming the first block of 1K words of 16 bits. The CS_1 output of the same address decoder would be used for the two devices forming the second block of 1K 16 bit words and so on (Figure 31(d)).

The diagrams of Figure 31 use the $\overline{WR}$ signal and correspond to the minimum mode; when the memory and input/output spaces are distinct and have identical addresses in this mode the M/$\overline{IO}$ signal must be included at the decoding level in order to distinguish between a memory and an input/output device. The M/$\overline{IO}$ signal is often included in the decoding as an enabling input of the address decoder. Hence in Figure 31(d) it is connected to input E_3 of the 8205 decoder. It follows that any memory package can be addressed only if M/$\overline{IO}$ is at the '1' level, which corresponds to an instruction requiring a memory access.

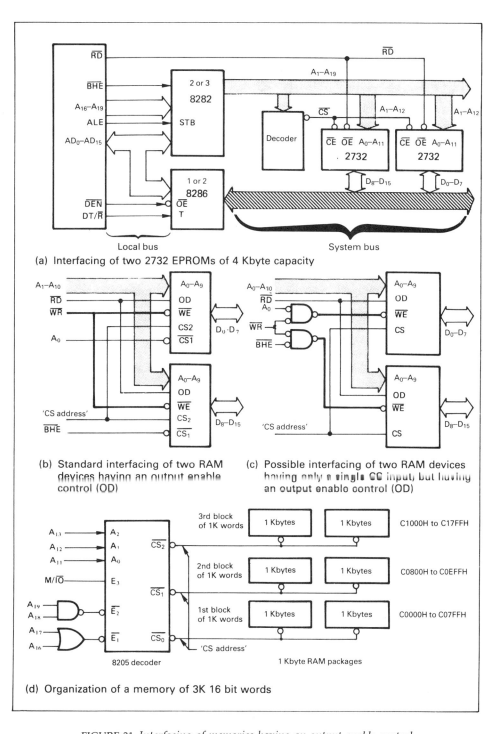

(a) Interfacing of two 2732 EPROMs of 4 Kbyte capacity

(b) Standard interfacing of two RAM devices having an output enable control (OD)

(c) Possible interfacing of two RAM devices having only a single CS input, but having an output enable control (OD)

(d) Organization of a memory of 3K 16 bit words

FIGURE 31 *Interfacing of memories having an output enable control*

■ Interfacing static RAM devices which do not have an
output enable control
With static RAM devices without control of output enable, it is necessary to include
the $\overline{RD}$ and $\overline{WR}$ signals in the decoding for the packages in order to avoid conflicts on
the bus, that is the simultaneous presence of two sets of data on the bus. Two possible
methods for including $\overline{RD}$ and $\overline{WR}$ in the decoding are shown in Figure 32. Here
again the methods are applicable in the minimum mode. But it is easy to transpose
them into the maximum mode by replacing $\overline{RD}$ and $\overline{WR}$ by $\overline{MRDC}$ and $\overline{MWTC}$
respectively and not including the M/$\overline{IO}$ signal, which can be achieved simply by
replacing this signal by the '1' logic level (+ Vcc) at the device inputs. Thus in the
maximum mode, pin E_3 of the 8205 of Figure 31(d) would be connected not to M/$\overline{IO}$
but to + Vcc.

■ Interfacing static RAM devices with separate inputs and outputs
Figure 32(c) shows one possibility for interfacing static RAM with separate inputs
and outputs. The bus receivers are permanently enabled. Enabling of the memory
outputs to the data bus is by the RD.'address CS' signal.

12.3 *Segmentation of the memory space*

■ The logical address and the physical address
The 8086 has an address bus of 20 bits. However, to reduce the length of instructions
by limiting the address field to 16 bits, the memory space is divided into *N* segments.
Each segment has a maximum capacity of 64 Kbytes and has a name which is a label.
The number *N* is fixed by the programmer depending on the application. The physical
locations in memory of four of the *N* segments, that is the first physical addresses of
these four segments, are indicated by the contents of four registers called 'segment
registers'. In this way the programmer has four segments available at any time; they
are also specialized. These segments are:

> The program segment, reserved for instructions.
> The data segment which will contain the program data.
> The stack segment reserved for this purpose.
> The supplementary data segment which is another memory space reserved for
> data under certain conditions.

The segment registers assigned to these four current segments are CS (code
segment), DS (data segment), SS (stack segment) and ES (extra segment) respectively.
If the programmer needs one or more segments other than the four current
segments which have been defined, it is sufficient to load the base addresses of the
new segments into the appropriate segment registers. In order to be able to write
these 20 bit base addresses into the 16 bit segment registers the four least significant
bits of these base addresses must be zeros. This is the only restriction imposed on
segments which can be adjacent or separate or overlayed either partially or totally
(Figure 33(a)). The address of a memory location within a segment is the relative
address (displacement) of this memory location with respect to the first memory

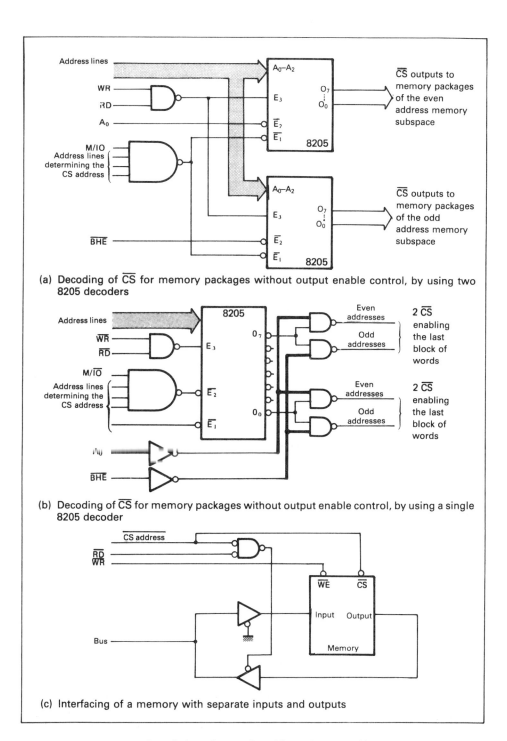

(a) Decoding of $\overline{CS}$ for memory packages without output enable control, by using two 8205 decoders

(b) Decoding of $\overline{CS}$ for memory packages without output enable control, by using a single 8205 decoder

(c) Interfacing of a memory with separate inputs and outputs

FIGURE 32 *Interfacing of memories without output enable control*

location of the segment. This relative address, expressed in 16 bits, is a logical address. The corresponding physical address is calculated by adding the logical address to the base address of the segment. The latter is easily obtained by adding four zeros on the right of the contents of the segment register. In this way in Figure 33(b), which shows calculation of the physical address, the contents of the segment register, hexadecimal 3256, give the hexadecimal address of the segment as 32560.

■ Managament of the segment register

For every memory access, the microprocessor automatically calculates the physical address by means of its integrated memory management unit using:

(a) The segment specified implicitly or explicitly in the instruction and whose base address is contained in the corresponding register segment;
(b) The displacement (offset) indicated in the address field of the instruction.

The segment register SS is initialized at the start by the programmer and subsequently updated automatically by stack read or write instructions. Only management of the segment registers DS and ES requires any attention on the part of the programmer. This is facilitated by the fact that the bus interface unit affects a segment register by default for every memory access. This signifies that if the program does not explicitly indicate a segment register, the microprocessor chooses one automatically. Thus when memory access concerns general data so that the programmer has not specified any segment register, the microprocessor takes the DS register as the segment register. But, in a program using assembler language pseudo-instructions, it is possible to choose one of the registers CS, ES and SS as indicated in Figure 33(c). The table in this figure shows that of the six types of memory access, three are always managed by the bus interface unit and the choice of pointer register which provides the displacement is implicit. After examining the instruction set of the 8086, the possibilities of accessing data by a segment register other than that which is chosen by default by the bus interface unit will be considered.

Two possibilities are offered to the programmer according to the size of the application. The first is valid for program and data files less than 64 and 128 Kbytes respectively. It consists of initializing the four segment registers once only without further attention. It is thus possible to use only a single data segment. In this first possibility, which can cover a reasonable number of applications, segmentation brings only one insignificant constraint for the programmer, the transfer to him of the security of memory areas protected by the microprocessor itself.

The second possibility involves the programmer partitioning his application into as many segments as he wishes and, of course, correctly managing them. To access a segment other than one of the four current ones, it is necessary to modify the contents of a segment register.

Comment. When a program contains no instructions for either loading or modifying the segment registers and no branch instructions to a segment other than the current program segment, it can be dynamically relocated anywhere in memory space with the one condition that the contents of the segment registers pointing to the new base addresses must be updated. For this it is necessary that all displacements

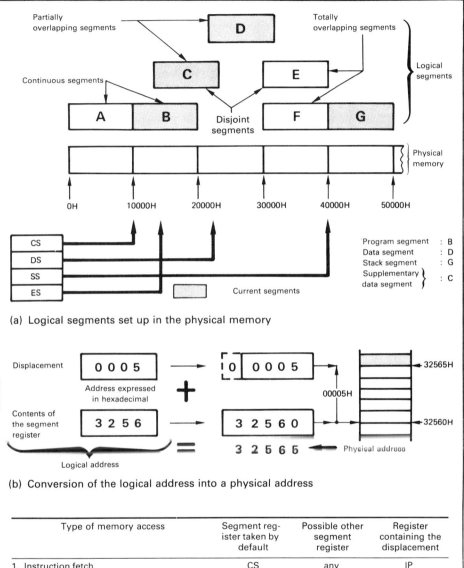

(a) Logical segments set up in the physical memory

(b) Conversion of the logical address into a physical address

Type of memory access	Segment register taken by default	Possible other segment register	Register containing the displacement
1. Instruction fetch	CS	any	IP
2. Stack operation	SS	any	SP
3. Access to data except 4, 5, 6	DS	CS,ES,SS	effective address
4. Access to the source data ⎫ of a string	DS	CS,ES,SS	SI
5. Access to the destination ⎬ of data ⎭ characters	ES	any	DI
6. Access to data with BP as base register	SS	CS,DS,ES	effective address

(c) Segment registers defined implicitly by the type of memory access or specified by the user in the program

FIGURE 33 *Segmentation of the 8086*

should be relative to the base addresses contained in the segment registers.

12.4 Loading the stack into RAM

The programmer can use as many stack segments as he wishes. The current stack segment is loaded into memory from the base address contained in the segment register. Since the stack extends towards lower addresses, writing into the stack (PUSH instruction) is always preceded by decrementing the stack pointer register by two. The latter is normally the SP register. When the BP register is used as an address register, the SS segment register is used by default.

Stack operations involve words and not bytes. The pointer register SP contains the address of the last word on the stack; so this register points to the top of the stack (TOS).

Figure 34 shows loading of the stack into memory and its operation by giving the states of the stack after execution of the PUSH AX instruction (write the contents of the AX register into the stack) then the two instructions POP AX and POP BX (read the contents into registers AX and BX from the stack).

12.5 Reserved memory locations for the 8086

Two memory areas are reserved for the processor at two extremities of the memory space. For execution of certain functions, in particular the vectoring of interrupts, the processor needs the two following memory areas:

From 00000H to 00013H which is 19 bytes.
From FFFF0H to FFFFBH which is 11 bytes.

In addition to these memory locations, Intel reserves other memory locations for the use of devices or software associated with the 8086. These reserved areas are:

From 00014H to 0007FH.
From FFFFCH to FFFFFH.

Figure 34(c) shows these reserved memory areas.

13. INPUT/OUTPUT DEVICES

The 8086 can interface up to 64K 8 bit ports or 32K 16 bit ports in the I/O structure using either I/O instructions (I/O space separated from memory space) or memory instructions (I/O space included in the memory space). In the first case the instructions are limited to two – IN and OUT – but they have the advantage of high speed. I/O transfers are made with accumulator AL for 8 bit ports and with AX for 16 bit ports.

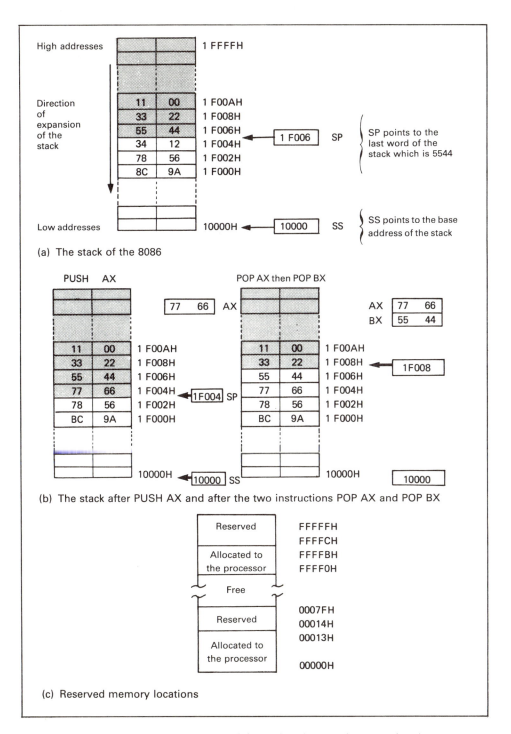

FIGURE 34 *Location in memory of the stack and reserved memory locations*

The first 256 bytes of the I/O space are directly addressable whereas the 64K bytes are addressable indirectly by the DX register. The 8 bit ports can be connected to either of the following:

Lines D_0 to D_7 of the data bus; their addresses are therefore even, represented by $A_0 = 0$.

Lines D_8 to D_{15} of the data bus; their addresses are therefore odd, represented by $A_0 = 1$.

It is of course desirable to balance the load between the low and high parts of the data bus. Choice of one of these two parts involves the need to include the A_0 and BHE lines in the decoding function. Figure 35 shows several techniques for generating the 'CS address' signals which allow the I/O device to be selected.

The technique of Figure 35(a) offers three possibilities:

(a) I/O transfer relative to an 8 bit port connected to the low half of the bus. The address is therefore even. The 8086 detects an even address and 8 bits of data (this information is contained in the transfer instruction). In consequence it sets A_0 to 0 and $\overline{\text{BHE}}$ to 1.

(b) I/O transfer relative to an 8 bit port connected to the high half of the data bus. The address is therefore odd. The 8086 detects an odd address and 8 bits of data (this information is again included in the transfer instruction) and sets A_0 to 1 and $\overline{\text{BHE}}$ pto 0.

(c) I/O transfer relative to a 16 bit port connected of course to 16 bits of the data bus. The information contained in the transfer instruction causes the microprocessor to set A_0 to 0 and $\overline{\text{BHE}}$ to 0.

The technique of Figure 35(b) offers the first two possibilities above but not the third since only one of the two 8205 decoders could be enabled during an I/O transfer on account of the cross connection of the A_0 and $\overline{\text{BHE}}$ lines to the $\overline{\text{E}}_2$ and E_3 inputs of the 8205 decoders.

In the arrangement of Figure 35(c) a single 8205 is used to generate four even 'CS address' and four odd 'CS address' signals for 8 bit ports. The $\overline{\text{BHE}}$ line is not involved, a transfer instruction containing an even address causes a transfer relative to an 8 bit port with an even address even if the instruction specifies 16 bits of data. The distinction between even and odd addresses is made by bit A_2 of the 8205 which is connected to address bit A_0.

The arrangement of Figure 35(d) offers only the possibility of addressing 16 bit ports since the 8205 is enabled only if $A_0 = 0$ and $\overline{\text{BHE}} = 0$.

Addressing of I/O ports is most often achieved by decoding; a decoder provides the 'CS address' signals at its outputs for the packages to be enabled. However, it is equally possible to use addressing by linear selection. This technique involves assigning an address bit to an I/O device exclusively. If the latter is an 8205 parallel interface, requiring bits A_1 and A_2 to select one internal register from four, the bit to be assigned exclusively must be chosen from bits A_3 to A_{15}, which allows 13 I/O devices to be addressed without decoding.

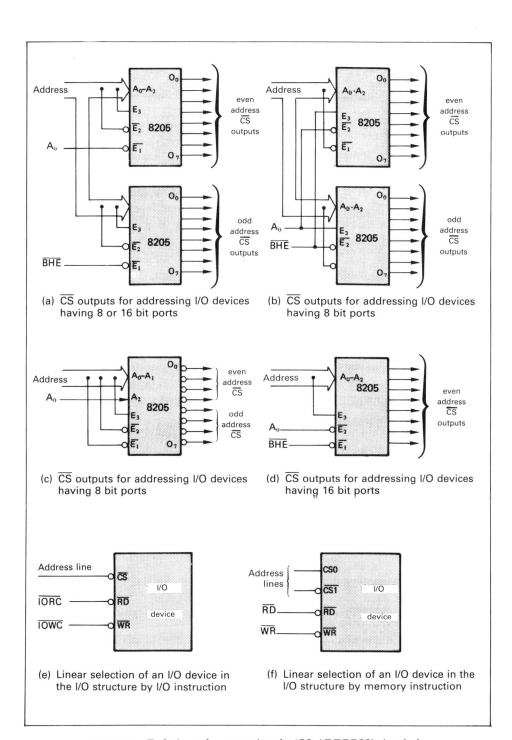

(a) $\overline{CS}$ outputs for addressing I/O devices having 8 or 16 bit ports

(b) $\overline{CS}$ outputs for addressing I/O devices having 8 bit ports

(c) $\overline{CS}$ outputs for addressing I/O devices having 8 bit ports

(d) $\overline{CS}$ outputs for addressing I/O devices having 16 bit ports

(e) Linear selection of an I/O device in the I/O structure by I/O instruction

(f) Linear selection of an I/O device in the I/O structure by memory instruction

FIGURE 35 *Techniques for generating the 'CS ADDRESS' signals for selecting I/O devices*

Addressing by linear selection in the I/O structure by I/O instruction (I/O space separated from memory space) does not pose any problems. Figure 35(e) gives an example of the 8086 in the maximum mode. In contrast, linear selection in the I/O structure by memory instructions is more difficult. In fact the 8086 uses addresses FFFF0H to FFFFFH during a reset, which prevents selection of an I/O device by a single address line at the '1' level. Also the 8086 uses the addresses 00000H to 00003H for interrupts, which precludes selection of an I/O device by a single address line at the '0' level. To avoid these situations where addresses would relate to memory and an I/O device at the same time, at least two address lines must be used: one at the '1' level and the other at the '0' level (Figure 35(f)). By choosing these two address lines from lines A_8 to A_{15}, erroneous addressing is no longer possible.

Figure 36(a) is a specific example of addressing 16 8255 parallel interfaces in the minimum mode and in the I/O structure by memory instructions. RA, ROM and I/O space are indicated in Figure 36(b) in addition to the addresses of each of the ports of the 8255s; each has four – A, B, C and the control register.

Figure 37(a) shows a possible addressing scheme for 16 8255 devices in the I/O structure using I/O instructions, still in the minimum mode. These two addressing schemes are easily converted into the maximum mode by replacing:

(a) $\overline{RD}$ by $\overline{MRDC}$ for the arrangement of Figure 36(a) and by $\overline{IORC}$ for the arrangement of Figure 37(a).
(b) $\overline{WR}$ by $\overline{MWTC}$ for the arrangement of Figure 36(a) and by $\overline{IOWC}$ for the arrangement of Figure 37(a).

and by connecting the $\overline{E_2}$ inputs of Figure 37(a) to ground or an address bit, the $M/\overline{IO}$ signal does not exist in the maximum mode. In the 64 Kbytes of I/O space some memory locations are reserved by Intel for possible future products (Figure 37(b)).

Comment. During transfers relating to an I/O device, bits A_{16} to A_{19} are at the zero level.

14. INTERRUPTS

This concept involves interrupting a program which is being executed by the processor in order to process a task which is considered to be more urgent. When execution of this task is finished, the processor returns to the halted program, it then continues from the point where it stopped. An interrupt can be initiated in either of the following ways:

(a) By an I/O device also called a peripheral. The interrupt is then 'external' and it must be sent either to the nonmaskable interrupt (NMI) input, which is an interrupt demand which cannot be masked by the program, or to the INTR input which can be masked by the program.
(b) By the 8086 processor itself. The interrupt is then 'internal'.

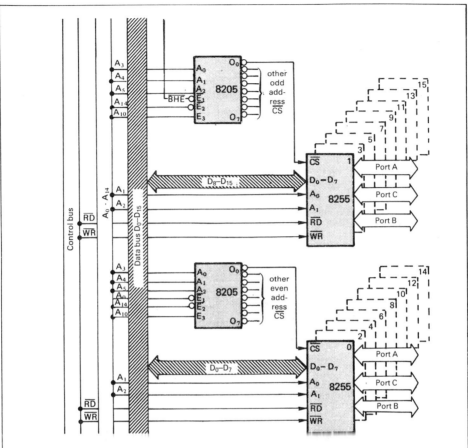

(a) Addressing of 16 8255 parallel interfaces in the I/O structure by memory instructions

| | FFFFFH |
	FFFF0H
Bootstrap	
User memory space (RAM and ROM)	
	FC000H
	0043FH
I/O space	
	00400H
Vector table	
	00000H

Port	Device	Port addresses	
A	0	00400H	
B	0	00402H	even
C	0	00404H	addresses
Control register	0	00406H	
A	1	00401H	
B	1	00403H	odd
C	1	00405H	addresses
Control register	1	00407H	

(b) Location of I/O space and I/O port addresses

FIGURE 36 *Example of addressing I/O devices when the I/O space is included in the memory space*

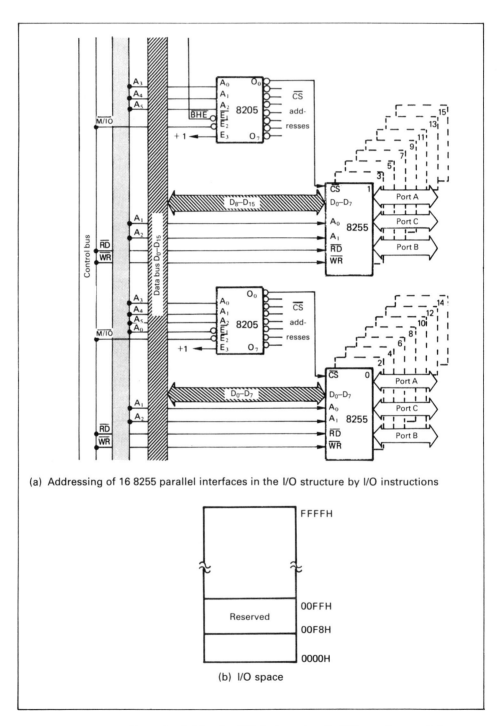

(a) Addressing of 16 8255 parallel interfaces in the I/O structure by I/O instructions

(b) I/O space

FIGURE 37 *Example of addressing I/O devices when the I/O space is separated from the memory space*

14.1 The vector table

Each accepted interrupt leads to the execution of a specific subroutine whose start address, called the 'pointer', is stored in four memory locations of a table. The first two contain the base address of the segment (or more precisely the 16 most significant bits of this base address); the last two contain the displacement expressed in 16 bits. When servicing an interrupt, the 8086 loads the base address into the CS register and the displacement into the program counter IP. The vector table can accept up to 256 interrupts each one being identified by a number called a 'vector'. Addresses 00000H to 003FFH are reserved for this vector table of capacity 1 Kbyte. In fact addresses 00014H to 00080H are reserved by Intel to ensure compatibility of future devices with the 8086. Taking account of this reserved space, which corresponds to vectors 5 to 31, 229 possible interrupts remain for the user which is more than necessary. Of these 229 vectors, five are obligatorily assigned to clearly specified interrupts; vectors 0, 1, 2, 3 and 4. Therefore the user chooses a vector number from numbers 32 to 255 for each internal and external interrupt of his application. Figure 38(a) shows the vector table.

14.2 External interrupts

There are three external interrupt lines in a hierarchy of decreasing priority: RESET, NMI and INTR.

■ RESET

This is a special external interrupt since on the one hand it cannot receive an interrupt demand originating from a peripheral and on the other hand the base address of the corresponding subroutine is not contained in the vector table.

The microprocessor is automatically diverted to address FFFF0H where the user has placed a JUMP instruction which branches the 8086 to the start of the program. Also, powering up of the 8086 and activation of the RESET input by applying the '1' level for at least four clock pulses causes all activity of the 8086 to stop. On the negative transition of the RESET signal the processor executes a specified sequence which lasts for about ten clock pulses.

This sequence puts the bus into the high impedance state and sets certain signals as indicated in Figure 38(b). After execution of this sequence the registers are initialized as follows:

flag register = 0000H which inhibits interrupts and single step operation
CS = FFFFH and IP = 0000H, the physical address pointed to is therefore FFF0H
DS = 0000H
SS = 0000H
ES = 0000H

The result of this sequence is that the microprocessor branches to the physical address FFFF0H where the programmer has previously placed an unconditional branch instruction to the start of the program. Since maskable interrupts are inhibited

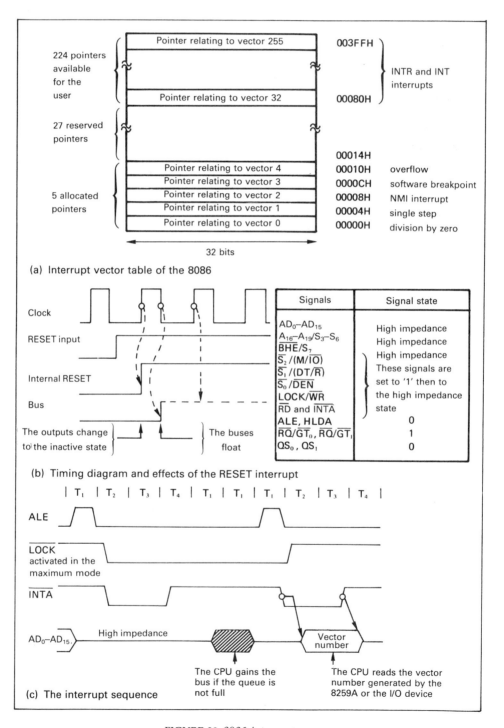

(a) Interrupt vector table of the 8086

(b) Timing diagram and effects of the RESET interrupt

(c) The interrupt sequence

FIGURE 38 *8086 interrupts*

by RESET, the programmer must enable them in the program. The states of the 8086 signals after activation of the RESET function are shown in Figure 38(b).

■ NMI

This input is activated by a rising edge; the '1' level must be maintained for a time greater than two clock pulses. The transition from level '1' to level '0' of the interrupt demand can occur before, during or after execution of the corresponding subroutine. However, this interrupt demand must be a signal free from transients and contact bounce since each rising edge arriving after the start of execution of the subroutine is interpreted as another interrupt demand which is stored and will be serviced. The nonmaskable interrupt is normally reserved for serious events such as accidental power failure, a memory error or a bus parity error. The associated vector number is 2. If the NMI pin is not used it must be connected to the '1' level. Activation of an interrupt demand on this input starts at the end of the instruction being executed. The 8086 saves the contents of the status register and then the CS and IP registers on the stack. It resets the status bits I and T to zero which inhibits interrupts and single step operation. Then it executes the branch process to the subroutine relating to vector 2 which consists of loading the pointer of this vector into the CS and IP registers.

■ INTR

An interrupt demand on this pin is maskable by setting the I bit of the status register to '0' or '1' by the CLI and STI instructions respectively. The interrupt demand signal is active at the '1' level and must be maintained active until the 8086 has generated the $\overline{\text{INTA}}$ signal. If the interrupts have been authorized by the program, the CPU terminates the instruction in course of execution and executes the sequence to service the interrupt. Exceptionally, when the current instruction is a MOV or POP relating to a segment register, the CPU does not start the interrupt sequence until after execution of the current instruction and the following one. This sequence consists of the following:

(a) Saving the contents of the status register and the return address as expressed by the contents of the CS and IP registers.
(b) Generating two $\overline{\text{INTA}}$ cycles of which the first contains two TI states (the bus interface unit is idle during TI states). During the first cycle the multiplexed bus is in the high impedance state. During the second cycle the CPU reads the vector, that is the interrupt number, on the data bus; this number must have been put there directly or indirectly by the peripheral which made an interrupt request (Figure 38(c)). The 8259A interrupt controller is specially designed to receive this vector (Figure 39). In the maximum mode the $\overline{\text{LOCK}}$ signal is activated.
(c) Multiplying the vector by four to obtain the first address of the interrupt pointer, that is the address of the subroutine relating to this interrupt. This 32 bit address is loaded into the CS and IP registers. The 8086 then executes the subroutine which ends with a specific IRET instruction whose execution restores the return address saved on the stack to CS and IP and the values of the flags to the status register. It is to be noted that this restoration involves automatic authorization of interrupts since it restores the value which it had before activation of the interrupt demand to the interrupt flag.

The 8259A interrupt controller has eight hierarchical interrupt levels but several

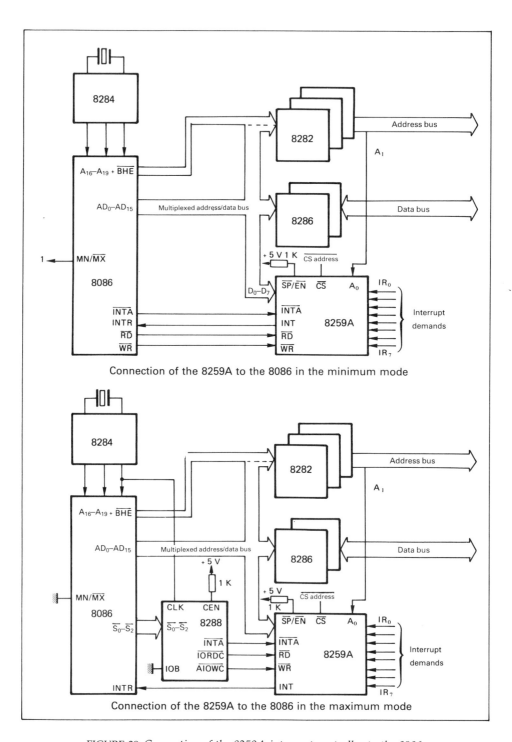

Connection of the 8259A to the 8086 in the minimum mode

Connection of the 8259A to the 8086 in the maximum mode

FIGURE 39 *Connection of the 8259A interrupt controller to the 8086*

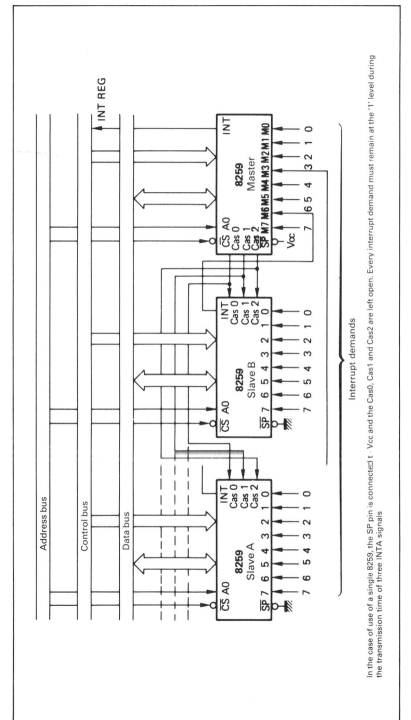

FIGURE 40 *Cascading of several 8259A interrupt controllers*

In the case of use of a single 8259, the SP pin is connected – Vcc and the Cas0, Cas1 and Cas2 are left open. Every interrupt demand must remain at the '1' level during the transmission time of three INTA signals

8259s can be cascaded which allows up to 64 levels of interrupt. Figure 39 shows interfacing of the 8259A to the 8086 in the two modes. Figure 40 is an example of cascading of several 8259As.

14.3 *Internal interrupts*

The 8086 has three internal interrupts which are generated automatically by the processor and software interrupts which can be inserted into the program.

14.3.1 Automatic internal interrupts

■ Interrupt 0: impossible division
This interrupt occurs when the quotient of a division is too large for the register provided; this occurs particularly in the case of a division by zero. This interrupt is not maskable.

■ Interrupt 1: single step operation
If the T (trace) bit of the status register is set to '1' by the programmer, the 8086 generates an internal interrupt at the end of execution of an instruction. The programmer can examine the contents of the registers in the subroutine associated with vector 1. This is single step operation.

When the 8086 accepts an interrupt 1, it carries out the following operations:

(a) It saves the contents of the status register and the return address (the contents of CS and IP).
(b) It resets status bits I and T to zero which inhibits interrupts and permits the subroutine of vector 1 to operate normally, that is without operating in single step.
(c) It loads the start address of the subroutine, contained in addresses 00004H to 00007H, into the CS and IP registers.

The subroutine ends with the instruction IRET which restores the contents of the status register saved on the stack in such a way that the T status bit is again set to '1'. Therefore single step operation continues.

The 8086 does not have instructions which permit the T status bit in the status register to be set directly to '0' or '1'; but it is possible to modify the T bit when the status word is saved on the stack.

(a) This bit is set to 1 by taking the logical OR of the status word on the stack and 0100H.
(b) It is set to 0 by taking the logical AND of the status word on the stack and FEFFH.

Restoration of the status word modified in this way, which is done by the POPF instruction, enables single step operation of the 8086.

■ Interrupt 4: overflow
This interrupt occurs if the O (overflow) status bit in the status register has been set to

'1' by an overflow and if an INTO instruction has been inserted into the program and executed. This instruction is specific to an overflow and is not maskable.

Although these three interrupts are automatic, the latter two require a deliberate action by the programmer.

14.3.2 Internal software interrupts

■ Interrupt 3: software breakpoint
This interrupt is generated by the 8086 during execution of the instruction INT 3 coded in a single byte. Insertion of this instruction into the program allows it to be debugged by the standard breakpoint technique.

■ Interrupt N: INT N (N ≠ 3)
This nonmaskable interrupt is expressed in two bytes; the second indicates the number of the interrupt, that is the vector. It does not generate $\overline{\text{INTA}}$ cycles since the vector is provided in the instruction itself. It resets the I and T bits to zero which inhibits interrupts and single step operation. The vector must be chosen by the programmer from vectors 32 to 255.

15. 8086 SOFTWARE

15.1 *Addressing modes*

The following are features of the 8086 instructions

■ Instructions without an explicit operand
These are the instructions for processor control (HLT, LOCK, WAIT), arithmetic adjustment (DAA, DAS), flag setting (CLI, STI, ...) and processing strings of characters for which the operands are implicit (MOVB, CMPW, ...).

■ Instructions with one explicit operand
These are the stack read and write, shift and rotate, increment and decrement, multiplication and division instructions.

■ Instructions with two explicit operands
These are the transfer, arithmetic calculation and logical instructions. The operations are made between registers or between registers and memory but never from memory to memory, except for strings of characters.
    In operations on 16 bits of data, the contents of one of the AX, BX, CX, DX, BP, SP, DI or SI registers can normally be involved as an operand with the exception of multiplication, division and certain instructions relating to strings of characters.

The addressing modes of operands are as follows.

■ Immediate addressing
The source operand is data expressed in 8 or 16 bits. Execution of an instruction of this kind is very rapid since it is done solely with information in the queue.

■ Register addressing
The operand or operands are contained in one or two registers. As for the previous addressing mode, execution of the instruction is very rapid. The length of the data is indicated by that of the registers.

ADD   AL,   BL   ;   addition of two 8 bit data elements
ADD   AX,   BX   ;   addition of two 16 bit data elements

In the case where the instruction contains two operands the lengths of the source and destination operands must be identical.

■ Direct addressing
The instruction directly contains the displacement of the data in the segment concerned. Recall that for each memory reference instruction there is a segment chosen by default when the programmer has not specified a segment register. The length of the data must be the same as that of the register; the displacement is expressed in 16 bits.

MOV AX, LABEL ; effective address EA = address represented by LABEL

In this instruction the name associated with the address of the data is represented by the general term LABEL which is an alphanumeric expression defined by the syntax of the assembler. Since the AX register is of 16 bits the 8086 fetches two data bytes from addresses LABEL and LABEL + 1. The low-order byte of the 16 bit data, located at address LABEL (which is normally an even address) is transferred into AL.

■ Indirect register addressing
The effective address of the displacement of the data, which will be denoted by EA, using Intel's symbols, is the contents of a register: BX, BP, DI or SI.

CMP   AX,   (BP)   ;   EA = contents of BP

The contents of the four registers involved in indirect register addressing can be modified by the LEA (load effective address) instruction for loading an effective address into a register. For example:

LEA   BX,   LABEL

When the BP register is used, the data is considered to belong to the stack segment if the program has not specified any segment register in the instruction.

■ Base addressing (indirect by base register)
The indirect address register for this mode is BX, assigned by default to segment

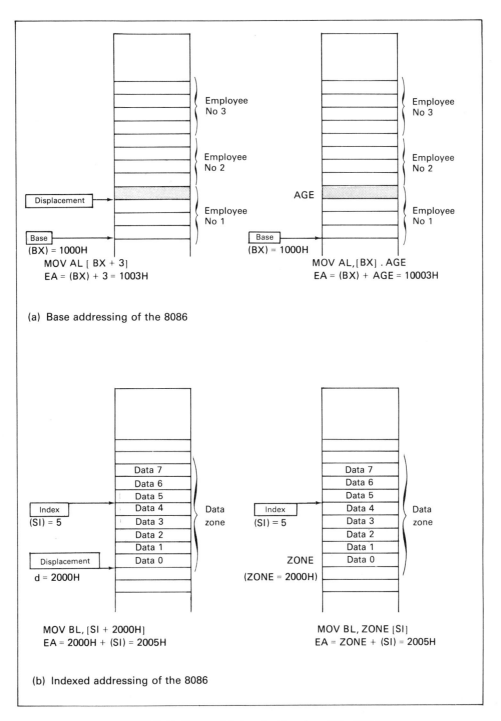

FIGURE 41 *Base and indexed addressing of the 8086*

register DS, or BP, assigned by default to segment register SS. A displacement may or may not exist.

```
ADD   BL,   (BX)          ;   EA = contents of BX
ADD   BL,   (BX + 8)      ;   EA = contents of BX incremented by 8
ADD   BL,   (BX).LABEL    ;   EA = contents of BX + LABEL
```

When a data file consists of items each containing numerous data bytes (for example in the personnel file of an organization, each salary is an item and much data is necessary per item) addressing by base register is practicable. Hence the base register BX can point to the first byte of the item (the first byte relating to the employee) and the displacement indicates the byte concerned in the item (for example the professional category of the employee) as shown in Figure 41(a). This mode is applicable within a segment.

■ Indexed addressing (indirect by index register)
In this mode, which exists within a segment, it is the displacement which points to the beginning of an area or item and the contents of the index register allow access to one data element of the item (Figure 41(b)).

```
AND   (SI + 100H),23H   ;   EA = contents of SI + 100H
```

The first data element of the area or item is pointed to when the index register contains zero. The displacement is of 8 or 16 bits.

■ Indexed base addressing
The effective address is the sum of the contents of the base register, the contents of the index register and the displacement if there is one. This mode is applicable within a segment.

```
MOV   (BX)(SI),       AL  ;  EA = contents of BX + contents of SI
MOV   (BX + 3)(SI),   AL  ;  EA = contents of BX + contents of SI + 3
```

This complex mode of addressing will be explained with the help of an example. Consider a data area consisting of N blocks of n items, each item containing p bytes. The first address of the area will be referred to by the name ZONE.

The first address of any block is accessed by the contents of a base register BX or BP, BX in this example. The first byte of any item of the block addressed is accessed by the contents of an index register SI or DI, SI in this example. Within an item any byte is accessed by the displacement indicated in the instruction (Figure 42). Assume

$N = 8$ (8 blocks), $n = 3$ (3 items per block)
$p = 4$ (4 bytes per item),   (DS) = 10000H, ZONE = 3000H

To access the 4th byte of the second item in block number 2 take

(BX) = 0CH, access to block 1, the length of each block is 0CH bytes
displacement = 08H, access to item 2, the length of each item is 04 bytes
(SI) = 03, access to byte 03 of item 2. For example:

ADD ZONE (BX)(SI + 8), 3 BH

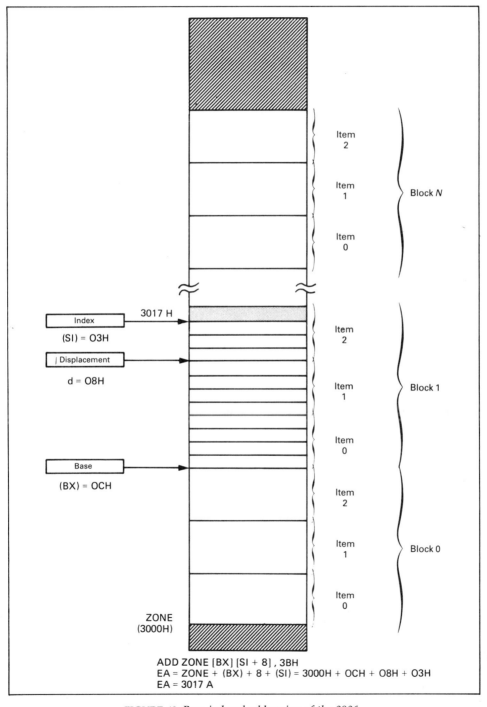

FIGURE 42 *Base indexed addressing of the 8086*

The effective address is

EA = ZONE + (BX) + 8 + (SI) = 3000H + 0CH + 08H + 03H
EA = 3017H

In this mode the indicated address is the displacement with respect to the program counter IP. This displacement is limited to −128/+127 for conditional branches and to −32768/+32767 for unconditional jumps and subroutine calls. The fact that the displacement is limited to −128/+127 for conditional jumps is a constraint at the programming level. It is, however, possible to avoid it by using two instructions instead of one. To realize the equivalent of the instruction JS JUMP with a displacement greater than −128 or +127, the following programming technique is used:

```
JNZ   NEXT
JMP   JUMP
NEXT  ...  ;  first instruction to be executed if Z = 0
  .
  .
  .
JUMP  ...  ;  first instruction to be executed if Z = 1
```

15.2 The instruction set

■ AAA
This is the ASCII correction for addition, that is correction for the addition of decimal numbers expressed by 8 bits (extended decimal numbers). It sets the four high order bits of the accumulator to zero in order to express a decimal number by eight bits.

■ AAD
This is the ASCII correction for division, that is correction for the division of extended decimal numbers. This instruction modifies the numerator in AL before dividing two decimal numbers expressed in 8 bits, for which the quotient is a decimal number expressed in 8 bits.

■ AAM
This is the ASCII correction for multiplication, that is correction for the multiplication of two extended decimal numbers. This instruction transforms the result of the multiplication into two decimal numbers each expressed in 8 bits.

■ AAS
This is the ASCII correction for subtraction, that is correction for the subtraction of two extended decimal numbers. This instruction transforms the result of the subtraction in register AL by putting the 4 high order bits to zero.

■ ADC
This is the addition with carry of two operands, signed or not, expressed in 8 or 16 bits. The result takes the place occupied by the destination operand.

■ ADD

This is the addition without carry of two operands, signed or not, expressed in 8 or 16 bits. The result takes the place occupied by the destination operand.

■ AND

This is the logical AND operation on two operands; the result takes the place occupied by the destination operand.

■ CALL

This is the calling instruction of a subroutine, also called a procedure. Although there is only a single mnemonic expression, the assembler generates a different operation code according to the location of the subroutine. Four cases can occur.

CALL direct intrasegment. The subroutine is stored in the same segment as the CALL instruction. It therefore involves a relative address instruction with a maximum displacement of ±32 Kbytes. The name of the subroutine is indicated in the instruction and the programmer must declare it NEAR.

CALL indirect intrasegment. This again involves calling a procedure declared NEAR, that is situated in the same segment as the calling instruction CALL and whose relative displacement is limited to ±32 Kbytes. This time the subroutine is no longer indicated by its name, but by a 16 bit register or memory location containing the address of the subroutine. For example:

CALL   AX
CALL   SUBROUT   (BX)

Execution of these instructions involves replacing the contents of the program counter IP with the contents of AX for the first example and with the contents of the 16 bit memory location designated by SUBROUT (BX) for the second.

CALL direct intersegment. This involves calling a subroutine declared FAR by the programmer, that is situated outside the current segment containing the calling instruction, and therefore anywhere in memory with no limit to the displacement. The name of the subroutine is indicated in the instruction. The CS and IP registers are both used and of course their previous contents are saved on the stack.

CALL indirect intersegment. This is the case of a FAR procedure indicated in the instruction by a memory location of 32 bits containing the total address of the procedure that is the new contents of CS and IP. The previous contents of these registers are of course saved on the stack.

■ CBW

This instruction extends the sign of the byte in register AL to each bit of register AH. For example:

contents of AX before execution of CBW 1011001001100111
contents of AX after execution of CBW 0000000001100111

■ CLC
This sets the CARRY flag to zero.

■ CLD
This sets the D (direction) command bit used in the manipulation of character strings to zero.

■ CLI
This sets the I (interrupt) command bit to zero.

■ CMC
The CARRY flag is complemented: $\overline{C} \to C$.

■ CMP
This is the comparison instruction. It subtracts the source operand from the destination operand without deleting these two operands but the flags are set.

■ CMPS and CMPB/CMPW
This is the comparison instruction for two character strings. It subtracts the destination operand pointed to by DI from the source operand pointed to by SI. The mnemonic expressions CMPB and CMPW can also be used for bytes and words respectively. These instructions can be used with REPE/REPZ or REPNE/REPNZ.

■ CWD
This is the instruction to extend the sign of a word contained in register AX to all the bits of register DX. This instruction can be used to obtain a double length (double word of 32 bits) dividend before realizing the division of two words.

■ DAA
This is the decimal correction for the addition of two decimal numbers, the destination operand must be the contents of register AL.

■ DEC
Decrements the operand by one.

■ DIV
This is the unsigned division of a dividend contained in accumulator A by a divisor which is the operand expressed in the instruction. If this operand is a byte, the dividend must be expressed in double length in AL and AH; the quotient and the remainder are expressed in 8 bits and stored in AL and AH respectively. If this operand is a 16 bit word, the dividend must be expressed in double length in AX and DX; the quotient and the remainder are expressed in 16 bits and stored in AX and DX respectively. If there is a quotient overflow or an attempted division by zero, a type zero internal interrupt is generated.

■ ESC
This instruction permits a processor other than the 8086 to obtain an operation code

and if necessary an operand from it. The operation code is an immediate value of 6 bits. It allows synchronization between the 8086 and another processor and taking of the bus by the latter. If the operand is in memory, the 8086 reads it, the operand is then put on the data bus and it is the external processor which accepts it.

■ HLT

The microprocessor stops and leaves this halt state following activation of the RESET line or receipt of an interrupt demand either on the NMI input or the INTR input if interrupts on this line have been enabled. This instruction can be used as an endless loop when the microprocessor must wait for an interrupt.

■ IDIV

This is the DIV instruction for signed numbers.

■ IMUL

This is signed multiplication of a first operand contained in accumulator A and a second operand expressed in the instruction. If the latter is a byte it is multiplied by the contents of AL and the result is sent to AH and AL. If it is a 16 bit word it is multiplied by the contents of AX and the result is sent to DX and AX. The C and O flags are set to 1 if the high order half of the result (AH for byte operands, DX for word operands) is different from zero.

■ IN

This is the read instruction for an I/O port, when the I/O space is separated from the memory space.

■ INC

Increments the operand by one.

■ INT N

This is an internal interrupt which initiates interrupt procedure N. If N = 3 the assembler generates an instruction code in a single byte.

■ INT O

This is the software interrupt generated automatically by the microprocessor in the case of an overflow. Placed after an arithmetic or logical operation, it permits the overflow to be processed in the interrupt subroutine.

■ JA/JNBE

All conditional branch instructions use relative addressing with respect to the contents of IP. The displacement is limited to −128 and +127. Two mnemonic expressions are often possible for these instructions, the assembler distinguishes them. Here they are separated by an oblique stroke. The instruction JA or JNBE causes a branch to the address indicated by the displacement if the result of a previous comparison of operands 1 and 2 gave operand 1 greater than operand 2. In this case flags C and Z are equal to zero.

■ JAE/JNB
Jump if greater or equal; C = 0.

■ JB/JNAE
Jump if less; C = 0.

■ JBE/JNA
Jump if less or equal; C + Z = 1.

■ JC
Jump if CARRY = 1.

■ JCXZ
Jump if the contents of CX are zero.

■ JE/JZ
Jump if equal/jump if equal to zero; Z = 1.

■ JG/JNLE
Jump if greater for signed numbers.

■ JGE/JNL
Jump if greater or equal for signed numbers.

■ JL/JNGE
Jump if less for signed numbers.

■ JLE/JNG
Jump if less or equal for signed numbers.

■ JMP
As for the CALL instruction there is only one mnemonic expression but different operation codes according to the jump. Several types of jump can be distinguished:

SHORT. The displacement is limited to −128/+127.

NEAR direct. The name is specified in the instruction. Example: JMP LOOP (relative addressing)

NEAR indirect by a 16 bit register. The branch address expressed in 16 bits is the contents of a register. Example: JMP BX.

NEAR indirect by a 16 bit memory location. The branch address expressed in 16 bits is the contents of a two byte memory location. Example: JMP LABEL; the memory locations at addresses LABEL and LABEL + 1 contain the branch address, which is loaded into IP after the contents of this register have been saved on the stack.

Long direct (FAR). This and the following involve a jump from one segment to another which requires the use of IP and CS. In the case of a long direct jump the name is indicated in the instruction. Example: JMP FAR.

Long indirect by a 32 bit memory location (FAR). The contents of CS and IP are saved on the stack and replaced by the four bytes in memory. Example: JMP.

■ JNC
Jump if CARRY = 0.

■ JNE/JNZ
Jump if not equal/jump if not equal to zero; Z = 0.

■ JNO
Jump if no overflow; O flag equal to zero.

■ JNP/JPO
Jump if no parity; P flag equal to zero.

■ JNS
Jump if positive; S flag equal to zero.

■ JO
Jump if overflow; O flag equal to one.

■ JP/JPE
Jump if parity; P flag equal to one.

■ JS
Jump if negative; S flag equal to one.

■ LAHF
This transfers the S, Z, A, P and C flags of the status register into positions 7, 6, 4, 2 and 0 of register AH.

■ LDS
This instruction specifies a general 16 bit register in the operand field which, with the DS register, makes a 32 bit register. The instruction involves loading a 32 bit pointer situated in memory at the address indicated in the instruction into this register. Example: LDS SI, LABEL. The four bytes pointed to by LABEL form a 32 bit pointer which will be loaded into DS and SI as follows:

the contents of LABEL are transferred into the low part of SI
the contents of LABEL + 1 are transferred into the high part of SI
the contents of LABEL + 2 are transferred into the low part of DS
the contents of LABEL + 3 are transferred into the high part of DS.

Hence the first two bytes of the pointer form the displacement and the latter two provide the base address or more exactly the sixteen high order bits of the base address.

■ **LEA**

This instruction loads a 16 bit address contained in memory (it is a displacement) into a 16 bit register indicated in the instruction. Example: LEA SI, LABEL. The two bytes pointed to by LABEL and LABEL + 1 are transferred into SI.

■ **LES**

This instruction specifies a general 16 bit register in the operand field which forms a 32 bit register with the ES register. The instruction involves loading a 32 bit pointer situated in memory at the address indicated in the instruction into this register. Example: LES DI, LABEL. The four bytes pointed to by LABEL form a 32 bit pointer which will be loaded into ES and DI as follows:

the contents of LABEL are transferred into the low part of DI
the contents of LABEL + 1 are transferred into the high part of DI
the contents of LABEL + 2 are transferred into the low part of ES
the contents of LABEL + 3 are transferred into the high part of ES.

■ **LOCK**

This prefix placed before an instruction activates the LOCK signal in the high configuration of the 8086 (maximum mode) throughout execution of the instruction.

■ **LODS**

This instruction, relating to the manipulation of character strings, transfers the operand pointed to by SI into AL (in the case of a byte) or AX (in the case of a word).

■ **LOOP**

This is a loop instruction which decrements CX by one and causes a short branch (-128 to $+127$) if the content of CX differs from zero.

■ **LOOPE/LOOPZ**

This is a loop instruction (displacement limited to -128 and $+127$) which decrements CX by one and which offers two possible exits from the loop:

if the contents of CX are equal to zero
or if the Z flag is at zero

Looping continues automatically if $(CX) \neq 0$ and the Z flag $= 1$.

■ **LOOPNE/LOOPNZ**

This is a loop instruction (displacement limited to -128 and $+127$) which decrements CX by one and which offers two possible exits from the loop:

if the contents of CX are equal to zero
or if the Z flag is at one

Looping continues automatically if $(CX) \neq 0$ and the Z flag $= 0$.

■ MOV
This transfers the source operand to the destination operand. The lengths of the two operands must be the same.

■ MOVS
This instruction, relating to the manipulation of character strings, transfers the source operand pointed to by SI into the destination memory location pointed to by DI. The transfer can be a byte or a word. The SI and DI registers are incremented for the next transfer if the D flag = 1 and decremented if D = 0. For example:

MOVS STRING 1, STRING 2

This instruction can be used with the prefix REP.

■ MOVSB/MOVSW
These two instructions effect a transfer of one byte (MOVSB) or word (MOVSW) in the case of a character string manipulation. These instructions do not involve any operand. The source and destination operands are implicitly pointed to by SI and DI. These instructions can be used with the prefix REP.

■ MUL
This is unsigned multiplication. It is identical to IMUL but for two unsigned operands.

■ NEG
The operand indicated in the instruction is replaced by its two's complement value.

■ NOP
No operation other than incrementing of the program counter.

■ NOT
The operand indicated in the instruction is replaced by its one's complement value.

■ OR
Logical OR function. The result is put in place of the destination operand.

■ OUT
This writes to an I/O port when the I/O space is separated from the memory space.

■ POP
The word pointed to by the SP register is transferred to the destination then SP is incremented by 2 to point to the new top of the stack.

■ POPF
The word pointed to by the SP register is transferred into the status register then SP is

incremented by 2. This instruction must be used to set the T (trace) command bit which cannot be directly set to zero or one.

■ PUSH

This instruction decrements the SP register by 2 then transfers the operand indicated in the instruction to the stack starting at the address pointed to by SP.

■ PUSHF

This instruction decrements SP by two then transfers the contents of the status register to the stack starting at the address pointed to by SP.

■ RCL

Rotation to the left by n bits, the CARRY being on the stack. If the number n is greater than 1, it is specified in the CL register. For example:

RCL MEM, CL with (CL) = 4.

This instruction effects a rotation to the left.

■ RCR

Rotation to the right by n bits, the CARRY being in the loop. If the number is greater than 1, it is specified in the CL register.

■ REP

This is a repetition prefix used in the manipulation of character strings.

■ REPE/REPZ

These are prefixes used with character strings for a repetition as long as two operands compared by the CMPS instruction are identical.

■ REPNE/REPNZ

These are prefixes used with character strings and associated with the CMPS instruction to cause repetition of the comparison as long as the two compared operands are not identical.

■ RET

This is the return from a subroutine.

■ ROL

Rotation to the left by n bits, the CARRY being outside the loop. If the number n is greater than 1, it is specified in the CL register.

■ ROR

Rotation to the right by n bits, the CARRY being outside the loop. If the number n is greater than 1, it is specified in the CL register.

■ SAHF

This is the transfer of bits 7 (MSB), 6, 4, 2 and 0 of AH to the corresponding positions of the low part of the status register, that is to the S, Z, A, P and C flags.

■ SAL/SHL

Shift to the left by n bits. If the number n is greater than 1, it is specified in the CL register.

■ SAR

Shift to the right by n bits. If the number n is greater than 1, it is specified in the CL register.

■ SBB

This is subtraction with borrow of two operands; the result takes the place of the destination operand.

■ SCAS

This is subtraction relating to the manipulation of a character string; the destination operand pointed to by DI is subtracted from the contents of AL in the case of a character string or the contents of AX in the case of a string of words. The DI register is used to point to the next character or word.

This instruction can be used with the prefixes REPE/REPZ and REPNE/REPNZ.

■ SHR

Shift to the right by n bits. If the number n is greater than 1, it is specified in the CL register.

■ STC

Sets the CARRY indicator to one.

■ STD

Sets the D (direction) command bit to one.

■ STI

Sets the I (interrupt) command bit to one.

■ STOS

In character string manipulation this transfers the contents of AL (byte) or AX (word) into the memory location pointed to by DI. This register is used for the next transfer. The STOS instruction can be used with the REP prefix.

■ SUB

This is subtraction without borrow of two operands; the result takes the place of the destination operand.

■ TEST

This is the logical AND function of two operands without changing them. The result is not sent anywhere but the flags are set.

■ WAIT

The processor enters the wait state for as long as the TEST input is not activated.

■ XCHG

This instruction exchanges the contents of the source and the destination. Used with the LOCK prefix this instruction permits a semaphore to be tested and set.

■ XLAT

This instruction replaces the contents of register AL with those of the memory location of a table pointed to by the address (BX) + (AL). The contents of AL therefore act as an index. This instruction is useful to carry out code conversions.

■ XOR

This is the exclusive OR of two operands; the result takes the place of the destination operand.

Tables 1–6 group the instructions in families and contain the information necessary for programming. Various symbols have been used which will now be defined:

R	designates a general register which can be 8 or 16 bits
R8	designates a general register of 8 bits
R16	designates a general register of 16 bits
R SEG	designates a segment register: CS, DS, SS or ES
R SOURCE	designates a source register
R DEST	designates a destination register
A	designates the accumulator AL or AX
MEM	is the memory location concerned in the instruction; it can be 8 or 16 bits
MEM 8	is the memory location of 8 bits whose address is provided in the instruction
MEM 16	is the memory location of 16 bits whose address is provided in the instruction
LABEL	is a general name designating a memory location
PORT	designates the address of an I/O port
brackets	symbolize the contents of a register or memory location; thus (R) designates the contents of R
double brackets	designate an indirect address; thus ((BX + AL)) designates the contents of the memory location whose address is (BX) + (AL)
C	designates the CARRY for additions and subtractions
DATA	designates data in immediate addressing mode

TABLE 1

	Dest.	Source	Operation performed	Example	D	IR	B	X	BX
			**Data transfer**		**Memory addressing modes**				
MOV	R	R	(Rsource) → (Rdest)	MOV AX, BX	•	•	•	•	•
	R	MEM	(MEM) → R	MOV BX, LABEL	•	•	•	•	•
	MEM	R	(R) → MEM	MOV [DI], CX	•	•	•	•	•
	R	DATA	DATA → R	MOV CL, 15 H					
	MEM	DATA	DATA → MEM	MOV [BX + 2], 2AH	•	•	•	•	•
	RSEG	R16	(R16) → RSEG	MOV ES, CX					
	RSEG	MEM16	(MEM) → RSEC	MOV DS, LABEL	•	•	•	•	•
	R16	RSEG	(RSEG) → R16	MOV BP, SS					
	MEM	RSEG	(RSEG) → MEM	MOV [BX].BLOC,CS	•	•	•	•	•
XCHG	R	R	(Rsource)→(Rdest) and (Rdest)→(Rsource)	XCHG AL, BL					
	MEM	R	(R) → MEM and (MEM) → R	XCHG LABEL, AX	•	•	•	•	•
XLAT	MEM		((BX + AL)) → AL	XLAT TABLE		•			
LAHF			Low order byte of the flag register → AH	LAHF					
SAHF			(AH) → low part of the flag register	SAHF	See note at foot of table				
LEA	R16	MEM16	(MEM) → R16	LEA BX, [BP]	•	•	•	•	•
LDS	R16	MEM32	(MEM) → R16 / (MEM + 2) → DS	LDS SI, pointer	•	•	•	•	•
LES	R16	MEM32	(MEM) → R16 / (MEM + 2) → ES	LDS DI, pointer	•	•	•	•	•
PUSH	R16		(R16) → stack	PUSH SI					
	RSEG		(RSEG) → stack	PUSH ES					
	MEM		(MEM) → stack	PUSH LABEL [SI]	•	•	•	•	•
PUSHF			(status register) → stack	PUSHF					
POP	R16		(stack) → R16	POP DX	See note at foot of table				
	RSEG		(stack) → RSEG	POP DS					
	MEM		(stack) → MEM	POP LABEL					
POPF			(stack) → status register	POPF					
IN	A	PORT	PORT → register A	IN AX, 1204H	•	•			
	A	DX	(DX) → register A	IN AL, DX	•	•			
OUT	PORT	A	(A) → PORT	OUT 32, AX	•	•			
	DX	A	(A) → (DX)	OUT DX, AX	•	•			

The above instructions do not affect the flags except for SAHF which affects the S, Z, A, P and C flags and POPF which restores the contents of the status register.

TABLE 2

Arithmetic instructions						Memory addressing modes				
	Dest.	Source	Operation performed	Example	Flags affected	D	IR	B	X	BX
ADD	R	R	(Rsource) + (Rdest) → Rdest	ADD CX,DX	O S Z A P C					
	R	MEM	(MEM) + (R) →	ADD DI, LABEL	O S Z A P C	•	•	•	•	•
	MEM	R	(R) + (MEM) → MEM	ADD LABEL,CL	O S Z A P C	•	•	•	•	•
	R	DATA	DATA + (R) → R	ADD CL, 23	O S Z A P C					
	MEM	DATA	DATA + (MEM) → MEM	ADD LABEL, 41	O S Z A P C	•	•	•	•	•
ADC	R	R	(Rsource)+ (Rdest) + C → Rdest	ADC AX, SI	O S Z A P C					
	R	MEM	(MEM) + (R) + C →	ADC BX, LABEL	O S Z A P C	•	•	•	•	•
	MEM	R	(R) + (MEM) + C → MEM	ADC LABEL,CL	O S Z A P C	•	•	•	•	•
	R	DATA	DATA + (R) + C → R	ADC AX, 300	O S Z A P C					
	MEM	DATA	DATA + (MEM) + C → MEM	ADC LABEL,84	O S Z A P C	•	•	•	•	•
DAA			Decimal correction for addition	DAA	O S Z A P C					
AAA			ASCII correction for addition	AAA	A C (O,S,Z,P = U)					
SUB	R	R	(Rdest)−(Rsource) → Rdest	SUB AX, CX	O S Z A P C					
	R	MEM	(R)−(MEM) → R	SUB BX,LABEL	O S Z A P C	•	•	•	•	•
	MEM	R	(MEM)−(R) → MEM	SUB [BP+ 4], CL	O S Z A P C	•	•	•	•	•
	R	DATA	(R)−DATA → R	SUB SI, 6040	O S Z A P C					
	MEM	DATA	(MEM)−DATA → MEM	SUB LABEL,850	O S Z A P C	•	•	•	•	•
SBB	R	R	(Rdest)−(Rsource) - C→Rdest	SBB CX,AX	O S Z A P C					
	R	MEM	(R)−(MEM)−C → R	SBB DI, LABEL	O S Z A P C	•	•	•	•	•
	MEM	R	(MEM)−(R)−C → MEM	SBB LABEL,BX	O S Z A P C	•	•	•	•	•
	R	DATA	(R)−DATA−C → R	SBB BX, 2	O S Z A P C					
	MEM	DATA	(MEM)−DATA−C → MEM	SBB LABEL, 10	O S Z A P C	•	•	•	•	•
DAS			Decimal correction for subtraction	DAS	S Z A P C (O = U)					
AAS			ASCII correction for subtraction	AAS	A C (O,S,Z,P= U)					
MUL (un-signed) or **IMUL** (signed)	R8		(AL) x (R8) → AH,AL	MUL BL	O,C					
	R16		(AX) x (R16) → DX,AX	IMUL CX	O,C S,Z,A,P					
	MEM8		(AL) x (MEM8) → AH,AL	IMUL LABEL	O,C = U	•	•	•	•	•
	MEM16		(AX) x (MEM16) → DX,AX	MUL LABEL	O,C	•	•	•	•	•
AAM			ASCII correction for multiplication	AAM	A C (O,S,Z,P = U)					
DIV (un-signed) or **IDIV** (signed)	R8		(AH,AL)/(R8) → AL	IDIV CL						
	R16		(DX,AX)/(R16) → AX	DIV BX	O,S,Z,A,P,C = U					
	MEM8		(AH,AL)/(MEM8) → AL	DIV LABEL		•	•	•	•	•
	MEM16		(DX,AX)/(MEM16) → AX	IDIV TABLE[SI]		•	•	•	•	•
AAD			ASCII correction for division	AAD	S Z P (O,A,C = U)					
CBW			Extension of sign of a byte	CBW	None					
CWD			Extension of sign for a 16 bit word	CWD	None					

TABLE 3

Logical instructions						Memory addressing modes				
	Dest.	Source	Operation performed	Example	Flags affected	D	IR	B	X	BX
OR	R	R	(Rsource) + (Rdest) ⟶ Rdest	OR BL, AL	S,Z,P					
	R	MEM	(MEM) + (Rdest) ⟶ R	OR BX, LABEL	S,Z,P O,C=0	•	•	•	•	•
	MEM	R	(R) + (MEM) ⟶ MEM	OR LABEL, CL	S,Z,P	•	•	•	•	•
	R	DATA	DATA + (R) ⟶ R	OR AL, 1AH	S,Z,P A = U					
	MEM	DATA	DATA + (MEM) ⟶ MEM	OR LABEL, 09	S,Z,P	•	•	•	•	•
XOR	R	R	(Rsource) ⊕ (Rdest) ⟶ Rdest	XOR BL, AL	S,Z,P					
	R	MEM	(MEM) ⊕ (R) ⟶ R	XOR BX, LABEL	S,Z,P O,C=0	•	•	•	•	•
	MEM	R	(R) ⊕ (MEM) ⟶ MEM	XOR LABEL,DX	S,Z,P	•	•	•	•	•
	R	DATA	DATA ⊕ (R) ⟶ R	XOR SI,00B3H	S,Z,P A = U					
	MEM	DATA	DATA ⊕ (MEM) ⟶ MEM	XOR LABEL,2CH	S,Z,P	•	•	•	•	•
AND	R	R	(Rsource) • (Rdest) ⟶ Rdest	AND AL, BL	S,Z,P					
	R	MEM	(MEM) • (Rdest) ⟶ R	AND CX, LABEL	S,Z,P					
	MEM	R	(R) • (MEM) ⟶ MEM	AND LABEL,BL	S,Z,P					
	R	DATA	DATA • (R) ⟶ R	AND AX, 21EH	S,Z,P					
	MEM	DATA	DATA • (MEM) ⟶ MEM	AND LABEL,7FH	S,Z,P					
NOT	R		$\overline{(R)}$ ⟶ R	NOT BX	None	•	•	•	•	•
	MEM		$\overline{(MEM)}$ ⟶ MEM	NOT LABEL						
NEG	R		0 − (R) ⟶ R	NEG AL	O,S,Z,A,P C	•	•	•	•	•
	MEM		0 − (MEM) ⟶ MEM	NEG MEM	O,S,Z,A,P =U					
INC	R		(R) + 1 ⟶ R	INC CL	O S Z A P	•	•	•	•	•
	MEM		(MEM) + 1 ⟶ MEM	INC LABEL	O S Z A P					
DEC	R		(R) − 1 ⟶ R	DEC AX	O S Z A P	•	•	•	•	•
	MEM		(MEM) − 1 ⟶ R	DEC LABEL	O S Z A P					
TEST	R	R	(Rsource) • (Rdest) _These instructions only affect the flags_	TEST SI, DI	S,Z,P					
	R	MEM	(MEM) • (R)	TEST SI,LABEL	S,Z,P O,C=0	•	•	•	•	•
	R	DATA	DATA • (R)	TEST AL,1BH	S,Z,P A =U					
	MEM	DATA	DATA • (MEM)	TEST LABEL,02	S,Z,P	•	•	•	•	•
CMP	R	R	(Rdest)−(Rsource) _These instructions only affect the flags_	CMP CX, AX	O S Z A P C					
	R	MEM	(R)−(MEM)	CMP DH,[BP-2]	O S Z A P C	•	•	•	•	•
	MEM	R	(MEM)−R	CMP LABEL,SI	O S Z A P C	•	•	•	•	•
	R	DATA	(R)−DATA	CMP AL, 04	O S Z A P C					
	MEM	DATA	(MEM)−DATA	CMP LABEL, 8	O S Z A P C	•	•	•	•	•

TABLE 4

	Dest.	Source	Operation performed	Example	Flags affected	Memory addressing modes D IR B X BX
			Shifting and rotation			
SAL /SHL	R	1	(R) shifted 1 bit to the left	SAL BL, 1	O, C	
	R	CL		SHL DI, CL	O, C	
	MEM	1	CY ← [ ] ← 0	SHL LABEL, 1	O, C	• • • • •
	MEM	CL	(MEM) shifted n bits to the left	SHL LABEL,CL	O, C	• • • • •
SAR	R	1	(R) shifted 1 bit to the right	SAR DX, 1	O,S,Z,P,C	
	R	CL		SAR DI, CL	O,S,Z,P,C	A
	MEM	1	sign bit → [ ] → CY	SAR LABEL,1	O,S,Z,P,C	=U • • • • •
	MEM	CL	(MEM) shifted n bits to the right	SAR LABEL,CL	O,S,Z,P,C	• • • • •
SHR	R	1	(R) shifted 1 bit to the right	SHR SI,1	O, C	
	R	CL	0 → [ ] → CY	SHR SI, CL	O, C	
	MEM	1		SHR LABEL,1	O, C	• • • • •
	MEM	CL	(MEM) shifted n bits to the right	SHR LABEL,CL	O, C	• • • • •
ROL	R	1	Rotation to the left of 1 bit of (R)	ROL BX, 1	O, C	
	R	CL	CY ← [ ] ←	ROL BX, CL	O, C	
	MEM	1		ROL LABEL,1	O, C	• • • • •
	MEM	CL	Rotation to the left of n bits of (MEM)	ROL LABEL,CL	O, C	• • • • •
ROR	R	1	Rotation to the right of 1 bit of (R)	ROR BL, 1	O, C	
	R	CL	→ [ ] → CY	ROR AX, CL	O, C	
	MEM	1		ROR LABEL,1	O, C	• • • • •
	MEM	CL	Rotation to the right of n bits of (MEM)	ROR LABEL,CL	O, C	• • • • •
RCL	R	1	Rotation to the left of 1 bit of (R)	RCL AX, 1	O, C	
	R	CL	CY ← [ ] ←	RCL AL, CL	O, C	
	MEM	1		RCL LABEL, 1	O, C	• • • • •
	MEM	CL	Rotation to the left of n bits of (MEM)	RCL LABEL,CL	O, C	• • • • •
RCR	R	1	Rotation to the right of 1 bit of (R)	RCR BX, 1	O, C	
	R	CL	→ [ ] → CY	RCR BX, CL	O, C	
	MEM	1		RCR LABEL, 1	O, C	• • • • •
	MEM	CL	Rotation to the right of n bits of (MEM)	RCR LABEL,CL	O, C	• • • • •

TABLE 5

Branch instructions				
	Condition	Unsigned numbers	Signed numbers	Explanation
Arithmetic	=	JE/JZ	JE/JZ	Jump if equal
	>	JA/JNBE	JG	Jump if greater
conditional	<	JB/JNAE	JL	Jump if less
	≥	JAE/JNB	JGE	Jump if greater or equal
branches	≤	JBE/JNA	JLE	Jump if less or equal
	≠	JNE/JNZ	JNE/JNZ	Jump if not equal
	Flag	Equal to 1	Equal to 0	Explanation
Branches	Zero	JZ	JNZ	Jump if contents = 0 or not
determined	Carry	JC	JNC	Jump if carry = 1 or not
by a single	Overflow	JO	JNO	Jump if overflow or not
	Sign	JS	JNS	Jump if sign = 1 or not
flag	Parity	JP	JNP	Jump if parity or not
	Type of branch	Operation performed	Limiting values of displacement	Example
	Short direct	(IP)=(IP)+DISP	−128/+127	JMP LABEL
	Near direct	(IP)=(IP)+DISP	−32768/+32767	JMP LABEL
JMP	Near indirect by 16 bit register	(IP) = (R16)	−32768/+32767	JMP CX
	Near indirect by 16 memory bits	(IP) = (MEM16)	−32768/+32767	JMP LABEL
	Far direct	CS is used (IP)=DISP	Access to all memory possible	JMP LABEL
	Far indirect 32 memory bits	(CS:IP)=(MEM32)	Access to all memory possible	JMP TABLE [BX]
	Type of branch	Operation performed	Limiting values of displacement	Example
	Near direct	IP=IP+DISP	−32768/+32767	CALL LABEL
	Near indirect by 16 bit register	IP = (R16)	−32768/+32767	CALL AX
CALL	Near indirect by 16 memory bits	IP =(MEM16)	−32768/+32767	CALL TABLE [SI]
	Far direct	CS is used (IP) = DISP	Access to all memory possible	CALL LABEL
	Far indirect by 32 memory bits	(CS·IP)=(MEM32)	Access to all memory possible	CALL TABLE [BX]
LOOP	(CX) = (CX)−1 then jump if (CX) ≠ 0; DISP: −128 to +127			LOOP LABEL
LOOPNE/LOOPNZ	(CX) = (CX)−1 then jump if (CX) ≠ 0 and Z = 0 DISP: −128 to +127			LOOPNE LABEL
LOOPE/LOOPZ	(CX) = (CX)−1 then jump if (CX) ≠ 0 and Z = 1 DISP: −128 to +127			LOOPE LABEL
JCXZ	jump if (CX) = 0 DISP: −128 to +127			JCXZ LABEL

TABLE 6

Character strings			LABELS = (SI) LABELD = (DI)	
		Operation performed	Example	Flags affected
REP	MOVS MOVS	(LABELS)⟶LABELD repetition as long as (CX) ≠ 0	MOVS LABELD,LABELS REP MOVS LABELD,LABELS	None None
REP	MOVSB/MOVSW MOVSB/MOVSW	((SI))⟶(DI) repetition as long as (CX) ≠ 0	MOVSB REP MOVSW	None None
REPE/REPZ REPNE/REPNZ	CMPS CMPS CMPS	(LABELS) — (LABELD) repetition as long as (CX) ≠ 0 and (LABELS) = (LABELD) repetn. if (CX) ≠ 0 and (LABELS) ≠ (LABELD)	CMPS LABELD,LABELS REPE CMPS LABELD,LABELS REPNZ CMPS LABELD,LABELS	O,S,Z,A,P,C O,S,Z,A,P,C O,S,Z,A,P,C
REPE/REPZ REPNE/REPNZ	SCAS SCAS SCAS	(A) — (LABELD) reptn. if (CX) ≠ 0 and (A) = (LABELD) reptn. if (CX) ≠ 0 and (A) ≠ (LABELD)	SCAS LABELD REPZ SCAS LABELD REPNE SCAS LABELD	O,S,Z,A,P,C O,S,Z,A,P,C O,S,Z,A,P,C
	LODS	(LABELS)⟶A	LODS LABELS	None
REP	STOS STOS	(A)⟶LABELD reptn. as long as (CX) ≠ 0	STOS LABELD REP STOS LABELD	None None

8086 Control instructions			
	Operation performed	Example	Flags affected
INT N	Software interrupt demand	INT 12	I = 0 T = 0
INTO	Internal interrupt if flag O = 1	INTO	I = 0 T = 0
IRET	Return from interrupt	IRET	The flags are restored
RET RET N	Return from subroutine Return from subroutine then (SP) = (SP) + N	RET RET 4	None None
ESC DATA,R ESC DATA,MEM	Transmission of an operation code (DATA) and an operand to an external processor either by a register or by a memory location	ESC 6, AL ESC20,LABEL	None None
HLT	Halt the processor	HLT	None
LOCK	Prefix prohibiting bus access	LOCK CLC	None
WAIT	Generation of wait states TW by the CPU as long as $\overline{TEST}$ = 1	WAIT	None
CLC	Set the CARRY flag to zero	CLC	C = 0
STC	Set the CARRY flag to one	STC	C = 1
CMC	One's complement of the CARRY	CMC	C = $\overline{C}$
CLI	Set the I flag to zero	CLI	I = 0
STI	Set the I flag to one	STI	I = 1
CLD	Set the D flag to zero	CLD	D = 0
STD	Set the D flag to one	STD	D = 1
NOP	No operation	NOP	None

15.3 Assembler syntax

In this section the principal directives (or pseudo-instructions) of the ASM86 assembly language are given which permit segments, variables and procedures to be defined. A name designating data in the general sense of the term (operand, address, pointer) or in a data table will be called a variable.

Segments are defined by the pseudo-instruction ASSUME. Variables are defined with the help of directives:

SEGMENT and ENDS
DB, DW, DD and EQU
STRUC and ENDS

Procedures (or subroutines) are defined by the PROC and ENDP directives.

15.3.1 Definition of segments

For each access to a variable the segment register must be known by the assembler. If this register is not indicated explicitly, one of the four registers CS, DS, ES and SS is taken by default, as mentioned in Part I.

(a) CS is essential for fetching instruction bytes. There is no other possible choice.
(b) SS is essential for memory access relative to the stack. There is no other possible choice.
(c) DS is taken by default for access to a variable except when BP is used as a base register (in this case it is SS which is taken by default) or when the variable belongs to the destination string in the manipulation of character strings (in this case it is ES which is taken by default).

Only the choice of segment register for a data area, or stack area with BP as base register, requires any attention on the part of the programmer. To impose a segment register other than that which would be taken by default by the assembler, the programmer has two possibilities:

(a) To indicate the segment register before the variable used. If DATA is a variable, the instruction MOV BL, DATA implies that the segment register is DS. To impose the register ES it is sufficient to write MOV BL, ES:DATA.
(b) To use the pseudo-instruction ASSUME. This allows a segment register to be associated with any segment.

Thus to impose ES as the register for the data segment which is called DATA-AREA it is sufficient to write:

DATA-AREA	SEGMENT		
	ASSUME	ES:DATA-AREA	
DATA	DB	1	Definition of all
.	.	.	the variables
.	.	.	belonging to the
.	.	.	DATA-AREA segment
DATA-AREA	ENDS		

All the variables defined between the lines ASSUME and ENDS will be considered by the assembler as having their base address contained in ES. If DATA is included in these variables, the instruction MOV BL, DATA implies ES as the segment register.

15.3.2 Definition of a variable

■ The DB, DW and DD directives

The length of the variable represented by a name is defined in a program with the help of three directives: DB (define byte), DW (define word) and DD (define double-word). These three directives are used to reserve memory locations, to give them a name called a label and possibly to load a value into these memory locations. If the value is not indicated in the directive, it is replaced by a question mark. These directives must be enclosed between the two pseudo-instructions SEGMENT and ENDS. Hence the above directives define the data segment called DATA-AREA. This segment contains data, in the proper sense of this term, addresses which are pointers and tables. The expression DUP ensures reservation of an area of memory.

```
DATA-AREA  SEGMENT
DATA1      DB    1            ;DATA1 is a byte of value 01
DATA2      DW    1A0EH        ;DATA2 is a word of value 1A0EH
MEM1       DB    ?            ;memory area of one byte not initialized
MEM2       DW    ?            ;memory area of two bytes
MEM3       DD    ?            ;memory area of four bytes
MEM4       DB    50DUP(?)     ;memory area of fifty bytes
MEM5       DW    20DUP(?)     ;memory area of twenty words
POINTER 1  DW    MEM1         ;memory area of 16 bits containing the offset of
                              MEM1
POINTER 2  DD    MEM2         ;memory area of 32 bits containing the address of
                              MEM2
POINTERS   DD    5DUP(?)      ;table of 5 pointers of 32 bits not initialized
TABLE 1    DB    10DUP(0)     ;table of 10 bytes initialized to zero
TABLE 2    DB    'MESSAGE'    ;table containing the ASCII codes of M, E, S, S, A,
                              G, E
TABLE 3    DB                 1 AH, 0FFH, 5, 0, 7, 24, 1
                              8, 7, 4, 13, 4AH, 0BBH, 18, 3
DATA-AREA                     ENDS
```

The directive EQU allows a value to be assigned to a variable.

Example: DATA   EQU   1AH

■ The attributes of a variable

Using the directives DB, DW and DD, the assembler calculates the attributes for each mnemonic expression representing a variable and saves them in memory. These are:

SEG	This is the name of the segment containing the variable.				
OFFSET	This is the displacement of the variable that is its address in the segment. The displacement of each of the variables is calculated step by step by the assembler.				
TYPE	This attribute defines the number of bytes of a simple variable (1 for a byte, 2 for a word, 4 for a double word) or of each element of a multi-element variable (in data processing such a variable is called an item or a record) or for each element of a table.				
LENGTH	This is the number of elements contained in the variable, that is the number of words represented by the variable. The LENGTH attribute is greater than 1 only for a multi-element variable or a table.				
SIZE	This is the total number of bytes of a variable, that is the product TYPE × LENGTH				

For the DATA-AREA segment:

DATA	SEG	OFFSET	TYPE	LENGTH	SIZE
DATA1	DATA-AREA	0	1	1	1
DATA2	DATA-AREA	1	2	1	2
MEM1	DATA-AREA	3	1	1	1
MEM2	DATA-AREA	4	2	1	2
MEM3	DATA-AREA	6	4	1	4
MEM4	DATA-AREA	A	1	50	50
MEM5	DATA-AREA	3C	2	20	40
etc.					

The last four attributes allow valid sections of program to be written for any type of data; byte, word or double word. An example program is given for the addition in AX of the contents of a table of 30 words of 16 bits defined as follows:

```
TABLE    DW    30 DUP(?)
```

As a result of this directive, LENGTH = 30 and SIZE = 60. The number of additions to be carried out is the value of LENGTH or 30; also the value of LENGTH for the data table TABLE, a value written as LENGTH TABLE, is loaded into the CX register which is serving as a counter. The addition will start with the last data of the table, the chosen index register is SI. The size of decrement is of course the TYPE attribute relating to TABLE or TYPE TABLE. Decrementing of the index value will be done by the instruction SUB SI, TYPE TABLE. Looping will be effected by the instruction LOOP BCL which decrements the counter CX by one and causes a branch to BCL as long as the contents of CX differ from zero.

The program is, therefore:

```
        SUB     AX,     AX
        MOV     CX,     LENGTH TABLE    ;initialization of counter
        MOV     SI,     SIZE TABLE      ;initialization of index
                                         register to the last address
                                         of the table + 1
BCL     SUB     SI,     TYPE TABLE      ;decrementing of the index
                                         register
        ADD     AX,     TABLE(SI)       ;addition in indexed
                                         addressing
        LOOP    BCL                     ;jump as long as (CX) ≠ 0
```

This program remains the same if the data table relates to bytes and is defined, for example, by:

```
TABLE   DB      25 DUP(?)
```

As a further example the initialization sequence of the segment registers will be taken. Apart from the program segment register CS which is automatically initialized to FFFFH, each segment register must be initialized.

The AX register serves as an intermediary, for example:

```
MOV     AX, DATASEG
MOV     DS, AX
```

These two instructions load the value of DATASEG into register DS. It is necessary to reserve memory locations for the stack and to initialize the SS and SP registers. As an example, the sequence for reserving 100 words for the segment STACKSEG is given below; the top of the stack is denoted by TOS (top of stack) using the LABEL directive.

```
STACKSEG        SEGMENT
                DW              100 DUP(?)
TOS             LABEL           WORD
STACKSEG        ENDS
```

The SS register must be initialized to the value of STACKSEG and the SP register to the relative address of TOS in the segment. This address is merely OFFSET of TOS. Hence the initialization sequence is:

```
MOV     AX,STACKSEG     ;the value of STACKSEG is loaded into AX
MOV     SS,AX
MOV     SP,OFFSET TOS,
```

This last instruction could be replaced by the instruction:

```
LEA     SP,TOS
```

Comment. For certain instructions the assembler cannot determine the TYPE attribute, that is the length of the data. This is the case for the instruction MOVE (BX), 5 since the assembler does not know if the address (BX) points to a byte, a word or a double word. There are three operators BYTE PTR, WORD PTR and DWORD PTR which overcome the ambiguity. When placed before the register concerned, an operator of this kind specifies the length of the data. In the present case, the data becomes a 16 bit word if the instruction is written:

MOVE   WORD   PTR (BX), 5

15.3.3 Definition of a procedure with parameter passing

■ The PROC and ENDP directives

The use of subroutines or procedures often requires the passing of parameters. This operation, also known as the 'transmission of arguments' can be done by means of registers, a memory area or the stack. The last possibility is the most useful and it permits programs to be reentrant.

In Figure 43 an example is given of the call of a procedure designated by SUBROUT. The following assumptions are made for this example:

(a) The context to be saved consists of registers SI and AX.
(b) The workspace necessary for execution of the procedure is two 16 bit memory locations.
(c) There are two parameters to be transmitted and they are stored in the 16 bit memory locations called PARAM 1 and PARAM 2. They must be loaded into SI and AX respectively.
(d) The content of SP before the calling sequence of the SUBROUT procedure is 1200I I.
(e) The SUBROUT procedure is stored in a segment other than the current segment (the one which contains the calling sequence) and it is declared FAR by the pseudo-instructions PROC and ENDP.

An encircled number has been indicated before each instruction which involves a stack operation. This number is also placed before the stack memory location concerned. The successive contents of the SP register, the values of BP, BP + 6 and BP + 8 are also indicated in this diagram. Since it is not possible to use SP as a base or index register, the contents of SP are transferred into BP and it is then possible to access any value on the stack in base addressing mode, BP being the base register. Hence the parameters are pointed to by (BP + 8) for the first and (BP + 6) for the second.

■ The STRUC and ENDS directives

Another way of organizing data on the stack is to define a structure by means of the pseudo-instructions STRUC and ENDS associated with the name of the structure. In this way, an area of memory on the stack can be defined, for example STACKAREA.

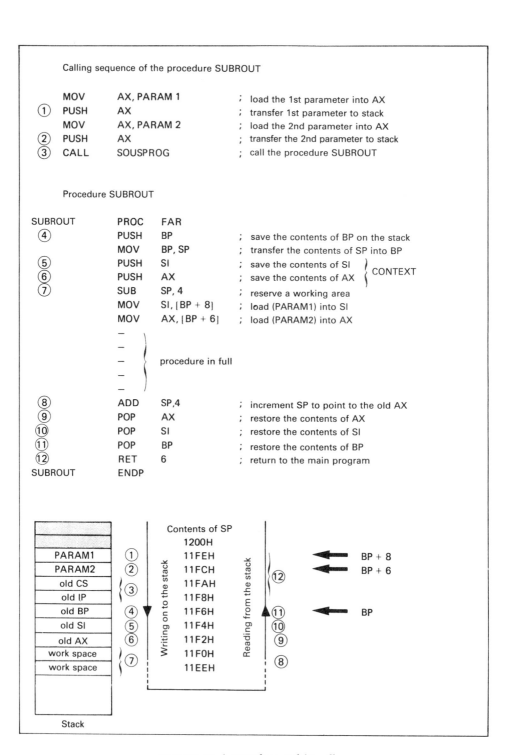

Calling sequence of the procedure SUBROUT

```
     MOV      AX, PARAM 1        ; load the 1st parameter into AX
①    PUSH     AX                 ; transfer 1st parameter to stack
     MOV      AX, PARAM 2        ; load the 2nd parameter into AX
②    PUSH     AX                 ; transfer the 2nd parameter to stack
③    CALL     SOUSPROG           ; call the procedure SUBROUT
```

Procedure SUBROUT

```
SUBROUT   PROC   FAR
④         PUSH   BP              ; save the contents of BP on the stack
          MOV    BP, SP          ; transfer the contents of SP into BP
⑤         PUSH   SI              ; save the contents of SI     ⎫
⑥         PUSH   AX              ; save the contents of AX     ⎬ CONTEXT
⑦         SUB    SP, 4           ; reserve a working area      ⎭
          MOV    SI, [BP + 8]    ; load (PARAM1) into SI
          MOV    AX, [BP + 6]    ; load (PARAM2) into AX
          —
          —
          —      procedure in full
          —
          —
⑧         ADD    SP, 4           ; increment SP to point to the old AX
⑨         POP    AX              ; restore the contents of AX
⑩         POP    SI              ; restore the contents of SI
⑪         POP    BP              ; restore the contents of BP
⑫         RET    6               ; return to the main program
SUBROUT   ENDP
```

		Contents of SP			
		1200H			
PARAM1	①	11FEH		←	BP + 8
PARAM2	②	11FCH		←	BP + 6
old CS		11FAH	⑫		
old IP	③	11F8H			
old BP	④	11F6H	⑪	←	BP
old SI	⑤	11F4H	⑩		
old AX	⑥	11F2H	⑨		
work space		11F0H			
work space	⑦	11EEH	⑧		

Writing on to the stack   Reading from the stack

Stack

FIGURE 43 *A procedure and its call*

For this it is necessary to give a name to each of the variables to be stored in this area of memory, for example OLDBP for the saved contents of BP, RETURN for the return address of the calling program, PARAMETER1 and PARAMETER2 for the two parameters. Figure 44 gives an example of the use of such a structure in a subroutine CALCUL situated in the segment where the subroutine call occurs (NEAR procedure). This subroutine consists of putting the larger of the two parameters into accumulator AX; the parameters are addressed in base addressing mode with BP since this register points to the base of the structure which is the top of the stack (that is the lowest stack address). Instead of using BP as the base register it is equally possible to define a pointer, called PT for example:

```
PT      EQU     (BP – OFFSET OLDBP)
```

The variables are then addressed from this pointer as follows:

```
MOV     AX,PT     PARAMETER1
```

This solution is to be used when the offset of OLDBP is not zero, as in the following structure:

```
STACKAREA       STRUC
DATA            DW      ?               ;   ←  SP
AREA            DW      10DUP(?)
OLDBP           DW      ?               ;   ←  BP
RETURN          DW      ?
PARAMETER2      DW      ?
PARAMETER1      DW      ?
STACKAREA       ENDS
;
PT              EQU     (BP  OFFSET OLDBP)
```

The offset of OLDBP, which is not zero, is subtracted from the value of BP since, for this structure, BP points to OLDBP and SP points to DATA.

```
; segment PROG is declared a program segment
PROG              SEGMENT
                  ASSUME          CS : PROG
SUBROUT           PROC            FAR
; if parameters 1 and 2 are stored in memory locations
; PARAM1 and PARAM2 the calling sequence of SUBROUT is:
;                 PUSH            PARAM1
;                 PUSH            PARAM2
;                 CALL            SUBROUT
; definition of the STACK AREA structure
STACK AREA        STRUC
OLD BP            DW              ? ; base of the structure
RETURN CP         DW              ? ; return address
RETURN CS         DW              ? ; return address
PARAMETER2        DW              ? ; second parameter
PARAMETER1        DW              ? ; first parameter
STACK AREA        ENDS
; save the contents of BP and transfer the contents of SP into BP
                  PUSH            BP
                  MOV             BP, SP
; save the contents of AX
                  PUSH            AX
; subroutine in full
                  MOV             AX, [BP] .  PARAMETER1
                  CMP             AX, [BP] .  PARAMETER2
                  JG              JUMP
                  MOV             AX, [BP] .  PARAMETER2
JUMP              POP             BP
                  RET             4
SUBROUT           ENDP
PROG              ENDS
```

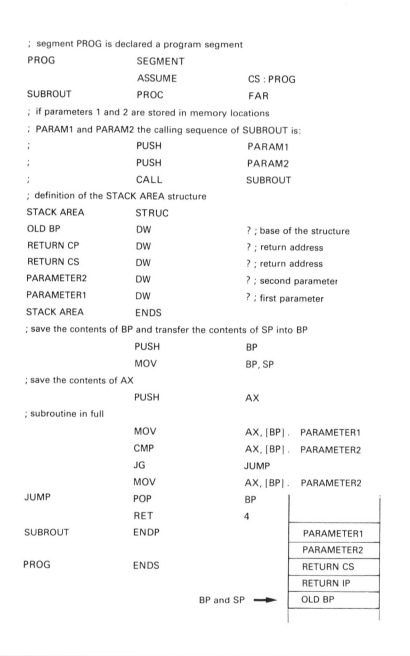

PARAMETER1
PARAMETER2
RETURN CS
RETURN IP
OLD BP

BP and SP ➡

FIGURE 44 *Procedure and definition of a structure*

PART III
THE 68000

16. INTERNAL AND EXTERNAL ORGANIZATION OF THE 68000

This microprocessor, introduced in 1979 and realized in HMOS technology, integrates more than 68000 transistors and is produced in a 64 pin package without multiplexed buses. It requires a single power source of +5 volts. Its general characteristics are:

(a) A 32 bit internal architecture although the external data bus is of 16 bits. This results in the possibility of performing arithmetic operations in 16 or 32 bits.

(b) An address bus of 23 lines, A_1 to A_{23}, together with bit A_0 which is used internally to distinguish a high order byte from a low order byte on the data bus. The program counter is therefore of 24 bits, which gives a direct address space of 16 megabytes (16,777,216 bytes) or 8 megawords (8,388,608 words) without the need for a memory management unit.

(c) Four separate address spaces – 'supervisor program', 'supervisor data', 'user program' and 'user data' – to which is added a space specially reserved for interrupts. These distinct spaces can be used without a memory management unit by decoding the three status bits provided by the processor: FC0, FC1 and FC2. These bits provide hardware security and also allow the address space to be increased from 16 to 64 million bytes with the use of a memory management unit.

(d) A data organization in memory of 16 bits with processing of the more significant byte first. The 16 bit data, or words, are aligned as has already been shown in Chapter 1 (see Figures 3 and 45(a)).

(e) Sixteen internal registers of 32 bits, consisting of 8 data registers designated D0 to D7 which can serve as operand or index registers and 8 address registers A0 to A7 which can be used as base registers, stack pointers or index registers.

(f) An I/O structure using memory instructions which means that the I/O devices are addressed as memory locations.

(g) The possibility of operating in single step by means of the 'trace' mode.

(h) Adaptation to a multiprocessor environment since specific dialogue signals are provided.

(i) A relative addressing mode with respect to the program counter. The displacement is expressed in 16 bits for both conditional and unconditional jumps; it is possible to access any memory location within a 64 Kbyte segment without having to reinitialize a register. This possibility facilitates writing of programs whose object code is independent of the physical location in memory.

16.1 Internal organization of the 68000

From the user's point of view, the 68000 consists of:

    8 data registers
    8 address registers
    a program counter
    a status register.

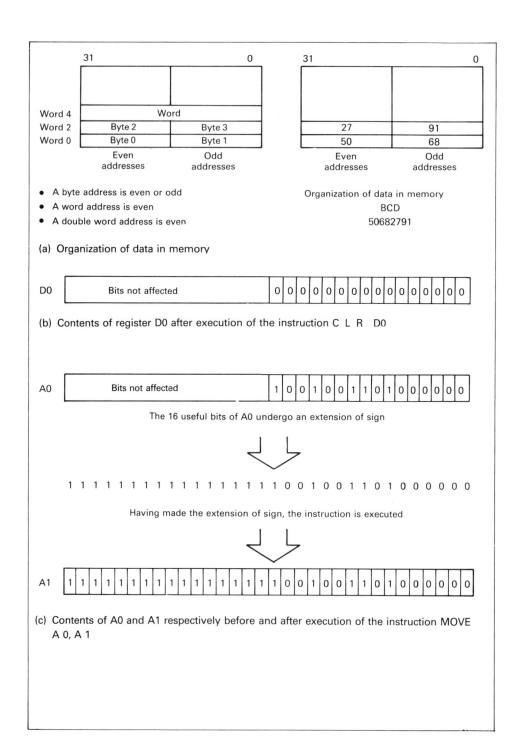

FIGURE 45 *The operands in memory and in the registers*

The eight data registers D0 to D7, of length 32 bits, can be used as accumulators or operand registers for data of 8, 16 or 32 bits. The length of the operand is specified in the instruction by the addition of the suffix B for byte (8 bits), W for word (16 bits) or L for long word (32 bits) to the mnemonic code. For example LDA.B, LDA.W and LDA.L. The suffix W is taken by default which means that the instruction LDA without a suffix is equivalent to LDA.W.

The 68000 is a two operand processor; the source operand is given first and the destination operand second. For example:

MOV   A4,D3

This instruction transfers the contents of register A4 into register D3. When a data register contains a source or destination operand only the area in the register specified by the length of the operand is affected; hence the instruction to reset to zero or 'clear', used with a 16 bit operand, affects only the first 16 bits of the data register concerned (Figure 45(b)). It is not possible, as is the case for the Z8000, to transform a 32 bit register into two 16 bit registers or four 8 bit registers. In contrast, this data organization, foreseen by Motorola, is one of the factors which makes orthogonality possible; this effectively permits standardization of registers with respect to data length. As specific instructions are provided, these registers can also be used to carry out operations at bit level.

■ **The address registers**

The seven general purpose registers A0 to A6 and the stack pointer A7, all of 32 bits, can be used as stack pointers controlled by software, as index registers or as base registers.

Register A7 is actually divided into two parts and consists of a system stack pointer (SSP) and a user stack pointer (USP). Both have a length of 32 bits and are hardware controlled. The choice of one or the other is determined by the mode of operation; supervisor or user. During a subroutine call, the return address is saved on the user stack. The return address and the contents of the status register are saved on the supervisor stack in the case of an interrupt.

If an address register An contains a source operand, only the area specified by the length of the operand (16 or 32 bits) is involved. In contrast, if a register An must receive a destination operand, the whole of the register is affected since if the source operand is of 16 bits the sign is extended before execution of the instruction. This consists of expressing the operand in 32 bits by writing the value of its sign bit in bit locations 2^{16} to 2^{31}. Figure 45(c) illustrates this case for the transfer instruction MOVE A0,A1; the length of the source operand is 16 bits.

■ **The program counter**

This register has a length of 32 bits but only 24 are used, which allows an address field of 16 million bytes. Motorola could, if necessary, extend the length of this register and hence the address field.

■ The status register

Taking account of the two operating modes of the 68000, supervisor and user, the 16 bit status word consists of a supervisor byte and a user byte as shown in Figure 46(a).

The supervisor byte, reserved for the system, includes the following:

(a) An interrupt mask consisting of the three bits I_0, I_1 and I_2. All interrupt demands of a level less than or equal to the value of the mask are ignored and therefore not taken into account by the 68000. Hence if the mask is programmed at 4, interrupt demands at level 1, 2, 3 and 4 are inhibited; only those at level 5, 6 and 7 are accepted. Level 7 has the highest priority and level 1 the lowest (Figure 46(b)).

(b) The status bit S which indicates the mode of operation of the 68000: supervisor if $S = 1$ and user if $S = 0$. Supervisor mode authorizes the operating system to access all the resources (that is the five address spaces, all of the status register and the two stack pointers SSP and USP) and to use all the instructions particularly those, called 'privileged', which are capable of modifying the mode of operation of the 68000. In user mode the 68000 can access only two user spaces and cannot use the privileged instructions. Any attempt to execute such an instruction is a 'violation of privilege' which results in an internal interrupt.

The processor changes from supervisor to user mode by setting the status bit S to 0. The only possibility offered to the programmer, after reset, to change from user to supervisor mode is to generate an internal interrupt called a 'trap' (or 'exception'). After execution of the interrupt subroutine in supervisor mode the 68000 returns to user mode.

(c) The status bit T which puts the microprocessor into the 'trace' mode if this bit is set to 1. The 68000 tests this bit after each instruction and if its value is 1, it is automatically diverted to the 'trace' interrupt subroutine after execution of each instruction. This option allows the programmer to operate in single step by displaying the contents of the registers in the 'trace' subroutine. The trace mode, essential for debugging a program, can be used in either user or supervisor mode.

The user byte contains the four standard flags of 8 bit microprocessors: carry (C), overflow (V), zero (Z) and negative or sign (N).

C is set to 1 if there is a carry for an addition or a borrow for a subtraction.
V is set to 1 by an arithmetic overflow, the result of the addition cannot be represented within the length of the operand.
Z is set to 1 if the result of the operation executed is zero.
N is set to 1 if the most significant bit of the result is 1.

These flags relate to the length of the operand, and hence to the processed part of the register or memory location concerned. Assume that the initial hexadecimal contents of register D2 are 11223344. The following transfer instruction

MOVE.B   #$85,D2

which consists of loading the hexadecimal value 85 into register D2, will set the flags

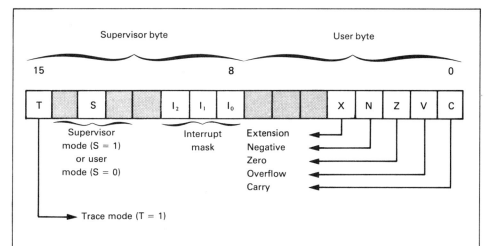

(a) The bits of the status register

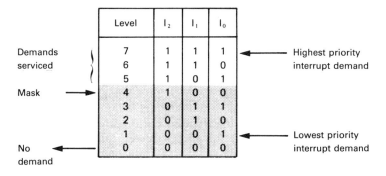

(b) Operation of the interrupt mask

Characteristics	Supervisor mode	User mode
Method of access to the mode	Reset or interrupt	Setting to zero of S bit
Hardware stack pointer	SSP	USP
Software stack pointers	USP and registers A0 to A6	Registers A0 to A6
Status bit FC2	1	0

(c) Distinction between the supervisor and user modes

FIGURE 46 *The bits of the status register SR of the 68000*

according to this value 85. After execution of this instruction one has:

hexadecimal contents of D2 = 11223385
flags: C = 0   V = 0   Z = 0   N = 1

The value 85 gives the value 1 to the most significant bit of the processed byte (10000101) and so the sign flag N is set to 1.

The flags are therefore linked to the processed part but only the latter can be modified. Consider the case of the addition of a byte of register D1 to a byte of register D2, as follows:

ADD.B   D1,D2

If the contents of the addition, which is transferred into D2, are greater than FF in hexadecimal, 10A for example, the carry and overflow flags will be set to 1 but the carry will not be propagated into the 2^8 bit position of register D2, since this bit belongs to the nonmodified part of the register (instruction operating on a byte). The same applies when shifting a byte or word to the left.

In addition to the four flags, C, V, Z and N, the user byte also has a flag called 'extension' and designated by X. This flag is the carry C limited to arithmetic operations only. It is therefore unaffected by transfers, logical operations and shifting. When it is affected it is identical to the C flag.

16.2 *External organization of the 68000*

The 68000 has 64 pins which include the data bus, the address bus, the groups of function signals, the clock and of course the power supply and earth (Figure 47).

■ D_0 to D_{15}
The 16 bit address bus can be used:

For the transfer of a 16 bit word.
For the transfer of a byte on the low part of the bus (D_0 to D_7).
For the transfer of a byte on the high part of the bus (D_8 to D_{15}).

During an interrupt cycle, the peripheral which raised an interrupt demand sends its number (for identification) on lines D_0 to D_7.

■ A_1 to A_{23}
The address bit A_0 is not an output. It would be insufficient to represent the three possible requirements:

Selection of a byte with an even address.
Selection of a byte with an odd address.
Selection of a word (address necessarily even).

However, A_0 is used internally to derive the $\overline{LDS}$ and $\overline{UDS}$ signals. To address

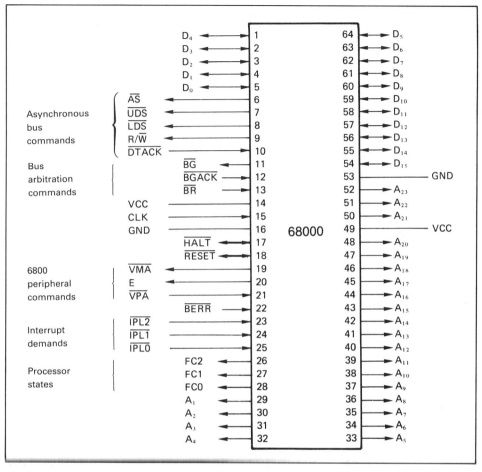

FIGURE 47 *Signals of the 68000*

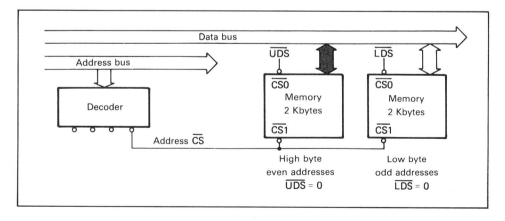

FIGURE 48 *Example of the use of $\overline{UDS}$ and $\overline{LDS}$*

memory or I/O devices associated with the 68000, bit A_1 of the microprocessor must be connected to bit A_0 of the memory or I/O device.

During an interrupt cycle lines A_1 to A_{23} are not normally used; bits A_1, A_2 and A_3 provide the number, in binary, of the interrupt being serviced and bits A_4 to A_{23} are in the high impedance state.

■ $\overline{UDS}$ (upper data strobe) and $\overline{LDS}$ (lower data strobe)

These two signals complete the address bus and replace bit A_0 which is insufficient. They control the data on the data bus by the following selection:

(a) $\overline{UDS}$ = 0 $\overline{LDS}$ = 1; selection of the high order byte that is enabling of lines D_8 to D_{15}. This case corresponds to $A_0 = 0$ and hence to an even address.
(b) $\overline{UDS}$ = 1 $\overline{LDS}$ = 0; selection of the low order byte that is enabling of lines D_0 to D_7. This case corresponds to $A_0 = 1$ and hence to an odd address.
(c) $\overline{UDS}$ = 0 $\overline{LDS}$ = 0; selection of a 16 bit word that is enabling of lines D_0 to D_{15}. This case corresponds to an even address.

Figure 48 shows the use of $\overline{UDS}$ and $\overline{LDS}$ for a memory of 2K words.

■ R/$\overline{W}$ (Read/Write)

This is the read/write signal. The 1 level defines a read and the 0 level a write.

■ $\overline{AS}$, $\overline{DTACK}$ (asynchronous bus commands)

These two signals, associated with $\overline{UDS}$, $\overline{LDS}$ and R/$\overline{W}$, ensure the correct execution of asynchronous transfers between the 68000 and slow memory or a slow peripheral. The address strobe signal $\overline{AS}$ indicates to the memory or peripheral that an address on the address bus is valid, that is it has been put on to the bus and latched so that it is stable. It is an address sampling signal. The data transfer acknowledge signal $\overline{DTACK}$ is the acknowledgement signal of data transfer. When the asynchronous data transfer on the bus has been executed, the memory or peripheral activates the $\overline{DTACK}$ signal, by setting it to the zero level, which informs the 68000 that the transfer has been effected. Hence, in the case of a read, activation of $\overline{DTACK}$ causes the microprocessor to read the data present on the data bus. In the case of a write, activation of $\overline{DTACK}$ informs the 68000 that writing is complete which causes the end of the write cycle.

■ $\overline{VPA}$, $\overline{VMA}$, $\overline{E}$ (6800 peripheral commands)

These command signals ensure interfacing and synchronization between the 68000 and devices of the 6800 family: PIA, ACIA and programmable timer. The valid peripheral address signal $\overline{VPA}$ is sent to the 68000 by the 6800 family device to inform the microprocessor that the address which it has just put on to the address bus relates to a synchronous device of the 6800 family. Thus informed, the microprocessor will generate the write or read cycle at the rate of a clock E of frequency one-tenth of that applied to the 'clock' input of the 68000 (clock H). In the case of an interrupt, an automatic vectoring system will be used, which means that

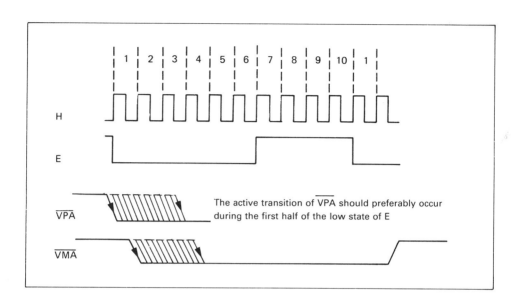

FIGURE 49 $\overline{VPA}$ and $\overline{VMA}$ signals

Signals	Input/output	Active level	Three state output
D_0–D_{15}	input/output	high	yes
A_1–A_{23}	output	high	yes
$\overline{AS}$	output	low	yes
$R/\overline{W}$	output	high/low	yes
$\overline{UDS}$, $\overline{LDS}$	output	low	yes
$\overline{DTACK}$	input	low	no
$\overline{VPA}$	input	low	no
$\overline{VMA}$	output	low	yes
E	output	high	no
FC0, FC1, FC2	output	high	yes
$\overline{BR}$	input	low	no
$\overline{BG}$	output	low	no
$\overline{BGACK}$	input	low	no
$\overline{IPL0}$, $\overline{IPL1}$, $\overline{IPL2}$	input	low	no
$\overline{RESET}$	input/output	low	no
$\overline{HALT}$	input/output	low	no
$\overline{BERR}$	input	low	no
CLK	input	high	no

FIGURE 50 *The signals of the 68000*

the numbers of the interrupting vectors will be attributed to demands coming from peripheral devices of the 6800 family. The $\overline{\text{VPA}}$ signal therefore ensures synchronization between the 68000 and the peripheral devices. It is obtained from the logical AND of AS (address strobe) and the decoded address signal.

As soon as the $\overline{\text{VPA}}$ signal is received, the microprocessor executes the transfer in synchronism with clock E. In particular, it puts an address on the address bus and, when it is stable, activates the $\overline{\text{VMA}}$ (valid memory address) signal used to generate the decoding signal of 6800 family peripherals.

If the active transition of $\overline{\text{VPA}}$ occurs during the first half of the low state of E, the 68000 activates $\overline{\text{VMA}}$ one period of its clock H after $\overline{\text{VPA}}$ (Figure 49). In the alternative case the 68000 activates $\overline{\text{VMA}}$ one period of clock E after $\overline{\text{VPA}}$.

Of the three signals $\overline{\text{VPA}}$, E and $\overline{\text{VMA}}$, only $\overline{\text{VMA}}$ is a three state output (Figure 50).

■ FC0, FC1, FC2 (selected address space)

These three output lines communicate the selected address space to the peripheral in accordance with the table of Figure 51. Bit FC2 indicates the operating mode of the 68000: supervisor if FC2 = 1 and user if FC2 = 0. Decoding of these three bits allows the programmer to obtain separate address spaces and the resulting security without the need for a memory management unit. This is useful for a small or medium size application in which security is vital. Figure 51 illustrates this simple but powerful possibility. When a memory management unit is used it decodes these three bits. Therefore they provide security of operation and the possibility of extending the addressing capacity of the 68000 from 16 to 64 million bytes.

■ $\overline{\text{BR}}$, $\overline{\text{BG}}$, $\overline{\text{BGACK}}$ (bus arbitration commands)

In the case of a direct memory access or a multiprocessor operation, the exchange protocol is ensured by three signals.

(a) $\overline{\text{BR}}$ (bus request) is the 'bus access demand' signal activated by the device which wishes to make use of the bus. Activation occurs by putting this signal to the zero level. When there are several devices able to take control of the bus, all 'bus access demand' signals are connected to a logical OR and the output of this OR is connected to the $\overline{\text{BR}}$ input of the 68000.

(b) $\overline{\text{BG}}$ (bus grant) is the 'bus allocation' signal generated by the 68000 when it has received a 'bus access demand'. This signal informs the devices able to take control of the bus that the 68000 will disconnect itself from the bus (high impedance state) at the end of the present bus cycle which is expressed by $\overline{\text{AS}} = 1$. If at this time $\overline{\text{DTACK}} = 1$ (no asynchronous transfer in progress), $\overline{\text{BGACK}} = 1$ (the 68000 has control of the bus), $\overline{\text{BG}} = 1$ (bus access demand), the 68000 puts the following into the high impedance state:

the data bus
the address bus
the $\overline{\text{UDS}}$, $\overline{\text{LDS}}$, $\overline{\text{AS}}$ and R/W signals
the status lines FC0, FC1 and FC2.

FC2	FC1	FC0	Selected address space
0	0	0	Undefined, reserved
0	0	1	User data space
0	1	0	User program space
0	1	1	Undefined, reserved
1	0	0	Undefined, reserved
1	0	0	Supervisor data space
1	1	0	Supervisor program space
1	1	1	Interrupt space

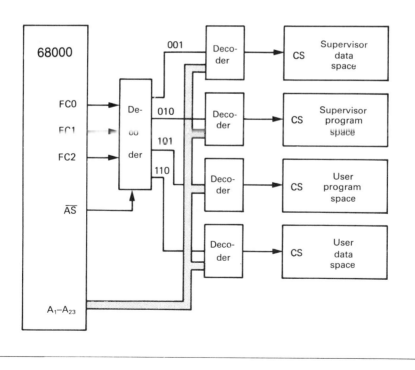

FIGURE 51 *The address spaces of the 68000 and the principle of their decoding without a memory management unit*

(c) $\overline{\text{BGACK}}$ (bus grant acknowledge) is the 'acknowledgement of taking the bus' signal sent by the demanding circuit which sees that it has been allocated control of the bus. The new bus master then activates $\overline{\text{BGACK}}$ by setting this signal to the low state and deactivating its bus access demand. It maintains $\overline{\text{BGACK}}$ at the low level as long as it has control of the bus. Deactivation of $\overline{\text{BR}}$ ($\overline{\text{BR}}$ = 1) by the demanding device leads to deactivation of $\overline{\text{BG}}$ ($\overline{\text{BG}}$ = 1) by the 68000.

When the present master no longer needs the bus, it de-activates $\overline{\text{BGACK}}$ and the processor retakes control of the bus at the beginning of the next bus cycle.

Comment. If the demanding device deactivates $\overline{\text{BGACK}}$ before it deactivates the bus access demand $\overline{\text{BR}}$, the 68000 generates another $\overline{\text{BG}}$. If the demanding circuit deactivates $\overline{\text{BR}}$ before activating $\overline{\text{BGACK}}$, the processor keeps control of the bus and continues execution of the current program.

■ $\overline{\text{IPL0}}$, $\overline{\text{IPL1}}$, $\overline{\text{IPL2}}$ (interrupt demands)
These three inputs indicate the priority level of the interrupt demand. There are eight hardware interrupt levels; the highest is level 7 but the zero level is not an interrupt demand, it is an indication that there is no demand. Many more than seven peripherals can be connected to the seven actual levels by the hardware technique of 'daisy chaining' or by software 'polling'. An interrupt demand can be serviced only if its coded level on the $\overline{\text{IPL0}}$, $\overline{\text{IPL1}}$ and $\overline{\text{IPL2}}$ inputs, from a priority encoder or other circuit, is greater than the value of the interrupt mask written into the status register by the programmer. Interrupts are serviced in supervisor mode using the SSP stack pointer.

■ $\overline{\text{RESET}}$, $\overline{\text{HALT}}$, $\overline{\text{BERR}}$ (system commands)
The $\overline{\text{RESET}}$ line is bidirectional. It becomes an input when it is initialized by an external signal. When this line is activated alone (the $\overline{\text{HALT}}$ line not being activated) the processor is initialized but the peripherals are not. Figure 52 shows this using a push button and an RS flip-flop to eliminate contact bounce.

When the $\overline{\text{RESET}}$ and $\overline{\text{HALT}}$ inputs are taken to the low state at the same time for a hundred milliseconds or more, the result is a global initialization of the processor and the peripheral devices whose $\overline{\text{RESET}}$ input is connected to the pin of the same name on the 68000. Figure 52 shows a circuit for this initialization which involves:

(a) Operation of the 68000 in supervisor mode.
(b) Inhibition of the trace mode (T = 0).
(c) Inhibition of interrupts (mask initialized to 7).
(d) Initialization of the supervisor stack pointer SSP with the contents of memory address locations $000000 to $000003 (vector zero).
(e) Initialization of the program counter with the contents of memory address locations $000004 to $000007 (vector one).

These eight memory address locations $000000 to $000007 are located in the

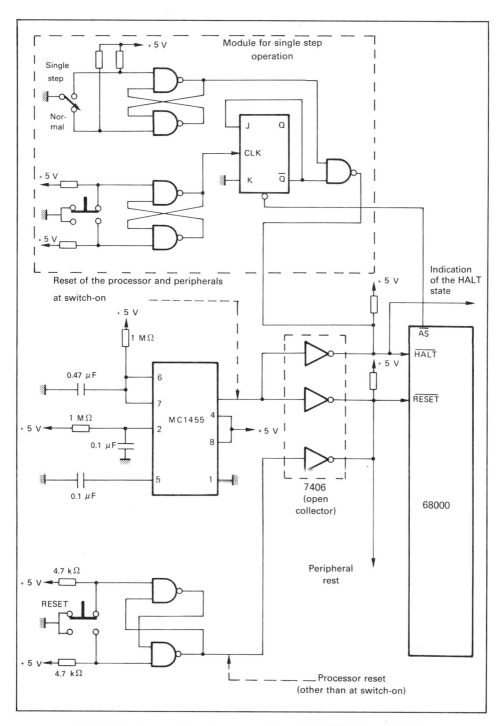

FIGURE 52 *The two bidirectional pins of the 68000:* $\overline{RESET}$ *and* $\overline{HALT}$

'supervisor program' address space. The status register, the program counter and the stack pointer SSP are the only registers of the 68000 which are affected by initialization.

During execution of the RESET instruction, the bidirectional $\overline{\text{RESET}}$ line becomes an output activated for 124 clock periods. It initializes all external devices which have a $\overline{\text{RESET}}$ input connected to the same pin of the 68000. The internal state of the latter is not affected.

When the bidirectional $\overline{\text{HALT}}$ line is put into the low state by an external device during a bus cycle, the processor stops at the end of the current bus cycle (a read or write cycle, for example). It puts all three state lines to high impedance notably the address and data buses and the $\overline{\text{UDS}}$, $\overline{\text{LDS}}$, $\overline{\text{AS}}$ and R/$\overline{\text{W}}$ signals. In contrast, the bus command arbitration signals $\overline{\text{BR}}$, $\overline{\text{BG}}$ and $\overline{\text{BGACK}}$ are available. This activation of the $\overline{\text{HALT}}$ line, as an input, allows single step and single cycle operation which is useful for debugging a design. Figure 52 shows a circuit for cycle by cycle operation. The strobe signal which is activated at the beginning of each cycle, causes a reset to zero of a flip-flop whose output, when in single step mode, activates the $\overline{\text{HALT}}$ input during each bus cycle. So the microprocessor stops at the end of the current bus cycle, which allows the programmer to confirm the state of the buses. Operation of the spring-loaded push button associated with the flip-flop deactivates the $\overline{\text{HALT}}$ input and the microprocessor, after a delay of two periods of its clock H, starts execution of a new bus cycle. For this it activates the $\overline{\text{AS}}$ signal which again activates the $\overline{\text{HALT}}$ input. Hence cycle by cycle operation is a succession of the following operations:

Activation of the $\overline{\text{HALT}}$ line by the $\overline{\text{AS}}$ signal.
Execution of the current bus cycle (generally read or write).
Confirmation of the state of the buses.
Deactivation of the $\overline{\text{HALT}}$ line.
Delay of two clock periods and start of a new bus cycle.

The single cycle mode is a useful tool for debugging hardware whereas the trace mode, which is operation instruction by instruction, is an effective aid to debugging software.

If an event occurs during the global initialization phase of the 68000 and associated circuits ($\overline{\text{RESET}}$ and $\overline{\text{HALT}}$ inputs to zero at the same time) which prevents the processor from terminating its sequence, it stops and informs external devices by setting the $\overline{\text{HALT}}$ pin as an output and activating it (double bus error). The same phenomenon occurs for the 'bus error' sequence which will now be examined. Only activation of the $\overline{\text{RESET}}$ and $\overline{\text{HALT}}$ lines allows the 68000 to leave this halted state.

The 68000 has been designed to allow an external device to inform of an anomaly during execution of the current bus cycle. This is the case when an addressed peripheral does not return the $\overline{\text{DTACK}}$ signal to signify that the transfer has been correctly effected. Detection of the anomaly involves examining the time interval between generation of the $\overline{\text{AS}}$ signal by the processor and the $\overline{\text{DTACK}}$ signal by the addressed peripheral. If $\overline{\text{DTACK}}$ is not generated at the end of a time greater than the normal delay, the external device causes a processor interrupt by activating the $\overline{\text{BERR}}$

pin. Similarly when an attempt to write into write-protected RAM is made, the processor can be informed by activation of the $\overline{\text{BERR}}$ line.

When alerted in this way, the 68000 executes one of the two following sequences according to the state of the HALT line:

(a) If the $\overline{\text{BERR}}$ input is activated but the $\overline{\text{HALT}}$ input is not, the processor terminates the current bus cycle, saves the contents of the program counter and the status register together with information which could help the programmer (address accessed, read or write, address space selected, etc.), finds the address of the subroutine for the 'bus error' exception in the vector table and executes it.

(b) If the $\overline{\text{BERR}}$ and $\overline{\text{HALT}}$ inputs are activated at the same time by the external device, the processor terminates the current bus cycle and causes a restart cycle. For this it puts the three state lines to high impedance, stops and does not restart until the external logic deactivates the $\overline{\text{HALT}}$ and $\overline{\text{BERR}}$ inputs.

The processor restarts at the preceding bus cycle with the same address, the same data and the same commands.

17. OPERATION OF THE BUS

17.1 Definitions

(a) A clock cycle is one period of clock H of the 68000. A half period is called a 'state' and designated by the letter S (state) followed by a number.

(b) A bus cycle is a sequence of clock cycles necessary for the execution of a fundamental operation such as a read or write operation; hence a read cycle or a write cycle.

(c) An instruction cycle is a sequence of bus cycles necessary for the execution of an instruction. Its length is often called the 'cycle time'.

17.2 Description of a read cycle

A cycle of this kind consists of a sequence of several states as follows:

STATE 0 (S_0). The address bus, A_1 to A_{23}, and the status lines FC0 to FC2 are in the high impedance state. The R/$\overline{\text{W}}$ signal is in the high state, which corresponds to a read operation.

STATE 1 (S_1). The address bus and status lines FC0 to FC2 leave the high impedance state, an address is placed on the address bus and the code provided on the status lines indicates the selected address space during the current bus cycle.

STATE 2 (S₂). The address strobe signal $\overline{AS}$ is activated to indicate that an address is available on the address bus. The $\overline{UDS}$ and $\overline{LDS}$ signals are set to the required logical values.

STATES 3 and 4 (S₃ and S₄). The processor waits for the $\overline{DTACK}$ signal. If this signal arrives before state 5, the 68000 detects it, otherwise it generates wait states S_w until $\overline{DTACK}$ is detected.

STATE 5 (S₅). No signal is generated or received during this state which is used to synchronize $\overline{DTACK}$.

STATE 6 (S₆). The data is taken from the bus by the 68000.

STATE 7 (S₇). The $\overline{AS}$, $\overline{UDS}$ and $\overline{LDS}$ signals are deactivated which causes the memory or peripheral addressed during the read cycle to no longer put data on the data bus and to deactivate $\overline{DTACK}$. This ought to occur less than one clock period after the transitions of $\overline{AS}$, $\overline{UDS}$ and $\overline{LDS}$.

Figure 53 shows the timing diagrams of the various signals involved in a fast read cycle (without wait states) and a slow read cycle for an odd byte and a word respectively.

17.3 Description of a write cycle

The various states of this cycle are as follows:

STATE 0 (S₀). The address bus and lines FC0, FC1 and FC2 are in the high impedance state. The $R/\overline{W}$ signal remains in the high state until state 2.

STATE 1 (S₁). The address bus and status lines FC0 to FC2 leave the high impedance state. An address is put on to the address bus and the code provided by the status lines indicates the selected address space during the current write cycle.

STATE 2 (S₂). The address strobe signal $\overline{AS}$ is activated to indicate that an address is available on the address bus. The $R/\overline{W}$ signal is set to the low state to execute a write cycle but the data to be written is not produced yet in anticipation of possible buffering of the data bus which necessarily causes a slight delay.

STATE 3 (S₃). The processor puts the data to be written on the data bus.

STATE 4 (S₄). The $\overline{UDS}$ and $\overline{LDS}$ signals are set to the required logical values and indicate to the peripheral that the data is stable and available for writing. The addressed memory or peripheral activates the $\overline{DTACK}$ signal.

STATES 5 and 6 (S₅ and S₆). No signal is generated during these states. If the

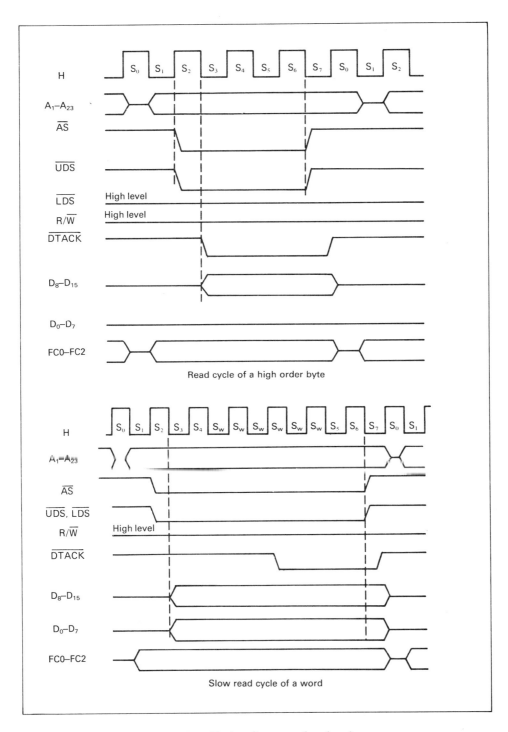

Read cycle of a high order byte

Slow read cycle of a word

FIGURE 53 *Timing diagrams of read cycles*

microprocessor receives the $\overline{\text{DTACK}}$ signal before state 7 it synchronizes this asynchronous signal in state 7. If it does not receive it, it generates wait states after state 6.

STATE 7 (S_7). Synchronization of the $\overline{\text{DTACK}}$ signal.

STATE 8 (S_8). Inactive.

STATE 9 (S_9). The $\overline{\text{AS}}$, $\overline{\text{UDS}}$ and $\overline{\text{LDS}}$ signals are deactivated. The address and data buses remain enabled together with the R/$\overline{\text{W}}$ signal and the status lines FC0 to FC2. The addressed memory or peripheral must deactivate $\overline{\text{DTACK}}$ less than one clock period after the transitions of the $\overline{\text{AS}}$, $\overline{\text{UDS}}$ and $\overline{\text{LDS}}$ signals. At the end of state 9 the data bus goes to the high impedance state. Figure 54 gives the timing diagrams of the various signals involved in a write cycle.

18. INTERFACING MEMORY AND PERIPHERALS

18.1 Interfacing ROM, PROM and EPROM

In the case of program memory, instructions are read as 16 bit words. As the most common memory devices have 8 data bits, they are used in pairs. One provides data for the low order part of the data bus and the other for the high part. Two packages are therefore selected at the same time. Figure 55 gives an example of interfacing four ROM packages each of 4 Kbytes. Total decoding controlled by $\overline{\text{AS}}$ is achieved by means of logic gates and a decoder type 74LS138.

Two outputs of the latter are used, outputs $\overline{\text{O}_4}$ and $\overline{\text{O}_5}$ which give the following word addresses:

$008000 to $009FFE for ROMs 1 and 2
$00A000 to $00BFFE for ROMs 3 and 4

The $\overline{\text{DTACK}}$ signal is generated by the first two D flip-flops of the 74LS175 connected as a shift register. This technique is a simple means of generating $\overline{\text{DTACK}}$ by delaying it one or more clock pulses with respect to the strobe signal $\overline{\text{AS}}$. The ROM $\overline{\text{CS}}$ signals are fed to a NAND gate which realizes the logical OR function of the two CS signals; that is CSROM = O_4 + O_5. As long as the address on the address bus does not concern the ROM, the CSROM signal is zero and the outputs of the D flip-flops are held at zero. The $\overline{\text{DTACK}}$ signal, connected to a $\overline{\text{Q}}$ output, is therefore at the inactive high level. As soon as the current address relates to the ROM, the CSROM signal takes the value 1 and the flip-flops are no longer held in the zero state. Since the D input of the first flip-flop is connected to the 1 level, it will take the value 1 on the rising edge of the first pulse of clock H. On the same edge of the

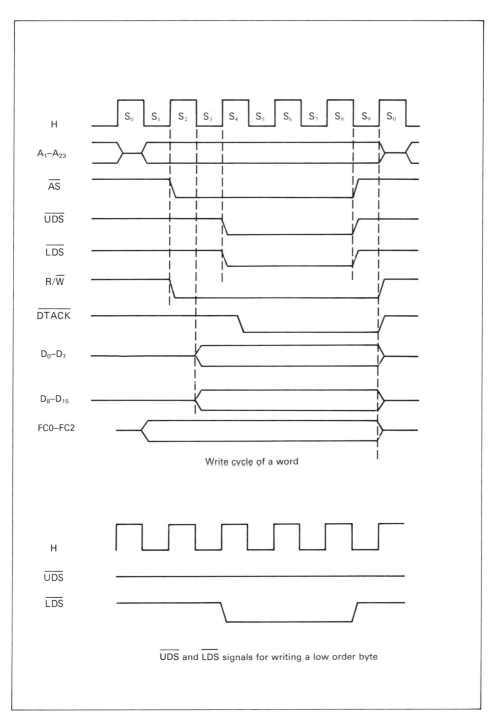

Write cycle of a word

$\overline{UDS}$ and $\overline{LDS}$ signals for writing a low order byte

FIGURE 54 *Timing diagrams of write cycles*

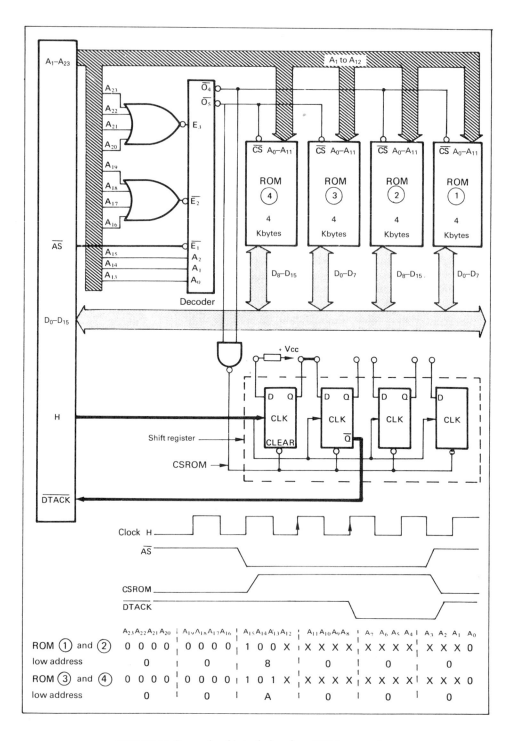

FIGURE 55 *Example of interfacing four ROM memories*

second clock pulse, the second flip-flop will take the value 1 which puts a 0 level on $\overline{DTACK}$. These two flip-flops retain the 1 state as long as CSROM = 1.

As soon as the strobe signal $\overline{AS}$ becomes deactivated, outputs $\overline{O_4}$ and $\overline{O_5}$ of the decoder will also be deactivated which implies resetting the CSROM signal and then the D flip-flops to zero and hence deactivation of $\overline{DTACK}$ as indicated in the timing diagram of Figure 55.

Notice that bit A_1 of the address bus is connected to bit A_0 of the ROMs and that calculation of addresses is made by assuming $A_0 = 0$ since word addresses are even.

18.2 Interfacing RAM

In the case of RAM it is possible to address the high order byte, the low order byte (odd address) or the word. The $\overline{UDS}$ and $\overline{LDS}$ signals make the distinction between the three possibilities. The same RAM decoding signal, therefore, involves two packages. Figure 56 gives an example of the interfacing of four RAM packages each of 2 Kbytes. Total decoding is provided in an identical manner to that described for the ROMs. The $\overline{O_1}$ and $\overline{O_2}$ outputs of the decoder are used to give the following addresses:

$001000 to $001FFF for RAMs 1 and 2
$002000 to $002FFF for RAMs 3 and 4

The $\overline{DTACK}$ signal is generated by two JK flip-flops connected as a shift register. The CLEAR inputs of these flip-flops are connected to the signal (UDS + LDS). CSRAM, the latter term being the logical OR function $O_1 + O_2$. As soon as a RAM address is put on the address bus, the CSRAM signal takes the value 1. As soon as the $\overline{UDS}$ and $\overline{LDS}$ signals are sent, the (UDS + LDS) signal takes the value 1. The logical AND of these two signals is therefore always at the zero level, which keeps the JK flip-flops at zero except when a RAM address is valid. In this case the first flip-flop changes to 1 on the falling edge of the next clock pulse, the second changes to 1 on the falling edge of the following clock pulse, which asserts $\overline{DTACK}$. The two flip-flops remain in the 1 state until deactivation of the $\overline{AS}$ signal which implies deactivation of CSRAM and hence $\overline{DTACK}$.

As for the ROMs, bit A_1 of the address bus is connected to bit A_0 of the RAMs. Bit A_0 of the address bus, which does not emerge from the 68000, is involved but it is the value of the $\overline{UDS}$ and $\overline{LDS}$ signals which selects the RAM packages.

18.3 Interfacing peripherals

Input/output devices, also called peripherals, are addressed as memory locations. It is possible, however, for peripherals having eight data bits, to use even addresses if $\overline{UDS}$ is included in the decoding function and odd addresses if $\overline{LDS}$ is included in the decoding function. It is, however, possible to use neither $\overline{UDS}$ nor $\overline{LDS}$ in the decoding function and in this case each peripheral register has two addresses; an even address and the following odd address.

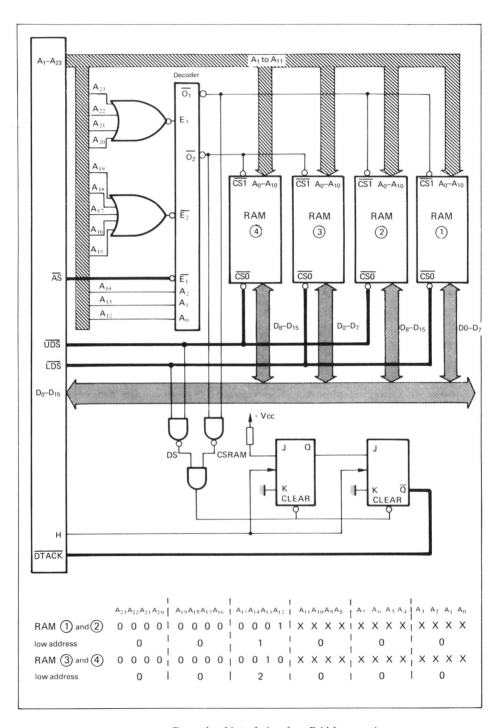

FIGURE 56 *Example of interfacing four RAM memories*

In addition to the possibility of even or odd addresses for 8 bit peripherals, there is the possibility of a synchronous command when the peripherals are those of the 6800 family (6821 PIA, 6850 ACIA, 6840 TIMER, etc.). In this case the $\overline{VPA}$, E and $\overline{VMA}$ signals are used. Figure 57 gives an example of a synchronous interconnection. Decoding is particularly simple in this diagram since the value 1 of bit A_{23} of the address bus is reserved for 6800 family peripherals. Generation of the $\overline{VPA}$ signal is therefore very simple since this signal is $\overline{VPA} = \overline{A_{23}.AS}$, AS being the address strobe signal. Selection of the PIA or ACIA is done in the addressing mode called 'linear selection', that is by assigning one of bits A_5 to A_{22} of the address bus to each I/O device exclusively; bits A_1 to A_4 are reserved for selection of one register from several within an I/O device. In Figure 57 bit A_{22} is assigned to the PIA and bit A_{21} to the ACIA. The $\overline{UDS}$ and $\overline{LDS}$ signals are not involved, each PIA and ACIA register has two adjacent addresses. The addresses of each of the four PIA registers are also given in this diagram by assigning the value zero to the unused address bits A_3 to A_{21}. Notice that it is bits A_1 and A_2 which are connected to inputs RS0 and RS1 of the PIA. The addresses are double but only the odd addresses can provide I/O transfers since the data is established on lines D_0 to D_7.

The addresses of the two ACIA registers are A00000 and A00001 for the control and status registers, A00002 and A00003 for the data register. Here, again, only the odd addresses can be used.

Figure 58 gives another possible synchronous interface of a PIA and an ACIA to the 68000. Selection of one of these devices is by means of a decoder, enabled only for odd addresses ($\overline{LDS} = 0$ and $\overline{UDS} = 1$). The $\overline{VPA}$ signal is enabled if $\overline{AS} = 0$ and if the PIA or ACIA is selected, that is $\overline{VPA} = \overline{AS.CS}$ with CS = CSPIA + CSACIA. Assuming the decoding to be carried out such that the CS address of the PIA is CSPIA = \$10000 and that of the ACIA is CSACIA = \$11000, the addresses of the registers of these interface devices are those indicated in Figure 58.

When two 8 bit peripherals are used, it is possible to combine them to form a 16 bit data bus. Figure 59 shows this technique applied to the interfacing of two MC6846 packages. These devices, called RIOT (ROM I/O timer), provide a 2 Kbyte ROM, an 8 bit I/O port and a 16 bit programmable timer in a single package.

Since ROM can be read only in 16 bit words, it is necessary to combine two MC6846s in order to use 2K words of ROM. The 8 data bits of the first device are therefore connected to lines D_0–D_7 of the 68000 and the 8 data bits of the second device are connected to lines D_8–D_{15} of the 68000.

The MC6846 has two enabling inputs CS, CS0 enables the ROM and CS1 enables the 8 bit port and the programmable counter. These enabling inputs are activated by two outputs of a decoder controlled by the VMA signal for synchronous communication with the 68000. Addressing conforms to the following:

	A_{23}	A_{22}	A_{21}	A_{20}	A_{19}	A_{18}	A_{17}	A_{16}	A_{15}	A_{14}	A_{13}	A_{12}	A_{11}	A_{10}	A_9	A_8	A_7	A_6	A_5	A_4	A_3	A_2	A_1
6846 ROM	0	0	0	0	0	0	0	1	0	0	0	0	X	X	X	X	X	X	X	X	X	X	X
6846 PORTS	0	0	0	0	0	0	0	1	1	0	0	0									X	X	X

ROM addresses \$010000 to \$010FFE

PORT addresses \$018000 to \$01800E

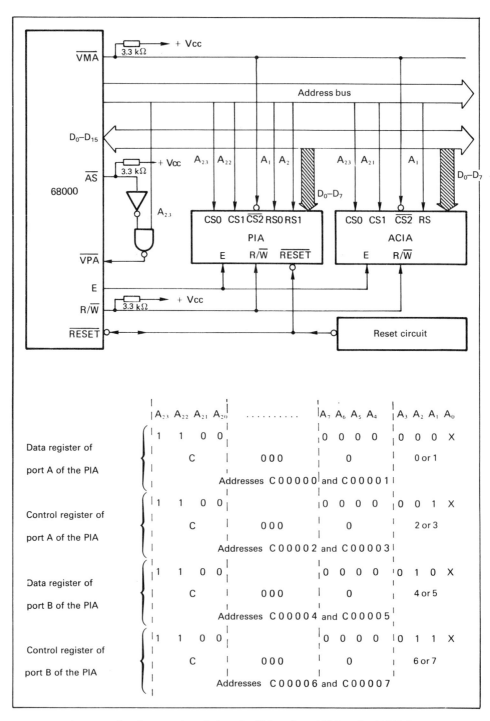

FIGURE 57 *Synchronous interfacing of a PIA and an ACIA to the 68000 for a case of very simplified addressing*

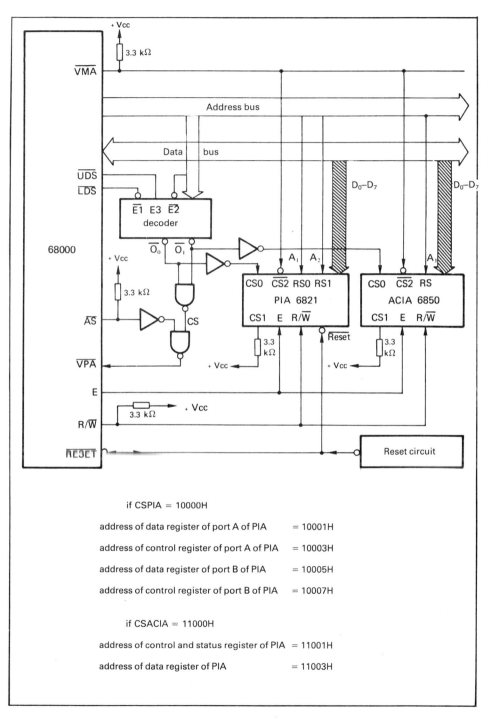

if CSPIA = 10000H

address of data register of port A of PIA   = 10001H

address of control register of port A of PIA = 10003H

address of data register of port B of PIA   = 10005H

address of control register of port B of PIA = 10007H

if CSACIA = 11000H

address of control and status register of PIA = 11001H

address of data register of PIA   = 11003H

FIGURE 58 *Synchronous interfacing of a PIA and an ACIA to a 68000 in the case of addressing by decoding*

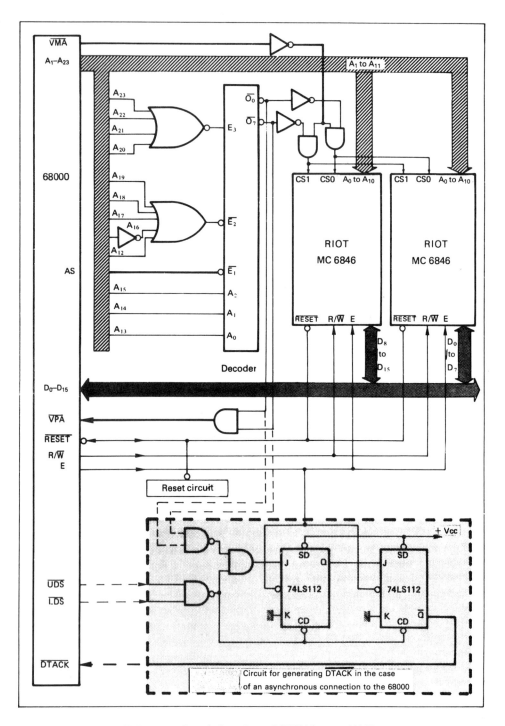

FIGURE 59 *Interfacing of two MC6846s to a 68000*

The $\overline{VPA}$ signal is the logical OR of the decoder outputs:

$$\overline{VPA} = O_0 + O_7$$

However, it is equally possible to realize an asynchronous interconnection of the MC6846 and the 68000. It is sufficient to remove the two AND gates providing the CS0 and CS1 signals, the AND gate providing $\overline{VPA}$ and to generate $\overline{DTACK}$. Figure 59 gives a possible circuit for generation of $\overline{DTACK}$. The two flip-flops are no longer latched in the zero state when at least one of the $\overline{UDS}$ and $\overline{LDS}$ signals is active (zero level).

Furthermore, if the MC6846s are addressed, the first flip-flop's J input is at the 1 level, which causes it to change to the 1 state on the first pulse of clock E. The second flip-flop changes to the 1 state on the second pulse of clock E which activates $\overline{DTACK}$. Changing of the $\overline{UDS}$ and $\overline{LDS}$ signals to the inactive state resets the flip-flops to zero and latches them in this state.

The 16 bit peripheral packages designed by Motorola for the 68000 generate the $\overline{DTACK}$ signal themselves.

19. EXCEPTIONS

The 68000 is always in one of the three following states:

(a) The normal state during which it executes instructions sequentially.
(b) The HALT state which results from a serious abnormal situation which prevents the microprocessor from operating correctly. This occurs in the case of a double bus error which, when detected by the 68000, causes it to stop. Only reinitialization by means of the reset button can restart the system.
(c) The exception state which is a generalization of the particular case of interrupts with an 8 bit microprocessor. With the 68000 this special situation occurs not only for external interrupts but also for internal interrupts. Any interrupt, external or internal, is called an 'exception'.

An 8 bit vector number is assigned to each exception which, when multiplied by four, gives the address where the exception vector is stored. The latter is the first address of 32 bits of the subroutine corresponding to the exception. The 68000 has 255 exception vectors grouped in memory in a table of 1024 bytes, that is 255 memory locations of 32 bits. Global initialization of the processor is a special external interrupt since it requires a 64 bit vector or 8 bytes. Furthermore, this vector, called the initialization vector, is stored in the 'supervisor program' space unlike all other vectors which are stored in 'supervisor data' space. Recall that every exception is processed in supervisor mode.

19.1 External interrupts

19.1.1 Global initialization or reset (vector number = 0)

This is brought about by holding the bidirectional $\overline{\text{RESET}}$ and $\overline{\text{HALT}}$ lines, acting as inputs, at the low level for 100 milliseconds. The result is as follows:

(a) A temporary copy of the contents of the status register into a register of the 68000 which is not accessible to the programmer.
(b) Setting of bit S of the status register to the 1 level, thereby putting the 68000 into supervisor mode.
(c) Setting of bit T of the status register to the 0 level, thereby inhibiting the trace mode.
(d) Assigning the value 7 to the interrupt mask, thereby inhibiting all interrupt demands.
(e) Internal generation of vector number zero and the address of the exception vector.
(f) Saving of the contents of the program counter and the copy of the contents of the status register on the stack.
(g) Reading the exception vector, that is:

   (i) loading the address stored in the memory locations with hexadecimal addresses 000000 to 000003 into the supervisor stack pointer SSP;
   (ii) and loading the address stored in the memory locations with hexadecimal addresses 000004 to 000007 into the program counter.

(h) Execution of the initialization interrupt subroutine whose address has just been loaded into the program counter.
(i) Return to the main program, which puts the 68000 back into user mode.

Comment. If an anomaly occurs during reading of the initialization vector, the 68000 puts itself in the HALT state, sets the bidirectional $\overline{\text{HALT}}$ line as an output and activates this line by putting it to the zero level (double bus error). A global initialization of the system is necessary to leave this state.

19.1.2 Bus error (vector number = 2)

In the case of abnormal operation at bus level (addressing of an absent or defective package, an attempt to write into a protected memory area, etc.), an external circuit for this purpose detects the anomaly and activates the $\overline{\text{BERR}}$ input by putting it to the low state. The 68000 detects this bus error at the end of the current clock cycle and executes the following sequence:

(a) Makes a temporary copy of the contents of the status register in an internal register of the 68000 which is not addressable by the user.
(b) Sets the S bit of the status register to 1 and the T bit to 0.
(c) Generates the number of the vector internally (number 2) and calculates the 'bus error' vector.

(d) Saves the copy of the contents of the status register and information likely to help the programmer to find the cause of the anomaly on the supervisor stack – the address placed on the address bus, the contents of the instruction register and program counter and the status bits FC0, FC1 and FC2.

(e) Reads the 'bus error' vector.

(f) Executes the 'bus error' subroutine.

(g) Returns to the main program which puts the 68000 back into user mode.

Comment. If an anomaly occurs during action of a 'bus error' exception, the 68000 puts itself into the HALT state, sets the bidirectional $\overline{\text{HALT}}$ line as an output and activates this line by putting it to the zero level (double bus error). A global initialization of the system is necessary to leave this state.

19.1.3 Interrupt demands

The three input lines $\overline{\text{IPL0}}$, $\overline{\text{IPL1}}$ and $\overline{\text{IPL2}}$ in conjunction with a priority encoder provide seven fixed levels of priority; level 7 is the level of highest priority. Programming of the interrupt mask in the status register permits interrupt demands of a level less than or equal to the contents of the mask to be inhibited. Several interrupt demands can be accommodated at each of the seven interrupt levels by the 'daisy chaining' technique, for example. Determination of priority of demands associated with the same level of $\overline{\text{IPL2}}$, $\overline{\text{IPL1}}$ and $\overline{\text{IPL0}}$ is by the order of insertion of demands in the 'daisy chain'. The result is that the total number of interrupt demands which the 68000 can receive is much greater than seven. Motorola has provided 199 vectors for external interrupt demands. Of these 199 vectors, seven are reserved for peripherals of the 6800 family, which the microprocessor recognizes due to the $\overline{\text{VPA}}$ input activated by them. In this case it is the 68000 itself which generates the vector number, which is called the 'autovector' and is specific to the priority level. There can, therefore, be only seven autovectors, one for each priority level of the $\overline{\text{IPL2}}$, $\overline{\text{IPL1}}$ and $\overline{\text{IPL0}}$ lines. Consequently one and only one 6800 family peripheral and several not belonging to this family can be assigned to each priority level on condition that a technique such as 'daisy chaining' is used to put the priorities in a hierarchy.

The 192 other vectors are reserved for peripherals which are capable of generating, directly or with the help of an associated device, their own specific vector number which is put on to the data bus. The process of servicing an interrupt is as follows:

(a) If, at the end of an instruction cycle, the 68000 detects a priority level different from zero on lines $\overline{\text{IPL2}}$, $\overline{\text{IPL1}}$ and $\overline{\text{IPL0}}$, it compares it with the value of the mask. If it is less than or equal to this value, the microprocessor ignores the interrupt demand and executes the following instruction. In the other case it carries out the following operations.

(b) It saves the low order word of the contents of the program counter on the stack.

(c) It makes a temporary copy of the status register in an internal register of the 68000.

(d) It sets bit S of the status register to 1 (supervisor mode) and bit T of the same register to 0 (trace mode inhibited).

(e) It copies the priority level provided by the $\overline{\text{IPL2}}$, $\overline{\text{IPL1}}$ and $\overline{\text{IPL0}}$ inputs into the status register and on to address lines A_1 to A_3 and then puts the R/$\overline{\text{W}}$ signal to 1. The 68000 can then be interrupted only by an interrupt demand of higher priority. External logic can decode the priority level of the interrupt demand being serviced from bits A_1 to A_3. The other bits of the address bus and lines FC2, FC1 and FC0 are put into the 1 state and lines $\overline{\text{AS}}$ and $\overline{\text{LDS}}$ are activated.

(f) It generates internally the number of the vector associated with the priority level if the peripheral concerned belongs to the 6800 family (the microprocessor is informed by $\overline{\text{VPA}}$) or reads from bits D_0 to D_7 of the data bus the number of the vector provided by the peripheral if this does not belong to the 6800 family (in this case it is the $\overline{\text{DTACK}}$ line and no longer $\overline{\text{VPA}}$ which is activated by the peripheral). The vector number enables the address of the vector to be calculated.

(g) It saves the copy of the status register and the high order word of the program counter on the supervisor stack.

(h) It reads the exception vector relating to the interrupt demand which is being processed.

(i) It executes the subroutine of the corresponding interrupt.

(j) It returns to the interrupted program and user mode.

Comment 1. If the addressed peripheral does not provide its vector number due to an omission by the programmer, the number provided is $0F if it is a 68000 peripheral since the latter is automatically initialized to this value when power is applied. The program is therefore diverted to exception number 15 (uninitialized interrupt vector).

Comment 2. If neither $\overline{\text{DTACK}}$ nor $\overline{\text{VPA}}$ is activated during action of an interrupt, this is an anomaly which causes activation of the $\overline{\text{BERR}}$ line if an external circuit is provided for this purpose. In this case the program is diverted to exception number 24 (spurious interrupt).

In the arrangement of Figure 57 the PIA and ACIA have two and one 'interrupt demand' outputs respectively. It is possible to make an autovector correspond to each of these three demands, as shown in Figure 60.

In order to show the required connections relating to interrupts, only those which are necessary have been shown. When at least one of the three interrupts $\overline{\text{IRQB}}$, $\overline{\text{IRQA}}$ and $\overline{\text{IRQ}}$ is activated, lines $\overline{\text{IPL2}}$, $\overline{\text{IPL1}}$ and $\overline{\text{IPL0}}$ provide a priority level different from zero which is detected by the 68000 at the end of the current instruction. If the value of the mask is less than this value, the processor enters the sequence to service an interrupt. This leads to activation of $\overline{\text{AS}}$ and to address bits A_1 to A_{23} being set to the 1 level. As a consequence, the $\overline{\text{VPA}}$ signal is activated which involves activation of $\overline{\text{VMA}}$ and the fetching of the autovector relating to the interrupt priority. The priority level, the vector number and the hexadecimal address are also given in Figure 60 for each interrupt.

In the arrangement of Figure 58 a PIA and an ACIA are again connected synchronously to the 68000 but the decoding is better than that of the arrangement of Figure 57. Actioning of interrupts for this arrangement is indicated in Figure 61. The

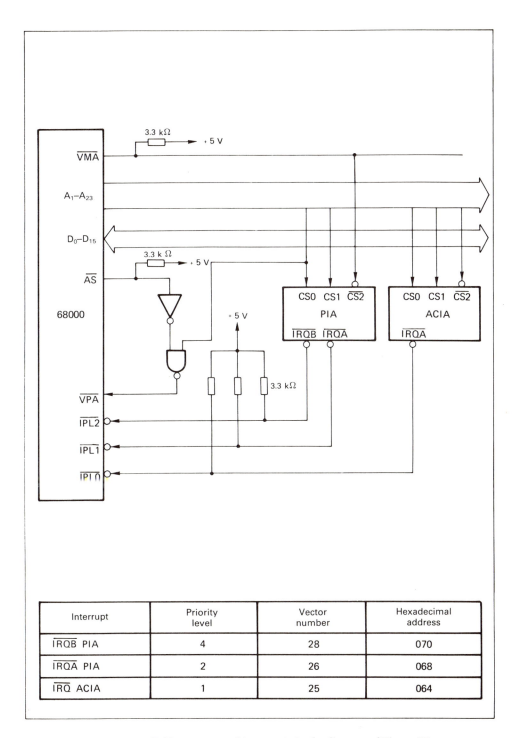

Interrupt	Priority level	Vector number	Hexadecimal address
$\overline{IRQB}$ PIA	4	28	070
$\overline{IRQA}$ PIA	2	26	068
$\overline{IRQ}$ ACIA	1	25	064

FIGURE 60 *Taking account of interrupts in the diagram of Figure 57*

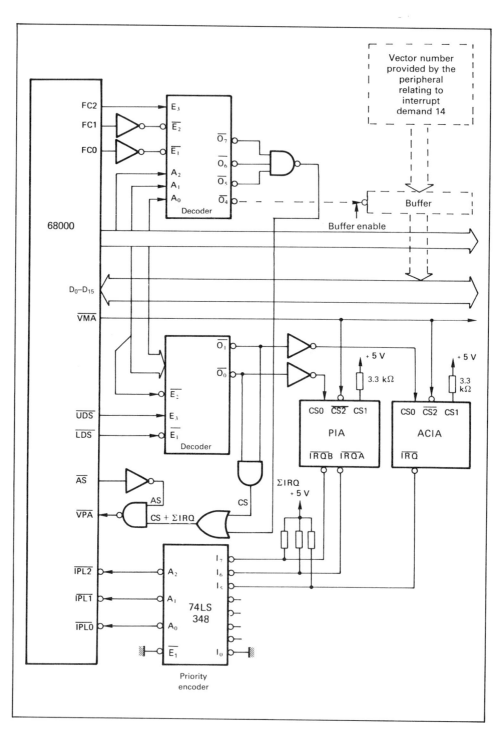

FIGURE 61 *Taking account of interrupts in the diagram of Figure 58*

three interrupt demands are applied to the inputs of a priority encoder whose outputs are connected to lines $\overline{IPL2}$, $\overline{IPL1}$ and $\overline{IPL0}$. The input of priority zero is permanently enabled, which ensures a zero level on lines $\overline{IPL2}$, $\overline{IPL1}$ and $\overline{IPL0}$ in the absence of all interrupt demands. As soon as a demand is activated, it is of higher priority than the zero level demand.

If the priority level of the demand is greater than the value of the mask, the 68000 enters the process to action the interrupt at the end of the current instruction cycle. During this process it puts the priority number of the interrupt demand being serviced on address bits A_1 to A_3. It puts lines FC2, FC1 and FC0 to the 1 level as evidence that the interrupt has been recognized. The decoder at the top of Figure 61 now decodes the recognized interrupt with the help of a NAND gate; the logical OR function of the three interrupt demands is generated and called ΣIRQ. The $\overline{AS}$ line is also activated by the 68000 during actioning of an interrupt, the $\overline{VPA}$ signal is then the product $\overline{AS}.\Sigma IRQ$. However, the $\overline{VPA}$ signal must also be activated, in the absence of any interrupt demand, when the PIA or ACIA is activated. Hence the logical equation of $\overline{VPA}$ is:

$$\overline{VPA} = \overline{AS}.(CS + \Sigma IRQ)$$

an equation in which the term CS is

$$CS = CSPIA + CSACIA$$

The arrangement given supports other interrupt demands. In particular, demands originating from peripherals not belonging to the 6800 family can be connected to inputs I_1 to I_4. They are not included in the function ΣIRQ which activates $\overline{VPA}$. But for each of these demands, there is an output of the decoder at the top of Figure 61 which enables the buffer by which the peripheral puts its vector number on to the data bus. This possibility is indicated in dotted lines in the figure for interrupt demand I_4 of the priority encoder.

In the case of an arrangement limited to the three demands $\overline{IRQB}$, $\overline{IRQA}$ and $\overline{IRQ}$, the priority encoder and the decoder at the top of Figure 61 will not be necessary. The three demands would be addressed by inputs $\overline{IPL2}$, $\overline{IPL1}$ and $\overline{IPL0}$. The ΣIRQ signal would be obtained by means of an AND and a NAND gate as follows:

$$\Sigma IRQ = (\overline{\overline{IRQB}.\overline{IRQA}.\overline{IRQ}}).FC2.FC1.FC0$$

19.2 Internal interrupts

Internal interrupts are debugging aids incorporated in the 68000 by Motorola. They are exceptions which are automatically initiated in the case of abnormal operation of a program.

■ Address error (vector number = 3)
This exception occurs when the processor attempts to access an odd memory address location to process an operand whose length is a word or double word, since such an operand must have an even address. The effect is similar to that of a 'bus error'

exception and the current bus cycle is interrupted to allow processing of the exception. This is identical to that which is executed during a 'bus error' exception, including the saving of information intended to help the programmer to detect the source of the anomaly, except for the vector number which is 2 for a bus error and 3 for an address error. If an 'address error' exception follows during processing of a bus or address error exception or during global initialization of the system, the processor puts itself into the HALT state (double bus error).

■ Invalid instruction (vector number = 4)
An instruction is considered to be invalid if its four most significant bits are not recognized by the processor as those of a valid instruction. The exception with vector number 4 is therefore generated.

■ Division by zero (vector number = 5)
This exception is initiated if a division by zero is attempted during execution of signed DIVS or unsigned DIVU instructions. The programmer can therefore take action by means of the corresponding subroutine which he can write.

■ CHK instruction (vector number = 6)
A 'CHK instruction' is initiated during execution of this instruction if the contents of the destination data register are less than zero or greater than a certain limit. This is the contents of another data register or a memory location, one of which constitutes the source of the instruction. The form of the latter is:

    CHK address, Dn or CHK Dm, Dn

where Dm is a data register other than Dn.

■ TRAPV instruction (vector number = 7)
A 'TRAPV instruction' exception is initiated if the overflow flag has the value 1 at the time of execution of this instruction. For this exception, as for all the others, it is for the programmer to determine and to write the corresponding subroutine which seems to be appropriate. Overflow, of course, concerns the instruction which precedes TRAPV.

■ TRAP #n instruction (vector numbers = 32 to 47)
This instruction unconditionally initiates diversion of the program to the subroutine relating to the TRAP #n instruction. The value of n can be 0, 1, 2, ... , 15; there are sixteen TRAP #n instructions. They are used to call the operating system, to put breakpoints into a program during debugging, to signal an error, etc.

■ Privilege violation (vector number = 8)
Privileged instructions are reserved for supervisor mode. Any attempt to execute such an instruction in user mode causes the 'privilege violation' exception.

■ Trace (vector number = 9)

In the trace mode (T bit of the status register = 1) the processor diverts to the trace exception after execution of each instruction. The programmer can then examine the display of the contents of the registers in the corresponding subroutine; this permits single step operation.

■ Emulation (vector numbers 10 and 11)

Instructions whose code starts with 1010 or 1111 are not part of the present instruction set of the 68000; they are reserved for future instructions for this processor. The programmer can take part in this by creating instructions or macroinstructions whose code starts with 1010 or 1111, since execution of these instructions causes diversion of the program to the exceptions with vector numbers 10 and 11. The subroutines relating to these exceptions can be primitives emulating instructions.

19.3 Hierarchy of priorities

The exceptions are classed into three groups, 0, 1 and 2 with the highest priority belonging to group 0. If several exceptions occur at the same time, that of the group of highest priority will be processed. But within groups 0 and 1, there is a hierarchy of priorities. It is not the same for exceptions of group 2 since only one can occur at a given time. Figure 62 illustrates the hierarchy of priorities for the various exceptions of the 68000 and gives the table of exceptions.

20. 68000 SOFTWARE

The basic 68000 instruction operates on two operands, a source operand and a destination operand. For the standard MOVE instruction, the general form of the instruction is:

MOVE.X   SOURCE,   DEST

X is a letter designating the length of the operand, B for a byte, W for a word and L for a long word. The suffix W is optional which means that without the suffix the length is taken to be 16 bits.

SOURCE and DEST are labels which represent the source and destination operands and can be data, a data register Dn, an address register An or an address. For 68000 instructions, only one of the SOURCE and DEST labels can represent an address, except for the MOVE instruction which can include two addresses. Of course the address can be expressed using the numerous addressing modes. The symbol EA will be used to represent the effective address, since this has been used by Motorola. Some examples of instructions follow:

Group	Exception	Decreasing priority	Serviced
0 (highest priority)	• Initialization • Bus error • Address error	↓	At the end of a clock cycle
1	• Trace • Interrupts ($\overline{IPL2}$, $\overline{IPL1}$, $\overline{IPL0}$)	↓	At the end of an instruction cycle
1	• Invalid instructions • Violation of privilege	↓	At the end of a bus cycle
2 (lowest priority)	• TRAP # n • TRAPV • CHK • Division by zero	Simultaneity impossible	By execution of the instruction

No	Address	Exception	No	Address	Exception
0	000	Initialization	25	064	Autovector 1
	004	Initialization	26	068	Autovector 2
2	008	Bus error	27	06C	Autovector 3
3	00C	Address error	28	070	Autovector 4
4	010	Invalid instruction	29	074	Autovector 5
5	014	Division by zero	30	078	Autovector 6
6	018	CHK instruction	31	07C	Autovector 7
7	01C	TRAPV instruction	32	080	Instructions TRAP # n
8	020	Violation of privilege	to	to	Instructions TRAP # n
9	024	Trace	47	0BF	Instructions TRAP # n
10	028	Emulation code 1010	48	0C0	Not assigned, reserved
11	02C	Emulation code 1111	to	to	Not assigned, reserved
12	030	Not assigned, reserved	63	0FF	Not assigned, reserved
to	to	Not assigned, reserved	64	100	Interrupts by $\overline{IPL2}$, $\overline{IPL1}$, $\overline{IPL0}$
23	05F	Not assigned, reserved	to	to	Interrupts by $\overline{IPL2}$, $\overline{IPL1}$, $\overline{IPL0}$
24	060	Spurious interrupt	255	3FF	Interrupts by $\overline{IPL2}$, $\overline{IPL1}$, $\overline{IPL0}$

FIGURE 62 *The 68000 exceptions*

NEG EA	the contents of the memory location with address EA are complemented
ADD # 1, D0	1 is added to the contents of register D0
ADD.W EA,A1	the contents of the memory locations with addresses EA and EA + 1 are transferred into register A1
AND.B D3,D1	the result of the logical AND (D3).(D1) is transferred into D1
SUB # D0, EA	the value of (EA) − (D0) is transferred into the memory location with address EA
MOVE EA1, EA2	the contents of the memory location with address EA1 are transferred into the memory location with address EA2 (the only instruction which can have two addresses).

An address is even or odd when the length of the operand (or operands) is a byte. It is exclusively even when this length is a word or double word; if this rule is not observed an 'invalid instruction' exception will be generated.

20.1 Addressing modes of the 68000

These few examples of instructions show that in general,

The SOURCE label represents data, a register or an address.

The DEST label represents a register or an address.

20.1.1 Case where the label (SOURCE or DEST) represents data or a register

In this case it is incorrect to refer to addressing since the label does not represent an address, nevertheless the term 'addressing mode' is commonly used.

20.1.1.1 Immediate addressing
The SOURCE label is data appearing directly in the instruction and the DEST label is one of the following.

A data register Dn. For example

MOVE.W   #$1000,D0

This instruction loads the hexadecimal data 1000 into register D0. There is no extension of the sign. The length of the data is 8, 16 or 32 bits.

An address register An. For example

MOVE.W   #$1000,A0

This instruction loads the hexadecimal data 1000 into register A0. Since the latter is an address register, there is always an extension of the sign to 32 bits which means that the bits not expressed in the data take the value of the most significant bit of the data. In this way the data 1000 becomes 00001000 before processing since the sign bit of 1000 is 0. Similarly the data 9000 becomes FFFF9000 before execution of the instruction since the sign bit of 9000 is 1. As the data is destined for an address register, its length can be only a word or double word.

A memory location. For example

ADD.B   #$C2,$2000

This instruction adds the operand $C2 to the contents of the memory location with address $2000 and transfers the result into this memory location.

■ Quick immediate addressing
This addressing mode involves only three instructions, ADDQ, SUBQ and MOVEQ, and contains several particular features which will be described. The instruction has a total length of one word.

ADDQ and SUBQ instructions. These allow an operand to be added to the contents of a data register. The operand has a value from 1 to 8 and is coded in three bits as follows:

000 for	8	100 for	4
001 for	1	101 for	5
010 for	2	110 for	6
011 for	3	111 for	7

For example ADDQ   #4,D0

The value 0000 0004 is added to the contents of D0.

MOVEQ instruction. The source operand must be one byte of data and the destination is a data register. There is an extension of sign of the data to 32 bits before transfer into register D*n*. For example

MOVEQ   #$90,D1

Before being transferred into register D1, the data undergoes an extension of sign and becomes FFFF FF90 since the most significant bit of 90 is 1.

20.1.1.2 Register addressing
In this mode the SOURCE label and/or the DEST label is a register.

■ Data register addressing
At least one of the SOURCE and DEST labels is a data register. The length of the operand is 8, 16 or 32 bits. For example:

MOV.B   D1,$1000 is a transfer of the 8 low order bits of D1 into the memory
                     location with address 1000

NOT D0   forms the one's complement of the contents of D0

EXG   D4, D3   exchanges the contents of registers D4 and D3, the exchange extends over 32 bits.

■ Address register addressing

At least one of the SOURCE and DEST labels is an address register which implies:

(a) That the length of the operand can be only 16 or 32 bits

(b) That in the case where the destination is an address register, the transfer of an operand to this register is preceded by an extension of sign of the operand to 32 bits.

For example:

MOVE A0, D0 transfers the 16 low order bits of A0 into D0 without extension of sign

MOVE D0, A0 transfers the 16 high order bits of D0 into A0 with extension of sign of the low order word of D0 without altering the high order word of D0

ADD D2, A1   adds the low order word of D2 extended to 32 bits to the contents of A1 with the result in A1.

■ Status register addressing

One of the SOURCE and DEST labels is the status register. For example:

AND #$00FF,SR   This privileged instruction sets all bits of the status register relating to the supervisor mode to zero. Notice that this instruction is accepted only if the processor is in supervisor mode, otherwise there is a violation of privilege.

MOVE $1000, SR

MOVE   SR,$1000

■ Implicit register addressing

For a number of instructions, one, two or three registers are implicit. The table of Figure 63 lists these instructions and the implicit registers.

20.1.2 Case where the label (SOURCE or DEST) represents an address

In this case the addressing modes are absolute. Recall that with the exception of the MOVE SOURCE, DEST instruction only one of the two labels SOURCE and DEST can be an address for 68000 instructions. In the following text the general case of a single address will be considered.

20.1.2.1 Absolute addressing

This is direct addressing in the data processing sense.

Instruction	Implicit registers		Instruction	Implicit registers
BCC	PC		MOVE CCR	SR
BRA	PC		MOVE SR	SR
BSR	PC, SP		MOVE USP	USP
CHK	SSP, SR		PEA	SP
DBCC	PC		RTE	PC, SP, SR
DIVS	SSP, SR		RTR	PC, SP, SR
DIVU	SSP, SR		RTS	PC, SP
JMP	PC		TRAP	SSP, SR
JSR	PC, SP		TRAPV	SSP, SR
LINK	SP		UNLK	SP

FIGURE 63 *List of instructions using registers implicitly*

■ Absolute short addressing
The address is expressed in, or extended to, 16 bits (extension of sign). For example

    ADD.B $1200,D0

The effective address is EA = $1200 and this instruction adds the byte contained in the memory location with address $1200 to the contents of D0 and transfers the result into D0.

■ Absolute long addressing
The address is expressed in, or extended to, 32 bits (extension of sign). For example

    CLR $10000

This instruction resets the contents of the memory location with address 0001 0000 to zero. Of course EA = $10000.

20.1.2.2 Indirect register addressing

■ Indirect addressing
In this standard mode, which is the basis of the instruction set of the Intel 8085A 8 bit microprocessor, the address is the contents of a register, in this case an address register, hence EA = (An). For example:

    ADD.B(A0),D0

The contents of the memory location whose address is the contents of A0 are added to the contents of D0 and the result is transferred into register D0. This operation can be written:

$((A0)) + (D0) \rightarrow D0$ and $EA = (A0)$

MOVE   D0,(A1)

The contents of register D0 are transferred into the memory location whose address is the contents of A1, that is:

$(D0) \rightarrow (A1)$ and $EA = (A1)$

MOVE   (A1),(A2)

This is the only instruction which can contain two addresses. The transfer can be written:

$((A1)) \rightarrow (A2)$ with $EA1 = (A1)$ and $EA2 = (A2)$

■ Indirect addressing with postincrementing
This is indirect addressing followed by incrementing of the contents of the address register by 1, 2 or 4 according to whether the length of the operand is a byte, a word or a double word. However, and this is exceptional, when the indirect register is the stack pointer and the length of the operand is a byte, the increment of the stack pointer is 2 and not 1. For example:

ADD.L   D0,(A1)+

The contents of register D0 are added to the contents of the memory location whose address is the contents of A1 and the result is transferred into this memory location. Then the contents of A1 are incremented by 4 since the length of the operand is a double word. Hence:

$EA = (A1); (D0) + ((A1)) \rightarrow (A1)$ then $(A1) + 4 \rightarrow A1$

■ Indirect addressing with predecrementing
This is indirect addressing preceded by decrementing of the contents of the address register by 1, 2 or 4 according to whether the length of the operand is a byte, a word or a double word. However, and this is exceptional, when the indirect register is the stack pointer and the length of the operand is a byte, the decrement of the stack pointer is 2 and not 1. For example:

CLR − (A1)

This instruction decrements the contents of A1 by two and resets the two memory locations whose addresses are (A1) and (A1) + 1 to zero. Thus, if the contents of A1 are 100 004 before execution of the instruction, the operations accomplished by the instruction are:

$(A1) = 100\,004 - 2 = 100\,002$ from which $EA = 100\,002$
$(100\,002) = 0$ and $(100\,003) = 0$.

■ Indirect addressing with displacement

The effective address is the sum of the contents of the address register and a signed displacement expressed in 16 bits and indicated in the instruction. There is an extension of sign of the displacement to 32 bits and the contents of the address register are unchanged. For example:

MOVE $FF00(A0),D1

The effective address is EA = (A0) + FFF F00.

■ Indirect addressing with displacement and index

The effective address is the sum of the following:

(a) The contents of the address register An.
(b) A signed displacement expressed in 8 bits and indicated in the instruction.
(c) The contents of an index register X, the latter being a data or address register. The length m of the contents is a word or a double word. Hence:

$$EA = (An) + (X.m) + d_8$$

There is an extension of sign to 32 bits for $(X.m)$ and d_8. For example:

MOVE $10 (A1, D0.W),A2.

The effective address is EA = (A1) + (D0) + $10.

$$\text{If } (A1) = 0000\ 4000 \text{ and } (D0) = 1234\ 5678$$
$$EA = 0000\ 4000 + 0000\ 5678 + 0000\ 0010$$
$$\text{hence} \quad EA = 0000\ 9688$$

In the calculation only 16 bits of D0 have been used and the sign has been extended to 32 bits.

20.1.2.3 Program counter relative addressing

■ Addressing relative to the program counter

The effective address EA is the sum of the contents of the program counter and a signed coded displacement of 16 bits and subjected to an extension of sign to 32 bits. All instructions using relative addressing must be situated in a program section declared 'RORG'.

The value of the displacement is calculated taking account of the fact that at the time of execution of an instruction in relative addressing, the value of the program counter is equal to the address of this instruction incremented by two. Designating this value by (PC) gives EA = (PC) + d_{16}.

The principle is identical to that of the 8 bit 6800 microprocessor but the displacement is expressed in 16 bits. This is important since it permits a program to be written whose object code is independent of its position in memory (PIC program). For this it is necessary that the whole program should be contained in the same block and that access to data or a working area is made through the stack so that there are no absolute addresses. The program block can then be translated without its contents requiring any modification; it can therefore be put into ROM or EPROM and located at any address. For example:

BNE LOOP

LOOP is a label whose displacement d with respect to (PC) is such that $-64K < d < +64K$.

MOVE LABEL,D1

The position of the label LABEL is expressed with respect to the value (PC), the instruction MOVE LABEL,D1 is situated in a program section declared RORG.

■ Indexed addressing relative to the program counter
The effective address is the sum of the contents of the PC, the contents of an index register and a signed displacement expressed in 8 bits. The index register X can be a data or address register of 16 or 32 bits.

$$EA = (PC) + (X.m) + d_8$$

$m = $ W for an index register of 16 bits, L for an index register of 32 bits.
(PC) again designates the address of the instruction being executed (and using relative addressing) incremented by two. For example:

MOVE LABEL(A1),D0

In this instruction the displacement d_8 is such that:

$$EA = \text{absolute address of LABEL} = (PC) + (A1) + d_8$$

The different modes of addressing a memory location are given in Figure 64.

20.2 *The instruction set of the 68000*

■ ABCD
This is decimal addition with carry, that is the addition of two operands expressed in BCD in one byte and with an extension bit X which takes the place of the carry. The operands are either the contents of two data registers or the contents of two memory locations specified in the indirect addressing mode with predecrementing.

■ ADD
This is binary addition without carry of the source operand to the destination operand, the result being transferred to the destination. The source is data, a data register or an address. The destination is a data register or an address. If the source is an address register the length of the operand is 16 or 32 bits.

Addressing mode	Effective address
• Absolute short	EA = 16 bit address
• Absolute long	EA = 32 bit address
• Indirect	EA = (An)
• Indirect with postincrementing	EA = (An) then incrementing of (An)
• Indirect with predecrementing	Decrementing of (An) then EA = (An)
• Indirect with displacement	EA = (An) + d_{16}
• Indirect with displacement and index	EA = (An) + (X.m) + d_8
• Relative to PC	EA = (PC) + d_{16}
• Indexed relative to PC	EA = (PC) + (X.m) + d_8

FIGURE 64 *Addressing modes of a memory location for the Motorola 68000*

■ ADDA

This is binary addition without carry of a source operand to the contents of an address register, the result being stored in this register. The length of the operand is a word or double word. In the first case there is an extension of sign to 32 bits, the addition being made over 32 bits.

■ ADDI

This is binary addition without carry of data in immediate addressing to the destination operand with storage of the result in the destination. The latter is a data or address register. The length of the immediate data is that of the destination operand, a byte, a word or a double word.

■ ADDQ

This is binary addition with carry of a number between 1 and 8 inclusive to a destination operand with storage of the result in the destination. The length of the destination operand can be a byte, a word or a double word.

■ ADDX

This is binary addition with carry of the source operand to the destination operand with storage of the result in the destination. The operands are either the contents of two data registers or the contents of two memory locations specified in indirect addressing mode with predecrementing.

■ AND

This is the logical AND function of the source operand and the destination operand, the result being transferred to the destination.

■ ANDI

This is the logical AND function between immediate data and a destination operand with storage of the result in the destination. The length of the immediate data corresponds to the length of the operation. When the destination is the status register and the length one word, the operation acts on the supervisor byte of the register; this is therefore a privileged instruction.

■ ASL

This is arithmetic shifting to the left of the bits of the destination operand.
    This operand is shifted a number of binary places equal to one of the following:

The immediate data which constitutes the source operand.
The contents of the source register which is a data register.
1 when the destination is a memory location.

■ ASR

This is arithmetic shifting to the right of the bits of the destination operand. The number of shifts is indicated as for the ASL instruction.

■ Bcc

This mnemonic expression represents numerous conditional branching instructions. The jump occurs if the condition is satisfied otherwise the program continues in sequence. The most common conditional branches of course relate to the value of a flag. Nevertheless there are other branches resulting from logical functions of two or more flags. The expression *cc* indicates one of the following conditions:

CC	carry equal to 0	*GT	greater than (signed numbers)
CS	carry equal to 1	HI	greater than (unsigned numbers)
EQ	zero flag equal to 1	GE	greater or equal
NE	zero flag equal to 0	*LE	less or equal (signed numbers)
MI	sign equal to 1	LS	less or equal (unsigned numbers)
PL	sign equal to 0	*LT	less than
*VS	overflow set	*VC	overflow clear

    The mnemonic expressions preceded by an asterisk involve signed numbers expressed in two's complement representation.

■ BCHG

This instruction tests one bit of the destination operand and writes the complemented value of this bit into both the Z bit of the status register and the place of the tested bit in the destination. The number of the bit concerned in the destination is either the value indicated in the source operand (immediate addressing) or the contents of the source register D*n*.

If the destination is a data register, the number of the bit is between 0 and 31 (modulo 32). If the destination is a memory location the number of the bit is between 0 and 7 (modulo 8).

■ BCLR

This instruction tests one bit of the destination operand, writes the complemented value of this bit into the Z flag of the status register and then sets the relevant bit in the destination to zero. The number of the bit concerned is indicated as for the BCHG instruction.

■ BRA

This is an unconditional branch in relative addressing mode; the displacement is signed and expressed in two's complement representation. The length of this displacement is 8 bits if this is sufficient and 16 bits if it is not, but in this case the 8 low order bits of the displacement must be zeros.

■ BSET

This instruction tests the specified bit of the destination operand, sets the Z flag to the complemented value of this bit and after the test, sets the relevant bit of the destination operand to 1. The number of the bit is specified as for the BCHG instruction.

■ BSR

This is the subroutine call in relative addressing, the displacement being signed and expressed in 8 or 16 bits. In the latter case the 8 low order bits are zeros. The return address is saved on the system stack.

■ BTST

This instruction tests the specified bit of the destination operand and sets the Z flag to the complemented value of this bit. The number of the bit is specified as for the BCHG instruction.

■ CHK

This instruction tests the contents of the destination register D*n* and generates the 'CHK instruction' exception if these contents are less than zero or greater than a limit defined in the source part of the instruction and being one of the following:

Data expressed in immediate addressing.
The contents of another data register.
The contents of a memory location specified in absolute, indirect or relative addressing mode.

These three possibilities allow data or an address to be tested.

■ CLR
This instruction sets the destination operand which is the contents of either a data register or a memory location to zero.

■ CMP
The source operand is subtracted from the contents of register Dn which is unchanged. The flags are set in accordance with the result of the subtraction.

■ CMPA
The source operand is subtracted from the contents of register An without transferring the result into the destination An which is therefore unchanged. The flags are set in accordance with the result of the subtraction.

■ CMPI
The immediate data is subtracted from the destination operand and the flags are set according to the result of the subtraction.

■ CMPM
The source operand is subtracted from the destination operand, both being expressed in indirect addressing mode with postincrementing. The result of the subtraction is not transferred into the destination but the status register flags are set.

■ DBcc
This instruction is a looping primitive containing three parameters:

(a) A condition cc relating to the flags. The expression cc represents the same conditions as for the Bcc instruction plus two others: T for 'always true' (which inhibits the loop) and F for 'always false' (which leads to a simple loop).
(b) The value of a loop counter which consists of a data register Dn specified in the instruction.
(c) The value of a displacement indicated in the instruction. Execution of this instruction involves testing of the condition cc. If it is true the processor continues to follow the program in sequence. If it is false the low order word of the loop counter is decremented by one and the processor branches to the address (PC) + displacement. The two operations 'decrementing of the contents of the counter' and 'jump to the branch address' are repeated until decrementing causes the contents of the counter to go from 0 to -1.

The form of the instruction is 'DBcc Dn, d_{16}', the displacement being signed and expressed in 16 bits. If the displacement is expressed as a byte it is extended to 16 bits with sign before calculation of the branch address.

In this way repetition N times of a process represented by a subroutine SRPROC is simply achieved by the following instructions:

```
        MOVE   N,D0
LOOP    BSR    SRPROC
        DBLT   D0,  LOOP
```

■ DIVS
This instruction carries out signed arithmetic division of the destination operand of 32 bits by the source operand of 16 bits. The quotient is transferred into the 16 low order bits of the destination register Dn. The remainder is transferred into the 16 high order bits of the same register. The remainder takes the same sign as the dividend. In the case of an attempt to divide by zero the corresponding exception is generated.

■ DIVU
This is division as before but unsigned.

■ EOR
This is the exclusive OR function of the source operand which is the contents of a data register and the destination operand; the result is transferred into the destination.

■ EORI
This is the exclusive OR function of immediate data and the destination operand; the result is transferred into the destination. The latter can be the status register and in this case it is a priviliged instruction if the length is a word since it affects the supervisor byte of the status register.

■ EXG
This is the exchange of the contents of two 32 bit registers. The exchange can be made in three modes:

    Exchange between two data registers.
    Exchange between two address registers.
    Exchange between a data register and an address register.

■ EXT
This is the extension of sign of a data register to 16 or 32 bits.

■ JMP
This is an unconditional jump to an address specified in one of the following addressing modes:

    Indirect without postincrementing or predecrementing.
    Indirect with displacement.
    Indexed indirect.
    Absolute.
    Relative.

■ JSR

This is a call of a subroutine with saving of the return address. The jump address can be expressed in the same addressing modes as the preceding instruction.

■ LEA

The effective address of 32 bits is loaded into the specified address register. Here again the address can be expressed in the same addressing modes as the JMP instruction. Notice that this instruction can be equivalent to a MOVE in immediate addressing. Hence the instruction 'LEA TABLE,A0' is equivalent to the instruction 'MOVE.L #TABLE,A0'.

This instruction is used particularly in relative addressing. For example:

LEA $30 (A1,D1.W),A0

Assuming (A1) = 0010 0000 and (D1) = 0000 A100.

Since the length of the index register is a word, there is an extension of sign of its contents to 32 bits giving FFFF A100. The sign of the displacement is also extended which gives 0000 0030. The effective address loaded into register A0 is therefore:

```
  0 0 1 0        0 0 0 0
+ F F F F        A 1 0 0
+ 0 0 0 0        0 0 3 0
_____
  1 0 0 0 F      A 1 3 0 hence the address 000F A130
```

The LEA instruction also serves the purpose of incrementing the contents of an address register. For example:

LEA 4(A7),A7.

This instruction increments the contents of A7 by 4. The register A7 is either the SSP if the processor is in supervisor mode or the USP if the processor is in user mode. The instruction of this example is equivalent to 'ADDQ # 4,A7'.

■ LINK and UNLK

These instructions will be examined together since together they form one function particularly in the case of reentrant subroutines. These are as follows:

(a) Reserving a working area on the stack specific to each calling program (the number of bytes is indicated in the instruction).
(b) Assigning a pointer for access to each 16 bit memory location of the reserved working area.
(c) Correct restoration of the contents of the stack pointer.

Reentrance of a subroutine has been explained in Part 1; this involves the following procedures:

(d) Sending the arguments to the subroutine via the stack.

(e) Saving the contents of the registers used in the subroutine on the stack. This saving can be done in the calling sequence of the procedure, and therefore in the calling program, or at the beginning of this procedure.
(f) Reserving a working area on the stack, this area being controlled by a register other than the stack pointer.
(g) Restoring the initial value of the stack pointer after return to the calling program.

The register used to point to any memory location of the working area or the space reserved for arguments is called the 'frame pointer' by Motorola and designated by FP. Here it will be called the 'working area pointer'. It is one of the registers A0 to A6 and is indicated in a LINK instruction of the form 'LINK A*n*, # d'. This instruction ensures the following:

(a) Saving the contents of the 'working area pointer' on the stack. It is possible to access memory locations of this area without changing the value of the working area pointer by using indirect addressing modes with displacement or an index.
(b) Reserving a working area of *d* bytes by decrementing the contents of the stack pointer by the value of *d*.

The LINK instruction is the first of the subroutine.
The instruction which precedes return from the subroutine is UNLK. It ensures the following:

(a) Loading the contents of the working area pointer into the stack pointer. This transfer implies that the first words to be read from the stack are the initial contents of register A*n* which has been used as a pointer to the working area.
(b) Restoration of its initial contents into this register A*n*, incrementing of the contents of the stack pointer so that the first two words to be read from the stack shall be the return address of the calling program.

To explain the role and use of the LINK and UNLK instructions, the twelve successive states of the stack and the two pointers are given in Figure 65 for the case of calling a multiplication subroutine called MUL and requiring the following:

(a) Prior transmission of the two 16 bit arguments; the multiplicand MCAND and the multiplier MLIER.
(b) Saving the contents of registers D0, D1 and D2 in the procedure itself.
(c) Reservation in this procedure of a working area of 8 bytes especially for storing the result of the multiplication.

A3 will be taken as the working area pointer and its contents will be assumed to be 0001 2000 immediately before execution of the LINK instruction. The stack pointer contents will be assumed to be 00001000 at the same time. The calling sequence of the

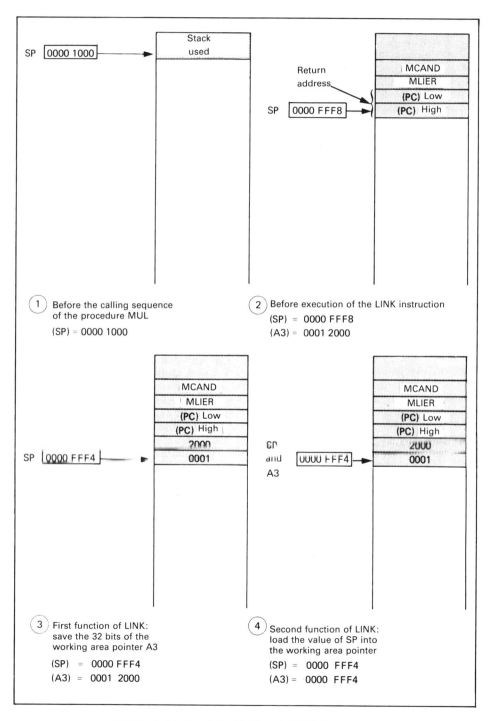

FIGURE 65 *(a) Use of the LINK and UNLK instructions*

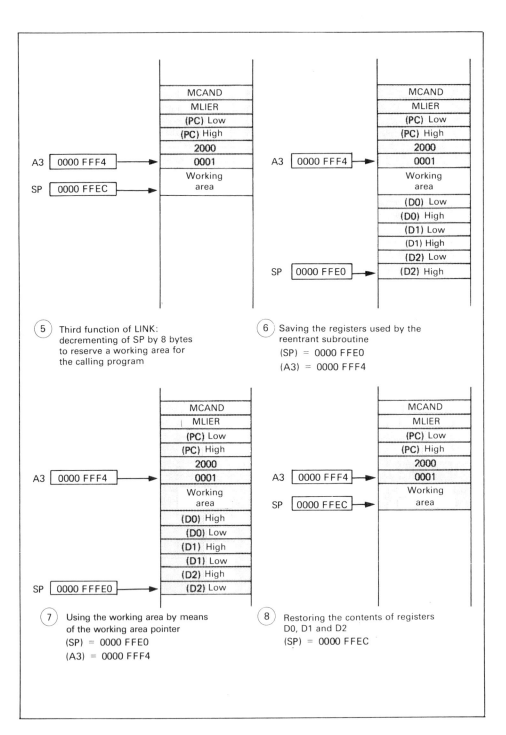

FIGURE 65 *(b) Use of the LINK and UNLK instructions*

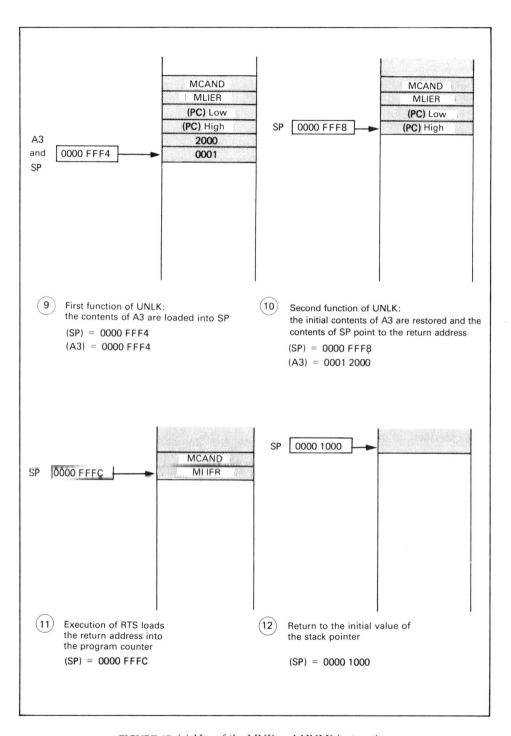

FIGURE 65 *(c) Use of the LINK and UNLK instructions*

procedure in the main program is then:

CALLING SEQUENCE OF THE PROCEDURE MUL
MOVE MCAND, −(SP)   ; transmission of MCAND to the stack
MOVE MLIER,   −(SP)   ; transmission of MLIER to the stack
JSR MUL   ; call the procedure
ADD # 4,SP   ; restoration of the initial value of the stack
                             pointer

.
.
.

16 × 16 MULTIPLICATION PROCEDURE
MUL LINK A3,8   ; reservation of an 8 byte working area
MOVEM.L D0/D1/D2, −(SP)   ; save the contents of registers D0, D1 and D2

.
. }   multiplication procedure itself
.

MOVEM.L (SP) + ,D0/D1/D2   ; restoration of the contents of D0, D1 and D2
UNLK A3   ; end of use of the working area
RTS   ; return to the calling program

The benefit of the LINK and UNLK instructions is that they allow the writing of reentrant procedures such as MUL above. Reentrance is assured by the fact that execution of the procedure can be interrupted by a subroutine interrupt which also calls the MUL procedure without the loss of information necessary for correct execution of the procedure called by the principal program. Figure 66 illustrates this case by giving the various information saved on the stack during execution of the MUL procedure when interrupted and called during interruption. This figure shows that each program calling the reentrant procedure has its own area on the stack and that all necessary information has been saved.

■ LSL
This instruction shifts the bits of the destination operand to the left. The number of basic shifts is one of the following:

The immediate data indicated in the instruction.
The contents of the source register (a data register).
1 when the destination is a memory location.

■ LSR
The same as the previous instruction except shifting is to the right.

■ MOVE
This fundamental instruction is the only one which can have two addresses.

■ MOVE from SR
The 16 bits of the status register are transferred to the destination.

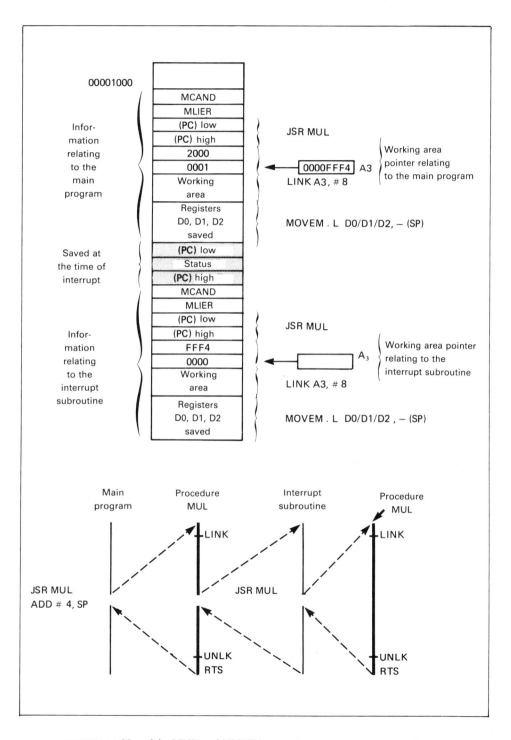

FIGURE 66 *Use of the LINK and UNLK instructions in a reentrant procedure*

■ MOVE to SR

The 16 bits of the source operand are transferred into the status register. This is a privileged instruction.

■ MOVE to CCR

The transfer is the same as for the preceding instruction but only the 8 low order bits of the source operand, which is of 16 bits, are transferred into the low part of the status register, which affects only the user byte.

■ MOVE USP

This is the transfer of the contents of an address register into the user stack pointer or the inverse. This is a privileged instruction.

■ MOVEA

This is the transfer of the contents of the source into a destination address register.

■ MOVEM

This is the transfer of a list of address or data registers to a memory area or the inverse. The list of registers is any combination of these registers; an oblique stroke (slash) separates two registers but a hyphen between two registers indicates a sequence of data registers or a sequence of address registers.

Several types of transfer are possible with this instruction.

Transfer of a list of registers to a memory area or the inverse in absolute, relative or indirect mode without postincrementing or predecrementing. In these modes the transfer is effected in the following order:

D0 – D1 – D2 – D3 – D4 – D5 – D6 – D7 – A0 – A1 – A2 – A3 – A4 – A5 – A6 – A7, for the registers.
By increasing address starting with the specified address for the memory area.

Hence the instruction MOVEM.W D0/D3/A2–A4, $10000 stores the 16 low order bits of D0 at addresses 10000 and 10001, those of D3 at addresses 10002 and 10003, those of A2 at addresses 10004 and 10005, those of A3 at addresses 10006 and 10007 and finally those of A4 at addresses 10008 and 10009 (Figure 67(a)).

Transfer of a list of registers to a memory area in indirect addressing mode with predecrementing. This transfer authorizes the stack pointer as a destination which permits writing the contents of registers to the stack. The contents of the registers are stored in memory by decreasing address starting from the specified address less two. The order of the registers is:

A7 – A6 – A5 – A4 – A3 – A2 – A1 – A0 – D7 – D6 – D5 – D4 – D3 – D2 – D1 – D0

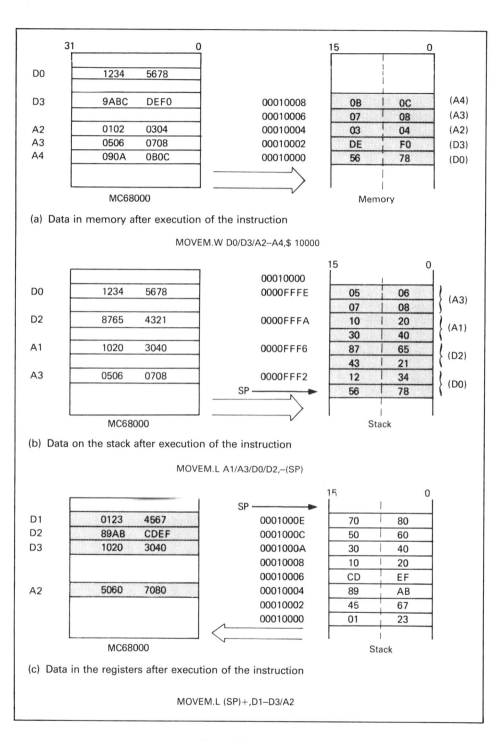

(a) Data in memory after execution of the instruction

MOVEM.W D0/D3/A2–A4,$ 10000

(b) Data on the stack after execution of the instruction

MOVEM.L A1/A3/D0/D2,–(SP)

(c) Data in the registers after execution of the instruction

MOVEM.L (SP)+,D1–D3/A2

FIGURE 67 *Use of the MOVEM instruction*

The address register used in the predecrementing mode is used to point to the address of the last word stored. For example:

MOVEM.L   A1/A3/D0/D2, −(SP)

The 32 bits of each register are transferred to the stack starting from address (SP) − 2. Figure 67(b) gives the state of the stack after execution of this instruction assuming the initial contents of the stack pointer SP to be 00010000.

Transfer of a memory area to a list of registers in indirect addressing with postincrementing. The registers are loaded by increasing memory address starting from the specified address. The order of loading of the registers is D0 to D7 then A0 to A7. The address register used for postincrementing is used to point to the address of the last word plus two. For example:

MOVEM.L(SP) + ,D1–D3/A2

The first four bytes of memory, starting from the address contained in SP, are transferred into D1. The four following into D2 and so on. The initial value of SP is taken to be 0001 0000. Figure 67(c) shows this type of memory area transfer into registers in indirect addressing with postincrementing.

■ MOVEP

This instruction is intended for transfers between a data register and registers of an I/O device of the 6800 family (6821 PIA, 6840 PTM, etc.) or 68000 family (68230 PI/T for example). It has been seen that the various registers of a PIA have alternate addresses, that is all even (in this case the data appears on bits D_8 to D_{15}) or all odd (in this case the data appears on bits D_0 to D_7).

Thus in Figure 58 the addresses of the registers of the PIA are 10001, 10003, 10005 and 10007. The instruction MOVEP is adapted to transfers with I/O devices for two reasons:

(a) It permits a transfer involving 2 or 4 registers belonging to an I/O device in a single instruction.
(b) It automatically increments the effective address by 2 after each transfer of a byte.

Assume that programming of the PIA requires FF,04,00,3C to be written into address registers at 10001, 10003, 10005 and 10007 respectively. Let address 10001 be designated by PIAAD. Programming is easily done by accessing the registers in indirect addressing mode with displacement. For this the base address PIAAD will be loaded into an address register; A0 will be taken as an example. The four data bytes will be loaded into a data register, D0 in this example. Hence:

```
PIAAD   EQU        $10001
        MOVE.L     #PIAAD,A0
        MOVE.L     #$FF04003C,D0
        MOVEP.L    D0,0(A0)
```

The transfer used as an example is writing to a peripheral; but it is equally possible to read from a peripheral and in this case the data is written into memory at alternate addresses. The size of the transfer is the word or double word.

■ MOVEQ

This is the transfer of immediate data into a data register. The data is expressed in 8 bits and receives an extension of sign to 32 bits before being transferred into the data register.

■ MULS

This is signed multiplication of two 16 bit operands; the result of 32 bits is stored in the destination which is always a data register. The destination operand is the low order word of the destination register.

■ MULU

This is unsigned multiplication of two 16 bit operands; the result of 32 bits is stored in the destination which is always a data register. The destination operand is the low order word of the destination register.

■ NBCD

This instruction produces the 10's complement of a number expressed by two BCD codes when the extension bit X is equal to zero. If this bit is equal to 1 the operation produces the 9's complement. Thus for an operand of 27, the result of the operation will be:

$$100 - 27 = 63 \quad \text{if } X = 0$$
$$99 - 27 = 62 \quad \text{if } X = 1$$

■ NEG

This is 2's complementing of the destination operand whose length can be a byte, a word or a long word.

■ NEGX

The operation accomplished is:

$$0 - \text{destination operand} - X$$

It is therefore 2's complementing with borrow.

■ NOP

This instruction does not effect any operation but the program counter is normally incremented.

■ NOT

This is 1's complementing of the destination operand.

■ OR

This is the (inclusive) OR function of two operands.

■ ORI

This is the (inclusive) OR function of immediate data, whose length is that of the operation, and a destination operand. The latter can be the contents of the status register SR. In this case the length of the operation is a byte, the instruction acts only on the 8 low order bits of the status register (user byte). If the length is a word, the instruction acts on the supervisor byte and it is therefore a privileged instruction.

■ PEA

This is the calculation over 32 bits of the effective address EA and writing of this address on to the stack.

■ RESET

The RESET line is activated which ensures initialization of I/O devices connected to this line. Program execution then continues with the following instruction. This is a privileged instruction.

■ ROL

This is rotation to the left by a number of shifts indicated as for the ASL instruction.

■ ROR

This is rotation to the right by a number of shifts indicated as for the ASL instruction.

■ ROXL

This is rotation to the left including the extend bit X in the loop. The number of shifts is indicated as for the ASL instruction.

■ ROXR

This is rotation to the right including the extend bit X in the loop. The number of shifts is indicated as for the ASL instruction.

■ RTE

This is the return from exception instruction. It restores the contents of the status register and the program counter. This is a privileged instruction.

■ RTR

This instruction restores the 8 low order bits of the status register then the contents of the program counter. The supervisor byte is not affected.

■ RTS

This is the instruction to return from a subroutine by restoring the contents of the program counter.

■ SBCD

This is decimal subtraction with borrow, that is subtraction of two operands expressed in BCD by one byte and the extend bit which is used for the borrow. The operands are:

(a) the contents of two data registers; or
(b) the contents of two memory locations specified in the indirect addressing mode with predecrementing; the latter mode permits decimal subtraction of numbers expressed in several bytes to be performed.

By way of example the following decimal subtraction will be performed:

$$
\begin{array}{r}
78\ \ 23\ \ 44\ \ 18\ \ 51 \\
-\ \ 50\ \ 19\ \ 33\ \ 65\ \ 28 \\
\hline
28\ \ 04\ \ 10\ \ 53\ \ 23
\end{array}
$$

The five bytes of these two numbers will be stored in memory starting with addresses which will be taken as $10000 for the first number and $10010 for the second number. Therefore bytes of value 78 will be stored at address $10000, 23 at address $10001 and 51 at address $10004. Similarly 50 will be stored at address $10010 and 28 at address $10014. Addresses $10005 and $10015 will be loaded into the two address registers A0 and A1 by the specific instruction LEA. As the number of bytes of each number is 5, it will be necessary to perform five subtractions and for this purpose register D0 will be used as a loop counter. This will be initialized to 5 by the instruction MOVEQ. The sequence of decimal subtractions will be performed by the SBCD instruction in a loop primitive without condition test (DBRA instruction).

```
          LEA      $10005, A0
          LEA      $10015, A1
          MOVEQ    #5, D0
LOOP      SBCD     -(A0),-(A1)
          DBRA     D0, LOOP
```

■ S*cc*

This instruction tests the condition *cc*, one of the 16 possible (the 14 given for the B*cc* instruction plus the particular conditions T and F). If the condition is true the value FF is loaded into the memory location whose address is indicated in the instruction. If the condition is false, the value 00 is written.

■ STOP

The immediate data indicated in the instruction is transferred into the status register. The program counter is incremented and points to the following instruction but the processor stops and restarts only after reinitialization, an interrupt or a trace exception. If the bit which corresponds to bit S of the status register in the immediate data is zero, there is a violation of privilege. This is a privileged instruction.

■ SUB

This is binary subtraction of two operands.

■ SUBA

This instruction subtracts the source operand from the contents of the destination address register. The length of the immediate data is that of the operation.

■ SUBI

This instruction subtracts immediate data from the destination operand.

■ SUBQ

Like the previous instruction, this is the subtraction of immediate data from the destination operand, but the immediate data is between 1 and 8 inclusive which enables the instruction to be coded in a single word.

■ SUBX

This instruction subtracts the source operand from the destination operand including the extend bit X.

The operands are either:

(a) the contents of two data registers; or
(b) the contents of two specified memory locations in indirect addressing mode with predecrementing, which permits binary subtraction of numbers longer than 32 bits to be performed.

■ SWAP

This is the exchange of low and high order words in a data register.

■ TAS

This is an instruction specific to multiprocessor operation. When several processors have requested use of the same hardware or software resource, it is necessary to assign to the latter several status indicators grouped in an 8 bit register or memory location called a semaphore. The most significant bit of the semaphore indicates, by the value 1 or 0, the availability or otherwise of the resource, a printer for example. The TAS instruction ensures:

(a) reading of the semaphore;
(b) testing of the value of the semaphore and the value of its most significant bit (resource available if this bit is equal to zero); the N and Z flags of the status register are consequently set;
(c) writing of a 1 into the most significant bit of the semaphore.

For correct operation of this instruction the read–modify–write cycle is indivisible, that is it cannot be interrupted.

This instruction is normally followed by an instruction which tests the zero flag so that the processor which demanded the resource awaits its availability. This is necessary since during execution of the TAS instruction the processor proceeds to the following instruction if the resource is occupied. After using the resource the most significant bit of the semaphore is reset to zero.

```
WAIT      TAS  SEMAPHORE
          BNE  WAIT
          .
          .
          .
          CLR  SEMAPHORE
          .
          .
          .
```

■ TRAP

Execution of this instruction involves generation of the exception whose vector number is indicated in the instruction by four bits.

■ TRAPV

This is a software exception which occurs if the 'overflow' flag is set to 1.

■ TST

This instruction compares the destination operand with zero and sets the status register flags in consequence.

■ UNLK

See the LINK instruction.

In Tables 7–12 the instructions of the 68000 are given, grouped by family. These tables have been devised to give the reader all the necessary programming information. The mnemonic expressions and conventions used will now be explained.

■ SOURCE and DESTination columns
   src signifies source when this can be a register or an address
   dst signifies destination when this can be a register or an address
   Dn signifies data register
   An signifies address register
   DATA signifies immediate data
   Dsrc signifies source data register
   Ddst signifies destination data register

Asrc signifies source address register
Adst signifies destination address register
Rsrc signifies source register (data or address)
Rdst signifies destination register (data or address)
EA signifies 'effective address of a memory location'
LABEL designates a label and hence an address
ROUTINE designates a subroutine
LOOP designates a label where the program loops.

■ LENGTH column
When the length is indicated by a letter, this must be associated with the instruction except for W which can be omitted. When the length is indicated by a number of bits, this is implicit.

■ EXAMPLE column
When an instruction has a special addressing mode (SR for example), the example given is expressed in this addressing mode.

■ ADDRESSING MODE column
(a) Dn signifies that the operand not defined in the instruction is the contents of a data register;
(b) An signifies that the operand is the contents of an address register. Thus, in the instruction ADDQ # DATA, dst, addressing mode An signifies that dst can be an address register.
(c) ABS signifies short or long absolute addressing.
(d) IND signifies indirect addressing with its variants.

■ NOTE column
This contains notes which are given after the instruction set tables.

■ Notes relating to the 68000 instruction set tables
(a) When the length of the operand is a byte the source cannot be an address register.
(b) In assembler language it is possible to write ADD for the four expressions ADD, ADDA, ADDI and ADDQ.
(c) When the length of the operand is a byte the destination cannot be an address register.
(d) The specified bit of the destination operand is that whose number is either the immediate data or the contents of the source register Dn. In the first case the number is from 0 to 7 (modulo 8), in the second it is from 0 to 31 (modulo 32).

■ List of privileged instructions

ANDI.W	#	DATA,SR
EORI.W	#	DATA,SR
MOVE		src,SR
MOVE.L		USP,An
MOVE.L		An,USP
ORI.W	#	DATA,dst
RESET		
RTE		
STOP		

204

TABLE 7 *Data transfers*

Instruction	Source	Dest.	Length	Operation performed	Example	Addressing modes Dn	An	ABS	IND	Flags X	N	Z	V	C	Note
MOVE	src	dst	B,W,L	(src) → dst	MOVE.L (A1), LABEL	All for src Dn, ABS and IND for dst					•	•	0	0	(a)
MOVE from SR	SR	dst	16 bits	(SR) → dst	MOVE SR, (A0)	X		X	X	None					
MOVE to SR	src	SR	16 bits	(src) → SR	MOVE D0, SR	All except An				•	•	•	•	•	
MOVE to CCR	src	CCR	16 bits	(src) → CCR	MOVE (A1), CCR	All except An				•	•	•	•	•	
MOVE USP	USP An	An USP	L	$\overline{\text{(USP)}}$ → An $\overline{\text{(An)}}$ → USP	MOVE.L USP,A0 MOVE.L A1, USP	—				None					
MOVEA	src	An	W,L	(src) → An	MOVEA.L LABEL, A0	All				None					
MOVEM	list src	list list	W,L W,L	(list of registers) → dst (src) → list of registers	MOVEM D0/D1,—(A2) MOVEM.L (A1)+, A2/A4	ABS and IND except (An)+ ABS, REL and IND except —(An)				None					
MOVEP	Dn d(An)	d(An) Dn	W,L W,L	$\overline{Dn}$ → EA = (An) + d $\overline{\text{(EA)}}$ → Dn	MOVEP D1, 09 (A1) MOVEP.L 0 (A2), D0	indirect with displacement				None					
MOVEQ	Data	Dn	32 bits	Data → Dn	MOVEQ # $2E, D3	X					•	•	0	0	
EXG	Rsrc	Rdst	32 bits	(Rsrc) → (Rdst)	EXG D0, A1	X	X			None					
SWAP	Dn		32 bits	Exchange the high and low order words of a register Dn	SWAP D7	—					•	•	0	0	
LEA	EA	An	32 bits	Address of MEM → An	LEA LABEL,A0	IND except postinc. and predec. ABSolute Relative				None					
PEA	EA	EA	32 bits	EA → Stack	PEA (A1)	IND except postinc. and predec. ABSolute Relative				None					

TABLE 8 *Arithmetic instructions*

Instruc-tion	Source	Dest.	Operation performed	Length	Example	Dn	An	ABS	IND	X	N	Z	V	C	Note
ADD	src	Dn	(src) + (Dn) ⟶ Dn	B,W,L	ADD.B D1, D0	All				•	•	•	•	•	(a)
	Dn	EA	(Dn) + (EA) ⟶ EA	B,W,L	ADD.W D2, LABEL			X	X	•	•	•	•	•	(b)
ADDA	src	An	(src) + (An) ⟶ An	W,L	ADDA.L (A0), A1	All				None					(b)
ADDI	Data	dst	Data + (dst) ⟶ dst	B,W,L	ADDI.B #$20, D1	X		X	X	•	•	•	•	•	(b)
ADDQ	Data	dst	Data (1 to 8) + (dst) ⟶dst	B,W,L	ADDQ.B #2, LABEL	X	X	X	X	•	•	•	•	•	(c) (b)
ADDX	Dsrc	Ddst	(Dsrc) + (Ddst) + X ⟶ Ddst	B,W,L	ADDX.L D1, D4		X	—	—	•	•	•	•	•	
	-(Asrc)	-(Adst)	(EAsrc) + (EAdst) + X⟶EAdst	B,W,L	ADDX.B -(A1),-(A5)			—	X	•	•	•	•	•	
SUB	src	Dn	(Dn) - (src) ⟶ Dn	B,W,L	SUB.B LABEL, D6	All				•	•	•	•	•	(a)
	Dn	EA	(EA) - (Dn) ⟶ EA	B,W,L	SUB.L D1,$1000			X	X	•	•	•	•	•	
SUBA	src	An	(An) - (src) ⟶ An	W,L	SUBA.W 6 (A2), A1	All				None					
SUBI	Data	dst	(dst) - (Data) ⟶ dst	B,W,L	SUBI.B #$18, D5	X		X	X	•	•	•	•	•	
SUBQ	Data	dst	(dst) - Data ⟶ dst	B,W,L	SUBQ.L #3, A2	X	X	X	X	•	•	•	•	•	(c)
SUBX	Dsrc	Ddst	(Ddst) - (Dsrc) - X ⟶ Ddst	B,W,L	SUBX.W D0, D1			—	—	•	•	•	•	•	
	-(Asrc)	-(Adst)	(EAdst) - (EAsrc) - X ⟶ EAdst	B,W,L	SUBX.B -(A1),-(A2)			—	—	•	•	•	•	•	

continued

Table 8 continued

Instruction	Source	Dest.	Operation performed	Length	Example	Addressing modes Dn	An	ABS	IND	Flags X	N	Z	V	C
EXT	Dn		Extension of sign to 16 or 32 bits	W, L	EXT.L D5	—	—	—	—		•	•	0	0
MULS	src	Dn	(src) x (Dn) ———→ (Dn)	16 bits	MULS $1000, D2	All except An					•	•	0	0
MULU	src	Dn	(src) x (Dn) ———→ (Dn)	16 bits	MULU #$20, D1	All except An					•	•	0	0
DIVS	src	Dn	(Dn) / (src) ———→ (Dn)	32/16	DIVS LABEL, D7	All except An					•	•	•	0
DIVU	src	Dn	(Dn) / (src) ———→ (Dn)	32/16	DIVU D1, D0	All except An					•	•	•	0
ABCD	Dsrc	Ddst	$(Dsrc)_{10} + (Ddst)_{10} + X$ ———→ Ddst	8 bits	ABCD D0, D2	—	—	—	—	•	U	U	U	•
	-(Asrc)	-(Adst)	$(EAsrc)_{10} + (EAdst)_{10} + X$ ———→ EAdst	8 bits	ABCD -(A0, - (A1)	—	—	—	—	•	U	U	U	•
SBCD	Dsrc	Ddst	$(Ddst)_{10} - (Dsrc)_{10} - X$ ———→ Ddst	8 bits	SBCD D2, D1	—	—	—	—	•	U	U	U	•
	-(Asrc)	-(Adst)	$(EAdst)_{10} - (EAsrc)_{10} - X$ ———→ EAdst	8 bits	SBCD -(A3), - (A6)	—	—	—	—	•	U	U	U	•
NBCD		dst	9's complement (if X = 1) and 10's complement (if X = 0)	8 bits	NBCD $A 0000	X		X	X	•	U	U	U	•
NEG		dst	2's complement	B,W,L	NEG.B D0	X		X	X	•	•	•	•	•
NEGX		dst	2's complement including X	B,W,L	NEGX.W (A1) +	X		X	X	•	•	•	•	•
CLR		dst	0 ———→ dst	B,W,L	CLR.L LABEL	X		X	X		0	1	0	0

TABLE 9 *Logical functions*

Instruction	Source	Dest.	Operation performed	Length	Example	Dn	An	ABS	IND	OTHER	X	N	Z	V	C
AND	src	Dn	(src) · (Dn) → Dn	B,W,L	AND.W D0, D2	All except An						•	•	0	0
	Dn	EA	(Dn) · (EA) → EA	B,W,L	AND.B D1, LABEL	All except An						•	•	0	0
ANDI	Data	dst	Data · (dst) → dst	B,W,L	ANDI.B #$7F, SR	X		X	X	SR		•	•	0	0
EOR	Dn	dst	(Dn) ⊕ (dst) → dst	B,W,L	EOR.L D0, D1	X		X	X			•	•	0	0
EORI	Data	dst	Data ⊕ (dst) → dst	B,W,L	EORI.B #04, SR	X		X	X	SR		•	•	0	0
NOT		dst	1's complement	B,W,L	NOT.W $2E000	X		X	X			•	•	0	0
OR	Dn	dst	(Dn) U (dst) → dst	B,W,L	OR.B D1, (A1)	All except An		X	X			•	•	0	0
	src	Dn	(src) U (Dn) → Dn	B,W,L	OR.L D1, D0	All except An		X	X			•	•	0	0
ORI	Data	dst	Data U (dst) → dst	B,W,L	ORI.B #01, SR	X		X	X	SR		•	•	0	0
CMP	src	Dn	(Dn) − (src)	B,W,L	CMP.W A0, D1	All						•	•	•	•
CMPA	src	An	(An) − (src)	W,L	CMPA.L A0, A2	All						•	•	•	•
CMPI	Data	dst	(dst) − Data	B,W,L	CMPI.B #$10, LABEL	X		X	X			•	•	•	•
CMPM	(Asrc)+	(Adst)+	(EAdst) − (EAsrc)	B,W,L	CMPM.W (A0)+, (A1)+							•	•	•	•
TST		dst	(dst) − 0	B,W,L	TEST.L D1	X		X	X			•	•	0	0

Addressing modes | *Flags*

TABLE 10 *Shifts and rotations*

Instruction	Source	Dest.	Operation performed	Length	Example	Addressing modes Dn	An	ABS	IND	Flags X	N	Z	V	C
ASL and ASR	Dsrc	Ddst	ASL [C] [X] ← Operand ← 0	B, W, L	ASL.L D1, D0	—				●	●	●	●	●
	Data	Dn	ASR [C] [X] Operand	B, W, L	ASR.W # 3, D2					●	●	●	●	●
	EA		Shifts the memory word one place	W	ASL.W LABEL			X	X	●	●	●	●	●
LSL and LSR	Dsrc	Ddst	LSL [C] [X] ← Operand ← 0	B, W, L	LSR.B D3, D1	—				●	●	●	0	●
	Data	Dn	LSR 0 → Operand [C] [X]	B, W, L	LSL.L # 1, D0					●	●	●	0	●
	EA		Shifts the memory word one place	W	LSR.W (A1)			X	X	●	●	●	0	●
ROL and ROR	Dsrc	Ddst	ROL [C] ← Operand	B, W, L	ROR.W D7, D6	—					●	●	0	●
	Data	Dn	ROR [C] Operand →	B, W, L	ROL.B # 8, D5						●	●	0	●
	EA		Shifts the memory word one place	W	ROL.W $ 10 (A2, D0)			X	X		●	●	0	●
ROXL and ROXR	Dsrc	Ddst	ROXL [C] [X] ← Operand	B, W, L	ROXR.L D1, D2	—				●	●	●	0	●
	Data	Dn	ROXR [C] [X] Operand	B, W, L	ROXR.B # 5, D0					●	●	●	0	●
	EA		Shifts the memory word one place	W	ROXL.W $10A00			X	X	●	●	●	0	●

TABLE 11 *Branch instructions*

cc	Condition	Unsigned numbers	Signed numbers	Operation	cc	Flag	= 1	= 0	Operation performed
	>	HI	GT	Jump if greater		Z	EQ	NE	Jump if contents = 0 or not
	≥		GE	Jump if greater or equal		C	CS	CC	Jump if carry = 1 or 0
	=	EQ	EQ	Jump if equal		V	VS	VC	Jump if overflow or not
	≤	LS	LE	Jump if less or equal		Sign	PL	MI	Jump if sign = 0 or 1
	<	CS	LT	Jump if less					

	Operation	Operation performed
Bcc LABEL	Jump to LABEL if condition cc is true	Relative for 8 or 16 bits
DBcc LOOP	Loop primitive with condition, condition = cc or T or F	Relative for 16 bits
Scc dst	(dst) = FF if condition true, otherwise (dst) = 00, condition = cc or T or F	Dn, ABS, IND
BRA LABEL	Unconditional jump to LABEL	Relative for 8 or 16 bits
BSR ROUTINE	Subroutine call in relative mode	Relative for 8 or 16 bits
JMP EA	Unconditional jump to address EA	• IND except postinc. and predec. • Absolute and relative
JSR ROUTINE	Subroutine call	
RESET	Initialization of I/O devices	
RTE	Restoration of the contents of SR and return from exception	
RTR	Restoration of the low byte of SR and return to main program	
RTS	Return from subroutine	
STOP # DATA	Load data into the SR register then halt the microprocessor	

TABLE 12 *Bit manipulation and exceptions*

Instruction	Source	Dest.	Operation performed	Length	Example	Dn	An	ABS	IND	X	N	Z	V	C	Note
BCHG	Dn	dst	Test the specified bit of the destination operand, change its value and write the complement into Z	8 bits if dst = memory	BCHG D0, LABEL	X		X	X			•			(d)
BCHG	Data	dst			BCHG #2, D1	X		X	X			•			
BCLR	Dn	dst	Write the complement of the specified bit of the dest. operand into Z and set the specified bit to 0	32 bits if dst = Dn	BCLR D1, D2	X		X	X			•			(d)
BCLR	Data	dst			BCLR #8, LABEL	X		X	X			•			
BSET	Dn	dst	Write the complement of the specified bit of the dest. operand into Z and set the specified bit to 1		BSET D3, (A0)	X		X	X			•			(d)
BSET	Data	dst			BSET #4, $2000	X		X	X			•			
BTST	Dn	dst	Set flag Z to the complemented value of the specified bit of the destination operand		BTEST D0, $1000	X		X	X			•			(d)
BTST	Data	dst			BTEST #1, D2	X		X	X			•			
TRAP	# NUMBER		Divert to the exception whose number is indicated in the instruction	—	TRAP #2			—		— None					
TRAPV	—		Divert to the 'overflow' exception if this flag is at 1	—	TRAPV			—		None					
CHK	src	Dn	Divert to the CHK exception if (Dn) < 0 or (Dn) > (src)	16 bits	CHK #$1000, D1	All except An					•	U	U		
NOP			No operation	—	NOP			—		None					

LINK, UNLK, TAS   see detailed explanations

INDEX